INTERNATIONAL FINANCIAL ORGANIZATIONS: A BIBLIOGRAPHY

INTERNATIONAL FINANCIAL ORGANIZATIONS: A BIBLIOGRAPHY

GEORGE B. GREY

NOVA SCIENCE PUBLISHERS, INC.
Huntington, NY

Editorial Production: Susan Boriotti
Office Manager: Annette Hellinger
Graphics: Frank Grucci and Jennifer Lucas
Information Editor: Tatiana Shohov
Book Production: Donna Dennis, Patrick Davin, Cathy DeGregory, and Lynette Van Helden
Circulation: LaToya Clay, Anna Cruz, Andre Tillman and Evelyn Woodberry

Library of Congress Cataloging-in-Publication Data
Available Upon Request

ISBN 1-56072-828-0.

227 Main Street, Suite 100
Huntington, New York 11743
Tele. 631-424-6682Fax 631-424-4666
e-mail: Novascience@earthlink.net
e-mail: Novascil@aol.com
Web Site: http://www.nexusworld.com/nova

Printed in the United States of America

CONTENTS

BIBLIOGRAPHY

50 years is enough: the case against the World Bank and the International Monetary Fund / edited by Kevin Danaher.
Boston, Mass.: South End Press, c1994.
Editor: Danaher, Kevin,
Description: xiii, 210 p.; 23 cm.
ISBN: 0896084965 (cloth) 0896084957 (pbk.)
Notes: Includes bibliographical references (p. 188-189) and index.
Subjects: World Bank. International Monetary Fund. Economic assistance. Structural adjustment (Economic policy)
Developing countries--Economic conditions.
LC Classification: HG3881.5.W57 A15 1994
Dewey Class No.: 332.1/52 20

A Brief History of Funny Money
Economist (London, England) Jan. 6, 1990, p21-24

A Continent in change: thirty years of the Asian Development Bank.
[Manila]: The Bank, 1997.
Description: 160 p.: chiefly col. ill.; 30 cm.
ISBN: 971561115X
Subjects: Asian Development Bank--History. Asian Development Bank--History--Pictorial works. Economic development projects--Asia. Economic development projects-Pacific Area. Economic development projects--Asia--Pictorial works. Economic development projects--Pacific Area—Pictorial works.
LC Classification: HG3881.5.A75 C66 1997

A Guide to Direction of trade statistics / [prepared by the Real Sector Division, IMF Statistics Department].
Washington, D.C.: International Monetary Fund, 1993.
Description: vii, 25 p.: ill.; 28 cm.

Notes: Includes bibliographical references.
Subjects: Commercial statistics--Handbooks, manuals, etc.
LC Classification: HF1016 .I652a Suppl.
Dewey Class No.: 382/.021 20

A mandate for development: the future of the World Bank : hearing before the Subcommittee on International Development Institutions and Finance of the Committee on Banking, Finance, and Urban Affairs, House of Representatives, Ninety-ninth Congress, first session, September 5, 1985.
Washington: U.S. G.P.O., 1986.
Description: iii, 41 p.; 24 cm.
Notes: Distributed to some depository libraries in microfiche. "Serial no. 99-42." Item 1013-A, 1013-B (microfiche)
Subjects: World Bank--Developing countries. Economic assistance, American--Developing countries.
LC Classification: KF27 .B547 1985h
Dewey Class No.: 332.1/532 19
Govt. Doc. No.: Y 4.B 22/1:99-42

A Study of the Soviet economy / International Monetary Fund ... [et al.].
Paris: OECD, c1991.
Description: 3 v.: ill.; 23 cm.
ISBN: 9264134689
Notes: "February 1991." Includes bibliographical references.
Subjects: Soviet Union--Economic conditions--1985-1991. Soviet Union--Economic policy--1986-1991.
LC Classification: HC336.26 .S793 1991
Dewey Class No.: 330.947/0854 20

A thousand flowers: social struggles against structural adjustment in African universities / edited by Silvia Federici, George Caffentzis, Ousseina Alidou.
Trenton, NJ: Africa World Press, 1999.
Description: p. cm.
ISBN: 0865437726 (HB) 0865437734 (PB)
Notes: Includes bibliographical references and index.
Subjects: World Bank. Education, Higher--Economic aspects--Africa. Structural adjustment (Economic policy)--Africa. Academic freedom--Africa.
LC Classification: LC67.68.A35 T56 1999
Dewey Class No.: 378.6 21

Abdallah, Makumulo.
IMF and the Third World: the case of Tanzania / by Makumulo Abdallah.
[Dar es Salaam]: Mozambique/Tanzania Centre or Foreign Relations, [1982]
Description: ii, 83 leaves; 32 cm.

Notes: "March 1982." Bibliography: leaf 83.
Subjects: International Monetary Fund. International Monetary Fund--Tanzania.
LC Classification: HG3881.5.I58 A33 1982
Dewey Class No.: 332.1/52 19

Adams, Patricia
The World Bank Is Not Financially Sound.
USA Today (Magazine) Sept. 1995, p28-30

Adams, W.M.
Peace without profit: How the IMF blocks rebuilding in Mozambique, by J. Hanlon
Environmental Values, 1999, Vol 8, Iss 1, pp 113-114

ADB quarterly newsletter.
Manila, Philippines: Asian Development Bank, [1974-1975].
Description: 8 v.: ill.; 28 cm. Jan. 1974-Oct. 1975. Continues: Asian Development Bank. Quarterly newsletter – Asian Development Bank (DLC) 76613476 (OCoLC)2277968
Continued by: Asian Development Bank. ADB quarterly review (DLC) 76642572 (OCoLC)2287317
ISSN: 0044-9199
Notes: from caption. SERBIB/SERLOC merged record
Subjects: Asian Development Bank--Periodicals. Loans, Foreign--Asia--Periodicals. Asia--Economic conditions--1945---Periodicals.
LC Classification: HG4517 .A83
Dewey Class No.: 332.1/53 19
Entry: ADB quarterly newsletter (Asian Development Bank). Manila, Philippines. 85-643422

ADB quarterly review.
[Manila, Information Office, Asian Development Bank], 1976-1994.
Description: 18 v. ill. 28 cm.
Jan. 1976-May 1994.
Current Frequency: Quarterly
Continues: Asian Development Bank. ADB quarterly newsletter (DLC) 85643422 (OCoLC)1831148
Continued by: ADB review (OCoLC)31125842 (DLC) 96647626
ISSN: 0115-074X
Notes: SERBIB/SERLOC merged record Indexed selectively by: Predicasts
Subjects: Asian Development Bank--Periodicals. Asia--Economic conditions--1945---Periodicals.
LC Classification: HG4517 .A83
Dewey Class No.: 332.1/53

Entry: Asian Development Bank. ADB quarterly review. 76-642572

ADB review / Asian Development Bank.
Manila: Information Office of the Bank, 1994-
Description: v.: ill.; 28 cm. Some issues combined. July-Aug. 1994-
Current Frequency: Bimonthly
Continues: Asian Development Bank. ADB quarterly review 0115-074x (DLC) 76642572 (OCoLC)2287317
Notes: from caption. Has supplement entitled: ADB review. Operations update. SERBIB/SERLOC merged record
Subjects: Asian Development Bank--Periodicals. Asia--Economic conditions--1945---Periodicals.
LC Classification: HG4517 .A83
Dewey Class No.: 332.1/53
Entry: ADB review. 96-647626

Adjustment crisis in the Third World / Richard E. Feinberg and Valeriana Kallab, editors.
New Brunswick, USA: Transaction Books, c1984.
Description: x, 186 p.; 24 cm.
ISBN: 0887380409 0878559884 (pbk.)
Notes: Includes bibliographies.
Subjects: International Monetary Fund. World Bank. Debts, External--Developing countries. Developing countries--Economic policy. Developing countries--Foreign economic relations.
Series: U.S.-Third World policy perspectives; no. 1
LC Classification: HC59.7 .A733 1984
Dewey Class No.: 337/.09172/4 19

Advances in international banking and finance.
Greenwich, Conn.: JAI Press, c1995-
Description: v.; 23 cm. Vol. 1 (1995)-
Current Frequency: Annual
Notes: SERBIB/SERLOC merged record
Subjects: International finance--Periodicals. Banks and banking, International--Periodicals.
LC Classification: HG3879 .A38
Dewey Class No.: 332.1/5/05 20
Entry: Advances in international banking and finance. 95-643950
Set 1-- Older Receipts: v.1-v.3 (1995-1998)

Advancing social development: a World Bank contribution to the social summit.
Washington, D.C.: World Bank, [1995]
Description: xii, 60 p.; 24 cm.
ISBN: 0821332082

Notes: "March 1995"--T.p. verso. Includes bibliographical references (p. 55-60).
Subjects: World Bank. Human capital. Economic development--Social aspects. Social planning.
LC Classification: HD4904.7 .A34 1995

Advancing sustainable development: the World Bank and Agenda 21.
Washington, DC: World Bank, 1997.
Description: x, 80 p.; 27 cm.
ISBN: 0821339745
Subjects: World Bank. Sustainable development. Economic development--Environmental aspects. Environmental policy--International cooperation.
Series: Environmentally sustainable development studies and monographs series; no. 19
LC Classification: HC79.E5 A354 1997
Dewey Class No.: 363.7 21

Africa in economic crisis / edited by John Ravenhill.
New York: Columbia University Press, 1986.
Editor: Ravenhill, John.
Description: xiii, 359 p.; 23 cm.
ISBN: 0231063822 0231063830 (pbk.)
Notes: Includes bibliographies and index.
Subjects: World Bank--Africa, Sub-Saharan. Africa, Sub-Saharan--Economic conditions.
LC Classification: HC800 .A557 1986
Dewey Class No.: 330.967 19

Africa, the World Bank, and the IMF: an appraisal : hearing before the Subcommittee on Africa of the Committee on Foreign Affairs, House of Representatives, Ninety-eighth Congress, second session, February 23, 1984.
Washington: U.S. G.P.O., 1984.
Description: iii, 103 p.; 24 cm.
Notes: Distributed to some depository libraries in microfiche. Item 1017-A, 1017-B (microfiche) Bibliography: p. 103.
Subjects: World Bank--Africa. International Monetary Fund--Africa. Africa--Economic conditions--1960- Africa--Economic policy.
LC Classification: KF27 .F625 1984d
Dewey Class No.: 330.96/0328 19
Govt. Doc. No.: Y 4.F 76/1:Af 8/26

Agreement of the International Monetary Fund and Agreement of the International Bank for Reconstruction and Development,
Cairo, Govt. Press. 1946.
Description: p. cm.

Subjects: International Monetary Fund. International Bank for Reconstruction and Development.
LC Classification: HG205.1944.A3 A77 1946

Agreements concluded at the Hague conference,
London, H. M. Stationery off., 1930.
Description: p. cm.
Subjects: European war, 1914-1918—Reparations Bank for international settlements.
LC Classification: D648 .A72 1930a

Agreements concluded at the Hague conference,
London, H. M. Stationery off., 1930.
Description: p. cm.
Subjects: European war, 1914-1918--Reparations. Bank for international settlements.
LC Classification: D648 .A72 1930a

Agricultural marketing: the World Bank's experience, 1974-85.
Washington, D.C.: Operations Evaluation Dept., World Bank, 1990.
Description: xv, 86 p.; 28 cm.
ISBN: 0821315358
Notes: Summaries in French and Spanish. Includes bibliographical references (p. 83-86).
Subjects: World Bank. Farm produce--Developing countries--Marketing. Produce trade--Developing countries. Agricultural development projects--Developing countries.
Series: A World Bank operations evaluation study, 1011-0984
LC Classification: HD9018.D442 A35 1990
Dewey Class No.: 380.1/41/091724 20

Agriculture in Asia.
[Manila]: Asian Development Bank, [1985]
Description: 2 v. in 1: ill.; 25 cm.
Contents: [1] Its performance and prospects the role of ADB in its development -- [2] Statistical appendices.
Notes: Cover title. Includes bibliographical references.
Subjects: Asian Development Bank. Agriculture--Economic aspects--Asia. Agricultural development projects--Asia. Agriculture--Economic aspects--Asia--Statistics. Agricultural development projects--Asia--Statistics.
Series: A bank staff working paper
LC Classification: HD2056 .A66 1985

Ajia-gata kaihatsu no kadai to tenb¯o: Ajia Kaihatsu Gink¯o 30-nen no keiken to ky¯okun / Kakazu Hiroshi, Yoshida Tsuneaki hen.
Edition Information: Shohan.
Nagoya-shi: Nagoya Daigaku Shuppankai, 1997.
Editor: Kakazu, Hiroshi,
Description: viii, 371 p.: ill.; 22 cm.
ISBN: 4815803196
Notes: Includes bibliographical references.
Subjects: Asian Development Bank--History. Asia--Economic conditions--1945-
LC Classification: HC412 .A2443 1997

Ali, `Ali `Abd Alli ah.
Some thoughts on the International Monetary Fund's relation with Third World countries / by Ali Abdalla Ali.
Khartoum: Development Studies and Research entre, Faculty of Economic & Social Studies, University of Khartoum, [1983]
Description: ii, 29 leaves; 29 cm.
Notes: "January 1983." Includes bibliographical references.
Subjects: International Monetary Fund.
Series: DSRC seminar series; discussion paper no. 3
LC Classification: HG3881.5.I58 A45 1983
Dewey Class No.: 332.1/52 19

Amadio, Mario.
Le Contentieux international de l'investissement privé et la convention de la Banque mondiale du 18 mars 1965.
Paris, Librairie générale de droit et de jurisprudence, 1967.
Description: 276 p. 24 cm.
Notes: Bibliography: p. [265]-268.
Subjects: World Bank. Investments, Foreign--Law and legislation. Arbitration, International.

Amin, Samir
Replacing the International Monetary System?
Monthly Review Oct. 1993, p1-12

An organizational survey of the International Bank for Reconstruction and Development.
Washington, U.S. Govt. Print. Off., 1953.
Description: iv, 10 p. 23 cm.
Notes: At head of 83d Congress, 1st session, Committee print.
Subjects: World Bank.
LC Classification: HG3881.I585 U6

Anderson, Dennis, 1937-
Rural enterprise and nonfarm employment.
Washington: World Bank, 1978.
Description: 87 p.; 22 cm.
Notes: Authors, D. Anderson and M. W. Leiserson.
Includes bibliographical references.
Subjects: World Bank. Rural development. Labor supply.
Series: A World Bank paper
LC Classification: HN17.5 .A55
Dewey Class No.: 309.2/63

Anderson, Jock R., 1941-
The World Bank, the grant program, and the CGIAR: a retrospective review / Jock R. Anderson, Dana G. Dalrymple.
Washington, DC: World Bank, 1999.
Description: p. cm.
ISBN: 0821345842
Notes: At head of World Bank Operations Evaluation Department.
Includes bibliographical references.
Subjects: Consultative Group on International Agricultural Research. World Bank. Agriculture--Research--International cooperation.
LC Classification: S540.8.C66 A63 1999
Dewey Class No.: 630/.72 21

Anderson, Robert S.,
The hour of the fox: tropical forests, the World Bank, and indigenous people in Central India / Robert S. Anderson and Walter Huber.
Seattle: University of Washington Press, c1988.
Description: xiii, 158 p., [16] p. of plates: ill.; 24 cm.
ISBN: 0295966033
Notes: Includes index. Bibliography: p. 155-156.
Subjects: World Bank. Forestry projects--India--Bastar (District)
LC Classification: SD646.B37 A53 1988
Dewey Class No.: 333.75/15/09543 19

Annual meeting [of the] boards of governors [of the]
International Monetary Fund [and of the] International Bank for Reconstruction and Development. Washington [etc.]
Description: p. cm.
Subjects: Foreign exchange. Currency question.
LC Classification: HG3881 .I613

Annual report for ... / Asian Development Bank.
[Manila]: The Bank, [1968-

Description: v.; 28 cm.
First report covers Nov. 24, 1966-Dec. 31, 1967. 1967-
Current Frequency: Annual
ISSN: 0066-8370
Notes: SERBIB/SERLOC merged record
Subjects: Asian Development Bank--Periodicals. Banks and banking--Asia--Periodicals. Economic assistance--Asia--Periodicals.
LC Classification: HG4517 .A8
Dewey Class No.: 332.1/53/095 19
Entry: Asian Development Bank. Annual report. Manila.
68-130307//r82

Annual report on portfolio performance.
Washington, D.C.: World Bank,
Description: v.; 28 cm. Began in 1992.
Current Frequency: Annual
Notes: Description based on: Fiscal 1993. SERBIB/SERLOC merged record
Subjects: World Bank--Periodicals. Portfolio management--Periodicals.
LC Classification: HG3881.5.W57 A557
Entry: Annual report on portfolio performance. 95-642197

Annual review of development effectiveness / World Bank Operations Evaluation Department.
Washington, D.C.: World Bank,
Description: v: ill.; 28 cm.
Current Frequency: Annual
Continues: Evaluation results for ... 1019-4363 (DLC) 90648363 (OCoLC)22496652
ISSN: 1520-9733
Notes: Description based on: 1997. SERBIB/SERLOC merged record
Subjects: World Bank--Periodicals. Economic development projects--Finance—Evaluation Periodicals.
Loans, Foreign--Developing countries—Statistics Periodicals.
LC Classification: HG3881.5.W57 E93
Dewey Class No.: 332.1/532/05 20
Repro./Stock No.: World Bank, 1818 H. St., NW, Washington, DC 20433
Entry: Annual review of development effectiveness. 98-645411

Annual review of project performance audit results.
Washington, D.C.: Operations Evaluation Dept., World Bank, -c1986
Description: 11 v.; 27 cm. Began in 1975. -12 (1985).
Current Frequency: Annual
Continued by: Project performance results for ... (DLC) 88650038 (OCoLC)18859544

ISSN: 0251-5261
Notes: varies slightly in 1985: Annual review of project performance results. Description based on: 6th, published in 1980.
Issued by: World Bank SERBIB/SERLOC merged record
Subjects: World Bank--Periodicals. Economic development projects--Evaluation--Periodicals.
LC Classification: HG3881.5.W57 A56
Dewey Class No.: 332.1/532/05 19
Entry: Annual review of project performance audit results.
Washington, D.C. 82-647135

Anulova, G. N.
Mezhdunarodnye valiutno-finansovye organizatsii I razvivaiushchiesia strany / G.N. Anulova.
Moskva: "Nauka," Glav. red. vostochnoi lit-ry, 1988.
Description: 182, [2] p.; 20 cm.
Notes: At head of Akademiia nauk SSSR. Ordena Trudovogo Krasnogo Znameni Institut mirovoi ekonomiki I mezhdunarodnykh otnoshenii. Bibliography: p. 176-[183].
Subjects: International Monetary Fund--Developing countries. World Bank--Developing countries. World Bank.
LC Classification: HG3881.5.I58 A47 1988

Anunobi, Fredoline O.
The implications of conditionality: the International Monetary Fund and Africa / Fredoline O. Anunobi.
Lanham, Md.: University Press of America, 1992.
Description: 338 p.: ill., maps; 24 cm.
ISBN: 0819187941 (cloth: alk. paper) 081918795X (pbk.: alk. paper)
Notes: Includes bibliographical references (p. [305]-333) and index.
Subjects: International Monetary Fund--Nigeria. International Monetary Fund--Africa. Conditionality (International relations) Nigeria--Economic policy. Africa--Economic policy.
LC Classification: HC1055 .A7 1992
Dewey Class No.: 338.9669 20

Araújo, Aloísio Barbosa de.
O governo brasileiro, o BIRD e o BID: cooperação e confronto / Aloísio Barboza de Araújo.
Brasília: Instituto de Pesquisa Econômica Aplicada, 1991.
Description: 122 p.: ill.; 21 cm.
Notes: Includes bibliographical references (p. 121-122).
Subjects: World Bank--Brazil. Inter-American Development Bank. Loans, Foreign--Brazil.

Series: Série IPEA; no. 131
LC Classification: HG3881.5.W57 A7 1991

Argoud, Jean.
La Banque des règlements internationaux dans le cadre de l'économie mondiale, Paris, Librairie de jurisprudence ancienne et moderne, Édouard Duchemin: L. Chauny & L. Quinsac, successeurs, 1931.
Description: 272 p., 1 l. tables. 25 cm.
Subjects: Bank for international settlements.
LC Classification: HG1997.I6 A75

Argoud, Jean.
La Banque des règlements internationaux dans le cadre de l'économie mondiale, Paris, Librairie de jurisprudence ancienne et moderne, Édouard Duchemin: L. Chauny & L. Quinsac, successeurs, 1931.
Description: 272 p., 1 l. tables. 25 cm.
Subjects: Bank for international settlements.
LC Classification: HG1997.I6 A75

Arneberg, Marie W.
Theory and practice in the World Bank and IMF economic policy models: case study Mozambique / Marie W. Arneberg. Oslo: Statistisk sentralbyrÂ, 1996.
Description: 28 p.: ill.; 29 cm.
ISBN: 8253742967
Notes: Includes bibliographical references (p. 24)
Subjects: International Monetary Fund. World Bank. Mozambique--Economic policy.
Series: Rapporter (Norway. Statistisk sentralbyrÂ); 96/13.
LC Classification: HC890 .A76 1996

Arrangements for borrowing by the International Monetary Fund.
London, H. M. Stationery Off., 1962.
Description: p. cm.
Subjects: International Monetary Fund.
Series: [Great Britain. Parliament. Papers by command[cmnd. 656.
LC Classification: HG3881 .I615

Arruda, Marcos.
External debt: Brazil and the international financial crisis / Marcos Arruda; translated by Peter Lenny.
Sterling, Va.: Pluto Press, in association with Christian Aid, 2000.
Description: p. cm.
Notes: Includes bibliographical references and index.
Subjects: International Monetary Fund--Brazil. Debts, External--Brazil. Debts,

External--Developing countries. Brazil--Economic conditions--1945-
LC Classification: HJ8579 .A77 2000
Dewey Class No.: 336.3/435 21

Articles of agreement of the International Bank for Reconstruction and Development, as amended effective December 17, 1965.
Washington: The Bank, 1972.
Description: 24 p.; 27 cm.
Notes: Includes index.
Subjects: World Bank.
LC Classification: K4451.A44 A2 1972
Dewey Class No.: 341.7/51

Arvin, M.
Assessing aid: What works, what doesn't, and why, by World Bank
Journal of Development Studies, 1999, Vol 35, Iss 6, pp 162-163

Asea Kaebal Unhaeng hyopchongmun.
Bank of Korea [1967]
Description: 141 p. 21 cm.
Notes: Romanized. ctl: lan-kor
Subjects: Asian Development Bank.
LC Classification: LAW <Korea I 968>

Asian Development Bank special funds. Hearing, Ninetieth Congress, first- session, on S. 2479 ...
Washington, U.S. Govt. Print. Off., 1967-
Description: v. 24 cm.
Subjects: Asian Development Bank.
LC Classification: KF26 .F6 1967C
Dewey Class No.: 332.1/53 19

Asian Development Bank special funds. Hearing, Ninety-second Congress, first session on S. 749, April 2, 1971.
Washington, U.S. Govt. Print. Off., 1971.
Description: iii, 42 p. 24 cm.
Subjects: Asian Development Bank.
LC Classification: KF26.F6 1971f
Dewey Class No.: 343/.73/074
Govt. Doc. No.: Y 4.F76/2:As4/6/971

Asian Development Bank.
[Washington, For sale by the Supt. of Docs. U. S. Govt. Print. Off., 1966]
Description: p. cm.

Subjects: Asian Development Bank.
Series: United States. Dept. of State. Treaties and other international acts series, 6103.
LC Classification: JX235.9 .A32 no. 6103

Asian Development Bank.
[Washington, For sale by the Supt. of Docs., U. S. Govt. Print. Off., 1968]
Description: p. cm.
Subjects: Asian Development Bank.
Series: United States. Dept. of State. Treaties and other international acts series, 6387.
LC Classification: JX235.9 .A32 no. 6385

Asian Development Bank: questions and answers.
[Manila: Information Office, Asian Development Bank], 1976.
Description: v, 51 p.: diagr.; 22 cm.
Subjects: Asian Development Bank.
LC Classification: HG4517 .A832 1976
Dewey Class No.: 332.1/53 19

Asian Development Bank: questions and answers.
[Manila]: The Bank, 1975.
Description: 55 p.; 23 cm.
Subjects: Asian Development Bank.
LC Classification: HG4517 .A832 1975
Dewey Class No.: 332.1/53 19

Assessing development effectiveness: evaluation in the World Bank and the International Finance Corporation.
Washington, D.C.: World Bank, [1994]
Description: vi, 37 p.: ill.; 23 cm.
ISBN: 0821328336
Notes: Includes bibliographical references.
Subjects: World Bank. International Finance Corporation. Economic development projects--Evaluation.
LC Classification: HC79.E44 A88 1994
Dewey Class No.: 332.1/532 20

Assessing development effectiveness: evaluation in the World Bank and the International Finance Corporation / World Bank Operations Evaluation Department.
Washington, D.C.: World Bank, 1998.
Description: vi, 79 p.: ill.; 26 cm.
Notes: Includes bibliographical references.
Subjects: World Bank. International Finance Corporation. Economic

development projects--Evaluation.
LC Classification: HC79.E44 A88 1998
Dewey Class No.: 332.1/532 21
Balance of payments yearbook.
Washington.
Description: v. 29 cm.
Current Frequency: Irregular
Continued by: SERLOC succeeding entry: Balance of payments tatistics. Yearbook
Subjects: Balance of trade.
LC Classification: HF1014 .I5
Entry: International Monetary Fund. Balance of payments yearbook
Balance of payments yearbook.
Washington.
Description: v. 29 cm.
Subjects: Balance of trade.
LC Classification: HF1014 .I5

Assetto, Valerie J.
The Soviet bloc in the IMF and the IBRD / Valerie J. Assetto.
Boulder: Westview Press, 1988.
Description: xi, 208 p.; 23 cm.
ISBN: 0813372364 (pbk.: alk. paper) :
Notes: Includes index. Bibliography: p. 195-202.
Subjects: International Monetary Fund--Europe, Eastern. World Bank--Europe, Eastern. Loans, Foreign--Europe, Eastern.
Series: Westview special studies in international economics
LC Classification: HG3881.5.I58 A76 1988
Dewey Class No.: 332.1/52 19

Auboin, Roger, 1891-
The Bank for International Settlements, 1930-1955.
Princeton, International Finance Section, Dept. of Economics and Sociology, Princeton University, 1955.
Description: 38 p. illus. 23 cm.
Subjects: Bank for International Settlements.
LC Classification: HG136 .P7 no. 22

Aufricht, Hans,
The Fund agreement: living law and emerging practice.
Princeton, N.J., International Finance Section, ept. Of Economics, Princeton University, 1969.
Description: 96 p. 23 cm.
Notes: Bibliographical footnotes.

Subjects: International Monetary Fund.
Series: Princeton studies in international finance, no. 23
LC Classification: HG3881 .A85
Dewey Class No.: 332.1/52

Aufricht, Hans,
The International Monetary Fund; legal bases, structure, functions.
New York, F. A. Praeger [1964]
Description: 126 p. 23 cm.
Notes: Bibliographical footnotes.
Subjects: International Monetary Fund.
Series: The Library of world affairs, no. 63
LC Classification: HG3881 .I639
Dewey Class No.: 332.15

Aufricht, Hans,
Central banking legislation; a collection of central bank, monetary, and banking laws.
Washington, International Monetary Fund, 1961-7.
Description: 2 v. 24 cm.
Contents: [v. 1] Statutes and related materials selected and annotated by Hans Aufricht. Pref. by Per Jacobsson. -- v. 2. Europe; statutes and related materials selected and annotated by Hans Aufricht with the assistance of Jane B. Evensen. Pref. by Pierre-Paul Schweitzer.
Notes: Includes bibliographies.
Subjects: Banks and banking, Central--Law and legislation.
Series: International Monetary Fund monograph series, no. 1,
LC Classification: LAW
Dewey Class No.: 340

Avramovic, Dragoslav.
Conditionality: facts, theory, and policy / Dragoslav Avramovic.
Helsinki, Finland: World Institute for Development
Economics Research, United Nations University, c1989.
Description: 33 p.; 25 cm.
ISBN: 9529011776
Notes: Includes bibliographical references.
Subjects: International Monetary Fund. World Bank. Loans, Foreign--Developing countries. Conditionality (International relations) Developing countries--Economic policy.
Series: WIDER research for action.
LC Classification: MLCM 92/14023 (H)

Awad, Mohamed Hashim.

The Sudan and the IMF / by Mohamed Hashim Awad.
[Khartoum]: Khartoum University Press, [1992]
Description: 193 p.; 23 cm.
Notes: Includes bibliographical references.
Subjects: International Monetary Fund--Sudan. International Monetary Fund--Egypt. Finance--Sudan. Privatization--Sudan.
Series: DSRC book series; no.6.
LC Classification: HG46 .A93 1992

Aylward, L.

Countries repayment performance vis-a-vis the IMF - A response to Backer
International Monetary Fund Staff Papers, 1999, Vol 46, Iss 2, pp 242-243

Aylward, L. and Thorne, R.

Countries' repayment performance vis-a-vis the IMF - An empirical analysis
International Monetary Fund Staff Papers, 1998, Vol 45, Iss 4, pp 595-618
While the literature oil external debt repayment performance by sovereign debtors is extensive, repayment performance vis-a-vis the International Monetary Fund has nor been dealt with separately. Given differences between the IMF and other providers of financial resources, this paper considers whether it is possible to distinguish through legit analysis between the countries that make timely repayments to the Fund and those that became overdue. The paper finds that the inclusion of IMF-specific financial variables and a small number of macroeconomic variables yields a highly significant Econometric model of the probability of a country incurring IMF arrears. [JEL F33, F34].

Ayres, Leonard Porter

The international monetary fund;
New York, N.Y., Economists' national committee on monetary policy [1944]
Description: 1 p.l., 5-14 p. 22 cm.
Subjects: International monetary fund (Proposed) [from old atalog]
LC Classification: HG255 .A86

Ayres, Robert L.

Banking on the poor: the World Bank and world poverty /
Robert L. Ayres.
Cambridge, Mass.: MIT Press, c1983.
Description: xiv, 282 p.; 24 cm.
ISBN: 0262010704
Notes: Includes bibliographical references and index.
Subjects: World Bank.
LC Classification: HG3881.5.W57 A96 1983

Dewey Class No.: 332.1/532 19

Azam, M. Z.
Bank operations in the fisheries sector.
Manila, Philippines: Asian Development Bank, [198-?]
Description: vii, 66 p.: col. maps; 22 cm.
Notes: "Prepared jointly by Messrs. M.Z. Azam, Richard E. Schatz, and Robert C. May"-T.p. verso.
Subjects: Asian Development Bank. Fisheries--Asia--Finance. Fisheries--Pacific Ocean--Finance.
Series: A Bank staff working paper
LC Classification: SH295 .A93 1980z
Dewey Class No.: 332.1/53 19

Backer, A.
Countries' repayment performance vis-a-vis the IMF - A comment on Aylward and Thorne
International Monetary Fund Staff Papers, 1999, Vol 46, Iss 2, pp 238-241

Badru, Pade.
International banking and rural development: The World Bank in Sub-Saharan Africa / Pade Badru.
Aldershot, Hants, England; Brookfield, Vt.: Ashgate, c1998.
Description: xi, 160 p.; 23 cm.
ISBN: 1840143053
Notes: Includes bibliographical references (p. 127-142) and index.
Subjects: World Bank--Africa, Sub-Saharan. Rural development projects--Africa, Sub-Saharan--Finance. Structural adjustment (Economic policy)--Africa, Sub-Saharan. Africa, Sub-Saharan--Economic conditions--1960-
Series: The making of modern Africa
LC Classification: HN780.Z9 C622 1998
Dewey Class No.: 307.1/412/0967 21

Baird, Vanessa
Money: Currencies of Desire.
New Internationalist (Oxford, England) Oct. 1998, p28-30

Baird, Vanessa
Money: Money, Markets and Madness.
New Internationalist (Oxford, England) Oct. 1998, p7-8

Banerji, D.
A fundamental shift in the approach to international health by WHO, UNICEF, and the World Bank: Instances of the practice of "intellectual fascism" and

totalitarianism in some Asian countries
International Journal of Health Services, 1999, Vol 29, Iss 2, pp 227-259
Navarro has used the term "intellectual fascism" to depict the intellectual situation in the McCarthy era. Intellectual fascism is now more malignant in the poor countries of the world. The Indian Subcontinent, China, and some other Asian countries provide the context. The struggles of the working class culminated in the Alma-Ata Declaration of self-reliance in health by the peoples of the world. To protect their commercial and political interests, retribution from the rich countries was sharp and swift, they "invented" Selective Primary Health Care and used WHO, UNICEF, the World Bank, and other agencies to let loose on poor countries a barrage of "international initiatives" as global programs on immunization, AIDS, and tuberculosis. These programs were astonishingly defective in concept, design, and implementation. The agencies refused to take note of such criticisms when they were published by others. They have been fascistic, ahistorical, grossly unscientific, and Goebbelsian propagandists. The conscience keepers of public health have mostly kept quiet.

Bank for international settlements.
[Geneva] Impr. Kundig, 1929.
Description: 18 p. 33 cm.
Subjects: Bank for international settlements.
LC Classification: HG1997.I6 L4 1920

Bank management in a changing domestic and international environment: the challenges of the eighties / edited by Donald E. Fair and François Léonard de Juvigny; with contributions from Raymond Bertrand ... [et al.].
The Hague; Boston: M. Nijhoff; Hingham, MA :
Distributor for the U.S.A. and Canada, Kluwer Boston, 1982.
Editor: Fair, Donald E. Juvigny, François Léonard de. Société universitaire européenne de recherches financières.
Description: xii, 342 p.: ill.; 25 cm.
ISBN: 9024726069 (U.S.: Kluwer Boston)
Notes: "Papers ... presented at the ninth colloquium arranged by the Société universitaire européenne de recherches financières (SUERF), which took place at Helsingør,
Denmark, in October 1980--P. ix.
Subjects: Banks and banking. Banks and banking, International. Bank management.
Series: Financial and monetary policy studies; 6
LC Classification: HG1591 .B34 1982
Dewey Class No.: 332.1/068 19

Banken: Erfahrungen und Lehren aus einem Vierteljahrhundert, 1958-1983 / [Herausgeber, Landesbank Rheinland-Pfalz, Girozentrale, Mainz].

Frankfurt am Main: Knapp, c1983.
Editor: Landesbank Rheinland-Pfalz Girozentrale.
Description: 216 p.; 25 cm.
ISBN: 3781902978 :
Notes: One article in English.
Includes bibliographical references and indexes.
Subjects: Landesbank Rheinland-Pfalz Girozentrale. Banks and banking—Germany (West) Banks and banking, International. Finance--Germany (West) International finance.
LC Classification: HG3048 .B27 1983

Bankers with a mission: the presidents of the World Bank, 1946-91 / Jochen Kraske ... [et al.].
New York: Oxford University Press, c1996.
Editor: Kraske, Jochen, 1932-
Description: ix, 333 p., [16] p. of plates: ill.; 24 cm.
ISBN: 019521112X
Notes: Includes bibliographical references (p. 289-322) and index.
Subjects: World Bank--Presidents--Biography. World Bank--History. Bankers--Biography.
LC Classification: HG3881.5.W57 B367 1996
Dewey Class No.: 332.1/532/0922 B 20

Banking in a global economy: economic benefits to the United States from the activities of international banks / Institute of International Bankers.
[New York, N.Y.]: The Institute, [1993]
Editor: Institute of International Bankers.
Description: iii, 78 p.: ill.; 28 cm.
Notes: Cover title. "September 1993." Includes bibliographical references.
Subjects: Banks and banking, International. Banks and banking--United States.
LC Classification: HG3881 .B3513 1993
Dewey Class No.: 332.1/5/0973 20

Banking in the 1970's: lectures and proceedings at the 23rd International Banking Summer School held at Christ Church, Oxford, July 1970.
London, Institute of Bankers, 1970.
Editor: Oxford. University. Christ Church.
Institute of Bankers, London.
Description: 170 p. illus., ports. 23 cm.
ISBN: 0852970064 :
Subjects: Banks and banking. Banks and banking, International.
LC Classification: HG1591 .I53 1970
Dewey Class No.: 332.1

Banking on poverty: the global impact of the IMF & World
Bank / edited by Jill Torrie; with a foreword by Mel Watkins.
[Toronto, Ont., Canada]: Between the Lines, [c1983]
Description: 336 p.; 24 cm.
ISBN: 0919946380 0919946399 (pbk.)
Notes: Papers of a conference held at the University of Toronto, Sept. 1982.
Bibliography: p. 330-336.
Subjects: International Monetary Fund--Congresses. World Bank--Congresses. International finance--Congresses. Developing countries--Economic conditions--Congresses.
Series: Perspectives on underdevelopment
LC Classification: HG3881.5.I58 B36 1983
Dewey Class No.: 332.1/52 19

Banking soundness and monetary policy: issues and experiences in the global economy: papers presented t the Seventh Seminar on Central Banking / editors, Charles Enoch, John H. Green.
Washington: IMF Institute and Monetary and exchange Affairs Dept., International Monetary Fund, 1997.
Editor: Enoch, Charles. Green, John Huss,
Description: xii, 542 p.: ill.; 23 cm.
ISBN: 1557756457
Notes: Includes bibliographical references.
Subjects: Banks and banking--Congresses. Monetary policy--Congresses. Banks and banking, Central--Congresses. Banks and banking--State supervision--Congresses.
LC Classification: HG1521 .C42 1997
Dewey Class No.: 332.4/6 21

Banks [sound recording].
Washington, D.C.: National Public Radio, p1980.
Description: 1 sound cassette (59 min.): analog.
Publisher Number: OP-801205 National Public Radio
Summary: Reporter David Selvin explores the banking industry by talking with people involved in banking, from the passbook holder to the director of policy planning for the World Bank, in an effort to clarify how banks work and how they are changing.
Notes: Originally broadcast Dec. 5, 1980, on the National Public Radio program entitled Options.
Cast: Producer, narrator, David Selvin.
Subjects: World Bank. Banks and banking.
LC Classification: HG1573 RYA 7192

Banks and bad debts: accounting for loan losses in international banking / Vivien A. Beattie ... [et al.].
Chichester [England]; New York: Wiley, c1995.
Editor: Beattie, Vivien A.
Description: viii, 201 p.; 24 cm.
ISBN: 0471953172
Notes: Includes bibliographical references and index.
Subjects: Loan loss reserves. Banks and banking, International.
LC Classification: HG1656.A3 B36 1995

Banks and money: international and comparative finance in history / edited by Geoffrey Jones.
London [England]; Portland, Or.: Frank Cass, 1991.
Editor: Jones, Geoffrey.
Description: ix, 198 p.: ill.; 23 cm.
ISBN: 0714634441
Notes: "First appeared in a special issue of Business history, vol. XXXIII, no. 3 (July 1991)"--T.p. verso. Includes bibliographical references and index.
Subjects: Banks and banking--History. Banks and banking, International--History.
LC Classification: HG1569 .B36 1991
Dewey Class No.: 332.1/09 20

Barratt Brown, Michael.
Africa's choices: after thirty years of the World Bank / Michael Barratt Brown.
Boulder, Colo.: Westview Press, 1996.
Description: xiv, 433 p.: map; 24 cm.
ISBN: 0813333334 (alk. paper) 0813333342 (alk. paper)
Notes: Includes bibliographical references (p. [369]-414) and indexes..
Subjects: World Bank--Africa. Africa--Economic conditions.
LC Classification: HC800 .B366 1996
Dewey Class No.: 338.96 21

Barratt Brown, Michael.
Short changed: Africa and world trade / Michael Barratt Brown and Pauline Tiffen; foreword by Susan George.
London; Boulder, Colo.: Pluto Press; Amsterdam : Transnational Institute (TNI), 1992.
Description: xix, 220 p.: ill., maps; 23 cm.
ISBN: 0745306942 (hbk) 0745306993 (pbk)
Notes: Includes bibliographical references (p. 143-155) and index.
Subjects: World Bank--Africa, Sub-Saharan. Exports--Africa, Sub-Saharan. Foreign trade promotion--Africa, Sub-Saharan. Structural adjustment (Economic policy)--Africa, Sub-Saharan. Natural resources--Africa, Sub-Saharan.

Series: Transnational Institute series
LC Classification: HF3876.5 .B37 1992
Dewey Class No.: 382/.0967 20

Barros, Henrique M. de.
Para compreender e dialogar com organismos internacionais : um guia sobre o Banco Mundial no Brasil e no mundo / Henrique M. de Barros, Michael Bailey.
Recife, PE: OXFAM Brasil; Brasília, DF: Instituto de Estudos Sócio-Econômicos, 1995.
Description: 62 p.; 30 cm.
Notes: "Setembro de 1995." Includes bibliographical references (p. 43-44).
Subjects: World Bank--Brazil.
LC Classification: HG3881.5.W57 B37 1995

Barth, Boris.
Die deutsche Hochfinanz und die Imperialismen: Banken und Aussenpolitik vor 1914 / Boris Barth.
Stuttgart: Steiner, 1995.
Description: 505 p.; 23 cm.
ISBN: 3515066659
Notes: Originally presented as the author's thesis (doctoral)--Universität Düsseldorf. Includes bibliographical references (p. [464]-491) and index.
Subjects: Banks and banking--Germany--History. Banks and banking, International--History. International finance--History. Germany--Foreign relations--1871-1918.
Series: Beiträge zur Kolonial- und Überseegeschichte; Bd. 61
LC Classification: HG3048 .B296 1995

Baru, R. and Jessani, A.
The role of the World Bank in international health: renewed commitment and partnership
Social Science & Medicine, 2000, Vol 50, Iss 2, pp 183-184

Baum, Warren C.
Investing in development: lessons of World Bank experience / Warren C. Baum and Stokes M. Tolbert.
New York: Published for the World Bank [by] Oxford University Press, c1985.
Description: xiv, 610 p.: ill.; 27 cm.
ISBN: 0195204751 019520476X (pbk.)
Notes: Includes bibliographical references and index.
Subjects: World Bank--Developing countries. Investments, Foreign--Developing countries.
LC Classification: HG3881.5.W57 B38 1985

Dewey Class No.: 332.1/532/091724 19

Beach, William W.

How realiable are IMF economic forecasts? / William . Beach, Aaron B. Schavey, and Isabel M. Isidro.

Wash., DC: Heritage Foundation, [1999]

Description: 21 p.: ill.; 28 cm.

Notes: "August 27, 1999"--P. [1]. "CDA99-05"--P. [1]. Includes bibliographical references.

Subjects: International Monetary Fund. Economic forecasting.

Series: Report of the Heritage Center for Data Analysis

LC Classification: HG3881.5.I58 B4 1999

Dewey Class No.: 330.9/001/12 21

Beeson, M.

Reshaping regional institutions: APEC and the IMF in East Asia

Pacific Review, 1999, Vol 12, Iss 1, pp 1-24

One of the most striking aspects of attempts to manage the crisis in East Asia has been the very different roles played by APEC and the IMF, Although both organizations have similar market-centred reform agendas, APEC has been conspicuous by its absence in the wake of the crisis. This paper considers the actions of both organizations and their very different approaches to institutional reform. It is suggested that the crisis in general and the actions of these two organizations in particular provides a timely opportunity to review the more influential varieties of institutional theory to see whether they provide either useful tools for understanding the roles and activities of APEC and the IMF, or plausible models of reform for policy-makers.

Behrendt, Jens Reiner, 1964-

Die Asiatische Entwicklungsbank: Organisation, Funktionsbedingungen, entwicklungspolitische Schwerpunkte / Jens Reiner Behrendt.

Hamburg: Institut für Asienkunde Hamburg, 1992.

Description: 117 p.; 21 cm.

ISBN: 3889101003

Notes: Summary in English. Includes bibliographical references (p. 111-117).

Subjects: Asian Development Bank.

Series: Mitteilungen des Instituts für Asienkunde Hamburg; Nr. 205

LC Classification: DS1 .I55 Nr. 205 HG3881.5.A75

Bello, Walden F.

Dark victory: the United States, structural adjustment, and global poverty / Walden Bello with Shea Cunningham and Bill Rau.

London: Pluto; Oakland: Food First; Amsterdam: TNI, 1994.

Description: xii, 148 p.: ill., map; 23 cm.

ISBN: 0745308333 0935028625 (pbk.) :
Notes: Includes bibliographical references (p. 142-143) and index.
Subjects: International Monetary Fund--Developing countries. World Bank--Developing countries. Structural adjustment (Economic policy)—Developing countries. Poverty--Developing countries. Supply-side economics--United States. Economic history--1971-1990. United States--Economic policy--1981-1993. United States--Foreign economic relations—Developing countries. Developing countries--Foreign economic relations—United States.
Series: Transnational Institute series
LC Classification: HC59.7 .B3873 1994
Dewey Class No.: 337.73 20

Bello, Walden F.

Development debacle, the World Bank in the Philippines / Walden Bello, David Kinley, Elaine Elinson.
San Francisco, CA: Institute for Food and Development Policy ; [Oakland, Calif.]: Philippine Solidarity Network, c1982.
Description: xvi, 256 p.; 22 cm.
ISBN: 0935028129 (pbk.) :
Contents: Introduction: cracking the World Bank -- Colonization without an occupation force / by Walden Bello, David Kinley and Elaine Elinson -- The making of McNamara's second Vietnam / by Walden Bello, David Kinley, and Elaine Elinson -- Containment in the countryside / by Walden Bello, David Kinley, and Vincent Bielski -- Counterinsurgency in the city / by Walden Bello and Vincent Bielski -- Export-oriented industrialization, the short-lived illusion / by Walden Bello, David O'Connor, and Robin Broad -- Structural and other adjustments / by Robin Broad and Walden Bello -- Technocrats versus cronies / by Walden Bello, David O'Connor, and Robin Broad -- Conclusion: development debacle.
Notes: Includes index. Bibliography: p. [243]-244.
Subjects: World Bank--Philippines. Economic assistance--Philippines. Investments, Foreign--Philippines. Philippines--Economic conditions--1946-1986.
LC Classification: HC455 .D487 1982
Dewey Class No.: 332.1/532/09599 19

Bench, Robert R.

A framework and new techniques for international bank supervision / by Robert R. Bench.
Washington, D.C.: Comptroller of the Currency, Administrator of National Banks, [1982]
Description: 1 v. (various pagings); 28 cm.
Notes: "Multinational Banking Division." "Presented at the Central Banking Seminar International Monetary Fund, Washington, D.C., June 28-July 1.

Includes bibliography.
Subjects: Banks and banking, International--State supervision.
LC Classification: HG1725 .B46 1982
Dewey Class No.: 353.0082/52043 19

Bergsten, Fred
The Dollar and the Euro C..
Foreign Affairs July/Aug. 1997,

Beyond Bretton Woods: alternatives to the global economic order / edited by John Cavanagh, Daphne Wysham, and Marcos Arruda; [foreword by Susan George]. London; Boulder, Colo.: Pluto Press; Washington, DC, USA: Institute for Policy Studies; Amsterdam : Transnational Institute (TNI), 1994.
Editor: Cavanagh, John,
Description: xviii, 238 p.; 22 cm.
ISBN: 0745308902 (cloth)
Notes: Commemorates the 50th anniversary of the Bretton Woods agreement, which established the World Bank, the IMF, and the international banking system. Includes bibliographical references and index.
Subjects: World Bank. International Monetary Fund. International finance. Sustainable development. Economic history--1990-
Series: Transnational Institute series
LC Classification: HG3881 .B49 1994
Dewey Class No.: 332.1/5 20

Bhattarai, M.
World Development Report, 1997: The state in a changing world by World-Bank
Journal of Economic Issues, 1999, Vol 33, Iss 1, pp 204-208

Binswanger, Hans P.
The World Bank's strategy for reducing poverty and hunger : a report to the development community / prepared by Hans P. Binswanger and Pierre Landell-Mills; foreword by Lewis T. Preston; preface by Ismail Serageldin..
Washington, D.C.: World Bank, c1995.
Description: xi, 56 p.; 29 cm.
ISBN: 0821331744
Notes: Includes bibliographical references (p. 55-56).
Subjects: World Bank--Developing countries. Food supply--Developing countries. Food relief--Developing countries. Poor--Developing countries.
Series: Environmentally sustainable development studies and monographs series; no. 4.
LC Classification: HG3881.5.W57 W696 1995
Dewey Class No.: 332.1/532 20

Bird, G.

Crisis averter, crisis lender, crisis manager: The IMF in search of a systemic role
World Economy, 1999, Vol 22, Iss 7, pp 955-975

Bird, Graham R.

IMF lending to developing countries: issues and evidence / Graham Bird.
London; New York: Routledge, 1995.
Description: x, 190 p.: ill.; 22 cm.
ISBN: 0415117003
Notes: Includes bibliographical references (p. 179-184) and index.
Subjects: International Monetary Fund. Debts, External--Developing countries. Loans, Foreign--Developing countries.
Series: Development policy studies
LC Classification: HG3881.5.I58 B525 1995
Dewey Class No.: 332.1/52 20

Bird, Graham R.

International financial policy and economic development : a disaggregated approach / Graham Bird.
New York: St. Martin's Press, 1987.
Description: xvi, 348: ill.; 23 cm.
ISBN: 031242213X :
Notes: Includes index. Bibliography: p. 338-343.
Subjects: International Monetary Fund--Developing countries. International finance. Finance--Developing countries.
LC Classification: HG3881 .B536 1987
Dewey Class No.: 332/.042/091724 19

Bird, Graham R.

The Bretton Woods institutions: a Commonwealth perspective: a paper prepared for the Commonwealth Secretariat / by Graham Bird and Tony Killick.
London: Commonwealth Secretariat, 1995.
Description: 46 p.; 28 cm.
ISBN: 085092443X
Notes: Includes bibliographical references (p. 43-46).
Subjects: World Bank. International Monetary Fund. Financial institutions, International.
Series: Commonwealth economic papers; no. 24
LC Classification: HG3881 .B5358 1995

Bird, Graham R.

The IMF and the developing countries: devolving relations, use of resources and the debate over conditionality / Graham Bird.
London: Overseas Development Institute, 1981.

Description: 37 p.; 30 cm.
ISBN: 0850030749 (pbk.)
Notes: Bibliography: p. 34-37.
Subjects: International Monetary Fund. Balance of payments--Developing countries. Finance--Developing countries. Conditionality (International relations)
Series: ODI working paper; no. 2
LC Classification: HG3890 .B57 1981
Dewey Class No.: 332.1/52 19

Birnbaum, Eugene A.
Changing the United States commitment to gold [by] Eugene A. Birnbaum.
Princeton, N.J., International Finance Section, Dept. of Economics, Princeton University [1967]
Description: 30 p. 23 cm.
Subjects: International Monetary Fund. Gold standard. Balance of payments—United States.
Series: Essays in international finance; no. 63.
LC Classification: HG136 .P7 no. 63
Dewey Class No.: 332.1/52

BIS economic papers.
Basle: Bank for International Settlements, 1979-
Editor: Bank for International Settlements. Monetary and Economic Dept.
No. 1 (Nov. 1979)-
Subjects: Banks and banking, International. International finance.
LC Classification: HG3879 .B57

Blair, Tony
A New International Financial System.
Vital Speeches of the Day Oct. 15, 1998, p2-4

Block, Fred
Controlling Global Finance.
World Policy Journal Fall 1996, p24-34

Born, Karl Erich.
Geld und Banken im 19. und 20. Jahrhundert / Karl Erich Born.
Edition Information: 1. Aufl.
Stuttgart: Kröner, 1977.
Description: 663 p.; 18 cm.
ISBN: 3520428016 :
Notes: Includes bibliographical references and indexes.
Subjects: Finance--History. Money--History. Banks and banking--History. Banks and banking, International--History.

LC Classification: HG171 .B67
Dewey Class No.: 332/.09

Born, Karl Erich.
International banking in the 19th and 20th centuries /
Karl Erich Born; translated from the German by Volker R. Berghahn.
Description: 353 p.; 23 cm.
ISBN: 0907582036 0907582044 (pbk.)
Notes: Includes indexes. Bibliography: p. 317-323.
Subjects: Finance--History. Money--History. Banks and banking--History. Banks and banking, International--History. International finance--History.
LC Classification: HG171 .B6713 1983
Dewey Class No.: 332/.09 21

Bortolani, Sergio.
Le funzioni monetarie della Banca dei regolamenti internazionali.
Milano, A. Giuffrè, 1968.
Description: 65 p. 25 cm.
Subjects: Bank for International Settlements.
Series: Milan. Università commerciale Luigi Bocconi. Istituto di economia aziendale. Pubblicazioni, ser. 6, n. 12.
LC Classification: HG1997.I6 B57

Bosch, Johannes Hendrik Otto van den, jonkheer, 1906-
Beschouwingen over de Bank voor internationale betalingen
Den Haag, N. v. de Zuid-hollandsche boek- en handelsdrukkerij, 1931.
Description: 4 p. l., 159 p. 24 cm.
Subjects: Bank for international settlements.
LC Classification: HG1997.I6 B6 1931

Böttger, Günter.
Das Recht der Auslandsbanken in den USA nach dem International banking act 1978, mit Übersetzung des International banking act 1978 / von Günter Böttger und Klaus Uebe.
Frankfurt am Main: F. Knapp, c1982.
United States. International banking act of 1978. 1982.
Description: 152 p.; 21 cm.
ISBN: 3781927105 :
Notes: Includes index. Bibliography: p. 147-149.
Subjects: Banks and banking, Foreign--Law and legislation—United States. Banks and banking, International.
Series: Schriften zum deutschen und ausländischen Geld-, Bank- und Börsenrecht; Bd. 1.
LC Classification: KF1001.5 .B67 1982

Dewey Class No.: 346.73/08215 347.3068215 19

Bouchet, Michel Henri.

Transnational banks and the external indebtedness of developing countries: impact of regulatory changes / United Nations Centre on Transnational Corporations.
New York: United Nations, 1992.
Centre on Transnational Corporations (United Nations)
Description: vi, 48 p.; 28 cm.
ISBN: 9211043883
Notes: "Prepared by Michel H. Bouchet and Azizul Islam"--P. iii. "ST/CTC/SER.A/22." "United Nations publication. Sales no. E.92.II.A.10"--T.p. verso. Includes bibliographical references (p. 41-46).
Subjects: Debt relief--Developing countries. Debts, External--Developing countries. Banks and banking, International.
LC Classification: HJ8899 .B68 1992
Dewey Class No.: 336.3/435/091724 20

Boughton, James M.

Fifty years after Bretton Woods: the future of the MF and the World Bank: proceedings of a conference held in Madrid, Spain, September 29-30, 1994 / James M. oughton and K. Sarwar Lateef, editors.
Washington, D.C.: International Monetary Fund, 995.
Description: xvi, 280 p.; 23 cm.
ISBN: 155775487X (pbk.)
Notes: Includes bibliographical references.
Subjects: World Bank. International Monetary Fund.
LC Classification: HG3881.5.W57 B68 1995
Dewey Class No.: 332.1/52 20

Boukrami, Sid-Ali.

Les mécanismes monétaires et financiers internationaux / Sid Ali Boukrami; préface de Boualem Benhamouda.
[Algiers]: Entreprise algérienne de presse: Entreprise nationale du livre, [1986]
Description: 319, [1] p.; 24 cm.
Notes: Cover Les mécanismes.
Bibliography: p. 312-[320]
Subjects: International finance. International economic relations. Banks and banking, International.
LC Classification: HG3881 .B626 1986

Boyce, James Edward,

Colombia's treatment of foreign banks: a precedent setting case? / James E. Boyce, François J. Lombard.

Washington: American Enterprise Institute for Public Policy Research, 1976.
Description: 56 p.: graphs; 23 cm.
ISBN: 0844732125 :
Notes: Includes bibliographical references.
Subjects: Banks and banking, Foreign--Colombia. Investments, Foreign--Colombia. Banks and banking, International.
Series: Foreign affairs study; 36
LC Classification: HG2905 .B68
Dewey Class No.: 332.1/5

Boyle, David
Money: Confessions of a Global Gambler.
New Internationalist (Oxford, England) Oct. 1998, p9-11

Brahmananda, P. R.
The IMF loan and India's economic future / P.R. Brahmananda.
Edition Information: 1st ed.
Bombay: Himalaya Pub. House, 1982.
Description: viii, 95 p.; 23 cm.
Notes: Includes bibliographical references.
Subjects: International Monetary Fund--India. Loans, Foreign--India. India--Economic conditions--1947-
LC Classification: HG3971 .B7 1982
Dewey Class No.: 338.91/0954 19

Branford, Sue.
The debt squads: the US, the banks, and Latin America / Sue Branford, Bernardo Kucinski.
London; Atlantic Highlands, N.J.: Zed Books, 988.
Description: xvii, 142 p.: ill.; 22 cm.
ISBN: 0862327903 0862327911 (pbk.)
Notes: Translation of: A ditadura da divida. Includes bibliographies and index.
Subjects: International Monetary Fund--Latin America. Debts, External--Latin America. Loans, Foreign--Latin America. Latin America--Economic conditions--1982- United States--Foreign economic relations--Latin America. Latin America--Foreign economic relations--United States.
LC Classification: HJ8514.5 .B7313 1988
Dewey Class No.: 336.3/435/098 19

Bretton Woods revisited: evaluations of the International Monetary Fund and the International Bank for Reconstruction and Development: papers delivered at a conference at Queen's University, Kingston, Canada [on 2nd and 3rd June 1969] / edited by A. L. Keith Acheson, John F. Chant, Martin F. J. Prachowny.
London: Macmillan, 1972.

Editor: Acheson, Keith,
Description: xxiv, 141 p.; 24 cm.
ISBN: 0333135865 :
Notes: Includes bibliographical references.
Subjects: International Monetary Fund. World Bank. International finance--Congresses.
LC Classification: HG3881 .B674 1972b
Dewey Class No.: 332.1/52

Bretton Woods: looking to the future.
Washington, DC 1990 M St., NW, Washington: Bretton Woods Commission, 1994
Description: 2 v.: ill; 28 cm.
Contents: v. [1]. Commission report; Staff review; Background papers -- v. [2]. Conference proceedings, Washington, DC, July 20-22, 1994.
Notes: At head of Bretton Woods Commission. "July 1994"--V. [1]. "September 1994"--V. [2], p. 4 of cover. Volume 1 is the final report of the Commission. "This volume contains the proceedings of a concluding conference hosted by the Commission in Washington, C on July 20-22, 1994 ... held on the fiftieth anniversary of the original Bretton Woods conference .... The volume ... marks the completion of the Commission's formal work program"--V. 2, p. iii. Includes bibliographical references--
Subjects: World Bank--Congresses. International Monetary Fund--Congresses. United Nations Monetary and Financial Conference (1944: Bretton Woods, N.H.)--Congresses. Monetary policy--Congresses. International finance--Congresses. Economic development--International cooperation Congresses.
LC Classification: HG3881.5.W57 B74 1994

Brimmer, Andrew F.
The world banking system: outlook in a context of crisis / Andrew F. Brimmer.
New York: New York University Press, 1985.
Description: 59 p.; 22 cm.
ISBN: 0814710689 :
Subjects: Banks and banking, International. Debts, External--Developing countries. Default (Finance)--Developing countries.
Series: The Joseph I. Lubin memorial lectures; no. 1
LC Classification: HG3881 .B677 1985
Dewey Class No.: 332.1/5 19

Broad, Robin.
Unequal alliance: the World Bank, the International Monetary Fund, and the Philippines / Robin Broad.
Berkeley: University of California Press, c1988.
Description: xxvii, 352 p.: ill.; 24 cm.

ISBN: 0520059050
Notes: Includes index. Bibliography: p. 239-337.
Subjects: World Bank--Philippines. International Monetary Fund--Philippines. Philippines--Economic policy.
Series: Studies in international political economy; 19
LC Classification: HG3881.5.W57 B76 1988
Dewey Class No.: 332.1/52 19

Broad, Robin.
Unequal alliance: the World Bank, the International Monetary Fund, and the Philippines / Robin Broad.
Berkeley: University of California Press, c1988.
Description: xxvii, 352 p.: ill.; 24 cm.
ISBN: 0520059050
Notes: Includes index. Bibliography: p. 239-337.
Subjects: World Bank--Philippines. International Monetary Fund--Philippines. Philippines--Economic policy.
Series: Studies in international political economy; 19
LC Classification: HG3881.5.W57 B76 1988
Dewey Class No.: 332.1/52 19

Brosset, Michel.
Multinationale Bankenverflechtungen: joint Ventures und Partnerschaften / von Michel Brosset.
Bern: P. Haupt, c1983.
Description: vii, 245 p.: ill.; 23 cm.
ISBN: 3258032750 :
Notes: Bibliography: p. 238-245.
Subjects: Banks and banking, International. Joint ventures. Investments.
Series: Bankwirtschaftliche Forschungen; Bd. 79
LC Classification: HG1526 .B27 Bd. 79 HG3881

Brown, Richard.
The IMF and Paris Club debt rescheduling: a conflicting role? / Richard Brown.
The Hague, Netherlands: Publications Office, Institute of Social Studies, [1990]
Description: 23 p.; 30 cm.
Notes: Includes bibliographical references (p. 22-23).
Subjects: International Monetary Fund. Paris Club. Debt relief--Developing countries. Debts, External--Developing countries.
Series: Working papers series (Institute of Social Studies (Netherlands)). Sub-series on money, finance, and development; no. 30.
LC Classification: HC59.69 .W654 no. 30 HJ8899

Dewey Class No.: 336.3/435/091724 20

Browne, Christopher, 1944-

Pacific island IMF member countries: recent economic developments and medium-term prospects / Christopher Browne.

Washington, D.C.: International Monetary Fund, 995.

Description: 20 p.; 23 cm.

ISBN: 1557754713

Notes: "Presented ... at the Seminar on Economic developments in the Pacific Island Economies and the Role of the Fund, Pacific Island Development Program, East-West Center, University of Hawaii, November 4, 1994."--P. 1.

Subjects: International Monetary Fund--Islands of the Pacific Economic assistance. Islands of the Pacific--Economic conditions.

LC Classification: HC681 .B763 1995

Brüll, Mária.

Nemzetközi pénzügyi intézmények és magyarországi kapcsolataik / Brüll Mária.

Budapest: Közgazdasági és Jogi Könyvkiadó, 1993.

Description: 281, [1] p.; 24 cm.

ISBN: 9632226143:

Notes: Table of contents in English. Includes bibliographical references (p. 281-[282]).

Subjects: Financial institutions, International. Banks and banking, International. Finance-Hungary. Banks and banking--Hungary.

LC Classification: HG3851 .B78 1993

Brunet Jailly, J.

Has the World Bank a strategy on health?

International Social Science Journal, 1999, Vol 51, Iss 3, pp 347+

Bank has gradually defined its doctrine on health. The doctrine proves to be far more interesting that one might think. But for this very reason, its practical application, i.e. The strategy involved, raises formidable problems which the World Bank clearly acknowledges in its internal evaluations of the effectiveness of its interventions and when it tries to determine the means to improve that effectiveness. However, it is also necessary for the purpose of external evaluation to take into account the context in which loans have been negotiated over the last two decades. It is then found that, given the funding needs linked to structural adjustment, health programmes have been an ideal opportunity for investing huge amounts in aid.

Brützel, Christoph.

Offshore-Banking deutscher Banken unter besonderer Berücksichtigung des Euro-DM-Marktes und der Möglichkeiten einer Rapatriierung / von Christoph Brützel.

Frankfurt am Main: Knapp, c1985.
Description: 456 p.: ill.; 21 cm.
ISBN: 3781921190
Notes: Bibliography: p. 401-451.
Subjects: Banks and banking, International. Banks and banking, West German. Money market--Germany (West) Euro-dollar market.
Series: Veröffentlichungen des Instituts für Bankwirtschaft und Bankrecht an der Universität Köln. Wirtschaftswissenschaftliche Reihe; Bd. 33
LC Classification: HG3881 .B72 1985

Bryant, Elizabeth and others.
The Bank and the Fund
Earth Times Oct. 1-15, 1996, p7-14

Budhoo, Davison L.
Enough is enough: dear Mr. Camdessus-- open letter of resignation to the managing director of the International Monetary Fund / Davison L. Budhoo ; foreword by Errol K. McLeod.
New York: New Horizons Press, c1990.
Description: xii, 115 p.: ill.; 28 cm.
ISBN: 0945257287
Subjects: International Monetary Fund. International Monetary Fund--Trinidad and Tobago. International Monetary Fund--Developing countries. Trinidad and Tobago--Economic conditions--Statistics.
Series: Documentary sources for social change
LC Classification: HG3881.5.I58 B83 1990

Buira, Ariel.
An alternative approach to financial crises / Ariel Buira.
Princeton, N.J.: International Finance Section, Dept. of Economics, Princeton University, c1999.
Description: 30 p.; 23 cm.
ISBN: 0881651192
Notes: Includes bibliographical references (p. 25-26).
Subjects: International Monetary Fund. International finance.
Series: Essays in international finance, 0071-142X; no. 212
LC Classification: HG136 .P7 no. 212 HG3881.5.I58
Dewey Class No.: 332/.042 s 332.1/52 21

Buira, Ariel.
Reflections on the international monetary system
Princeton, N.J.: International Finance Section, Dept. of Economics, Princeton University, c1995.
Description: 46 p.; 23 cm.

ISBN: 0881651028 (pbk.)
Notes: Includes bibliographical references (p. 40-41).
Subjects: International Monetary Fund. International finance.
Series: Essays in international finance, 0071-142X; no. 195
LC Classification: HG136 .P7 no. 195 HG3881.I58
Dewey Class No.: 332.1/52 20

Burgers, I. J. J.

Taxation and supervision of branches of international banks: a comparative study of banks and other enterprises / I.J.J. Burgers.
Haren: I.J.J. Burgers, c1991.
Description: xx, 570 p.; 22 cm.
ISBN: 9070125579
Notes: "The commercial version of a Ph.D. study entitled The allocation of fiscal profits of internationally operating banking enterprises ... "--T.p. verso.
Includes bibliographical references (p. 535-554) and index.
Subjects: Banks and banking, International. Banks and banking, Foreign--Taxation. Banks and banking--Europe--State supervision. Banks and banking--United States--State supervision.
LC Classification: HG3881 .B85 1991
Dewey Class No.: 332.1/5 20

Burk, Kathleen.

Goodbye, Great Britain: the 1976 IMF crisis / Kathleen Burk & Alec Cairncross.
New Haven: Yale University Press, 1992.
Description: xix, 268 p.: ill.; 25 cm.
ISBN: 0300057288
Notes: Includes bibliographical references (p. 254-259) and index.
Subjects: International Monetary Fund--Great Britain. Monetary policy--Great Britain. Great Britain--Economic policy--1964-1979. Great Britain--Politics and government--1964-1979.
LC Classification: HG939.5 .B87 1992
Dewey Class No.: 332.4/941 20

Burnham, J.B.

The IMF and world banks: Time to merge
Washington Quarterly, 1999, Vol 22, Iss 2, pp 101-111

Buscemi, Salvatore.

Le banche multinazionali / Salvatore Buscemi.
Roma: Bulzoni, [1975]
Description: 230 p.; 22 cm.
Notes: "Appendice" (p. 187-223): Notizie sull'attività bancaria internazionale nel 1973. Bibliography: p. 225-230.

Subjects: Banks and banking, International.
LC Classification: HG3881 .B86
National Bib. No.: It75-May

Buse, K. and Walt, G.
Role conflict? The World Bank and the world's health
Social Science & Medicine, 2000, Vol 50, Iss 2, pp 177-179

Butler, Nick.
The IMF, time for reform / Nick Butler.
London: Fabian Society, [1982]
Description: 29 p.; 22 cm.
ISBN: 0716320509 (pbk.)
Notes: Cover title. "January 1982"--Verso t.p.
Subjects: International Monetary Fund.
Series: Young Fabian pamphlet; 50
LC Classification: HX11 .F35 no. 50 HG3881.5.I58
Dewey Class No.: 300 s 332.1/52 19

Cahiers BEI / Banque européenne d'investissement = EIB papers / European Investment Bank.
[Luxembourg]: La Banque, 1986-
Description: v.; 30 cm. Issues for févr. 1986-sept. 1987 are unnumbered; numbering began with no. 5, févr. 1988. Févr. 1986- Ceased in 1996.
Current Frequency: Irregular
Continued by: EIB papers (DLC) 97641353 (OCoLC)36368159
ISSN: 0257-7755
Notes: English and French. SERBIB/SERLOC merged record
Subjects: Capital investments--European Economic Community countries Periodicals. Capital investments--European Union countries Periodicals. International finance--Periodicals. Banks and banking, International--Periodicals.
LC Classification: WMLC 93/2814
Entry: Cahiers BEI. sf93-95293

Caiola, Marcello.
A manual for country economists / Marcello Caiola.
Washington, D.C., U.S.A.: IMF Institute and Research Dept., International Monetary Fund, 1995-
Description: v. 1: ill.; 28 cm.
ISBN: 1557754608 (v. 1: alk. paper)
Notes: Includes bibliographical references.
Subjects: International Monetary Fund--Handbooks, manuals, tc. Finance, Public--Handbooks, manuals, etc. Finance--Handbooks, manuals, etc.
Series: Training series (International Monetary Fund); no. 1.

LC Classification: HJ131 .C34 1995
Dewey Class No.: 332.1/52 20

Cal, Marie-Line.
La banque des banques: l'assurance de liquidité: la fonction de prêteur en dernier ressort des banques centrales / [Marie-Line Cal; préface de Henri Bourguinat; postface de Robert Raymond].
Mont de Marsan [France]: Editions InterUniversitaires, c1995.
Description: 492 p.: ill.; 23 cm.
ISBN: 2878170482
Notes: Statement of responsibility from jacket. Includes bibliographical references (p. 433-454).
Subjects: Liquidity (Economics) Lenders of last resort. Banks and banking, International.
LC Classification: HG1656.A3 C26 1995

Calomiris, Charles W.
How to Invent a New IMF.
International Economy Jan./Feb. 1999, p32+

Calvo, Sara.
Capital flows to Latin America: is there evidence of contagion effects? / Sara Calvo and Carmen M. Reinhart.
Washington, DC: The World Bank, Economic Development Institute, Macroeconomic Management and Policy Division and International Monetary Fund, Western Hemisphere Dept., [1996]
Description: 20, [7] p.: ill.; 28 cm.
Notes: "June 1996"--Cover. Includes bibliographical references (p. 18-20).
Subjects: Investments, Foreign--Latin America. Stock exchanges--Latin America. Capital movements--Latin America.
Series: Policy research working papers; 1619.
LC Classification: HG3881.5.W57 P63 no. 1619

Camdessus, Michel,
Economic transformation in the fifteen republics of the former U.S.S.R.: a challenge or an opportunity for the world? / Michel Camdessus.
Washington, D.C.: International Monetary Fund, 1992]
Description: v, 10 p.: map; 28 cm.
ISBN: 1557753016
Notes: "Address to Georgetown University, School of Foreign Service, April 15, 1992."
Subjects: Economic forecasting--Former Soviet Republics. Former Soviet Republics--Economic policy.
LC Classification: HC336.26 .C36 1992

Dewey Class No.: 338.947 20

Camdessus, Michel, 1933-

Facing the globalized world economy: the IMF experience : four addresses / by Michel Camdessus.
Washington, D.C.: International Monetary Fund, Publication Services, [1996]
Description: vi, 52 p.; 23 cm.
ISBN: 1557756163
Contents: The dollar, the yen, and European currencies – adjustment to the global economy: lessons from Argentina -- Africa's recent accomplishments and future challenges - The Group of Seven in 1996: what is at stake.
Notes: "October 1996." Includes bibliographical references.
Subjects: International economic relations. International finance.
LC Classification: HF1359 .C35 1996

Camdessus, Michel, 1933-

Navigating stormy, uncharted waters: five addresses by Michel Camdessus.
Washington, D.C.: International Monetary Fund, Publication Services, 1998.
Editor: International Monetary Fund.
Description: vii, 54 p.; 23 cm.
ISBN: 1557757623
Contents: Crisis in emerging market economies: the road to recovery -- Toward a new financial architecture for a globalized world -- The IMF and good governance – Rebuilding confidence in Asia -- Africa: a continent on the move.
Notes: "October 1998." Includes bibliographical references.
Subjects: International economic relations. International finance.

Camdessus, Michel, 1933-

The IMF and the challenges of globalization: three addresses / by Michel Camdessus.
Washington, D.C.: International Monetary Fund, Publications Services, 1995.
Description: v, 29 p.; 23 cm.
ISBN: 1557755302
Contents: Minimizing risks to sustainable growth -- Drawing lessons from the Mexican crisis: preventing and resolving financial crises: the role of the IMF – Addressing Africa's economic challenges.
Notes: "October 1995."
Subjects: International Monetary Fund. International finance. Monetary policy. Mexico--Economic conditions. Africa--Economic conditions.
LC Classification: HG3881.5.I58 C35 1995
Dewey Class No.: 332.1/52 20

Campos, Ricardo (Campos Alvarez Tostado)

El Fondo Monetario Internacional y la deuda externa mexicana: crisis y

estabilizaciûn / Ricardo Campos.
Edition Information: 2. ed.
[Mexico, D.F.]: Plaza y Valdès Editores, 1993.
Description: 276 p.: ill.; 21 cm.
ISBN: 9688562904
Notes: At head of Universidad Autûnoma del Estado de Mexico, UAEM.
Rev. ed. of: Fondo Monetario International, deuda externa mexiana [sic] y la administraciûn p˙blica. 1. ed. 1991; originally presented as the author's thesis (Ph.D.)--Universidad Nacional Autûnoma de Mexico. Includes bibliographical references (p. 269-273).
Subjects: International Monetary Fund--Mexico. Debts, External--Mexico. Debts, External--Latin America. Mexico--Economic policy. Latin America--Economic conditions--1945-
LC Classification: HC135 .C2137 1993

Campos, Ricardo (Campos Alvarez Tostado)
Fondo Monetario Internacional, deuda externa mexiana sic] y la administraciûn p˙blica / Ricardo Campos.
Edition Information: 1a. ed.
Toluca, Estado de Mèxico: Universidad Autûnoma el Estado de Mèxico, 1991.
Description: 283 p.; 21 cm.
ISBN: 9688351024
Notes: Includes bibliographical references (p. 247-283).
Subjects: International Monetary Fund--Mexico. Debts, External--Mexico. Debts, External--Latin America. Mexico--Economic policy. Latin America--Economic conditions--1945-
Series: Colecciûn Ciencias y tècnicas; 22
LC Classification: HC135 .C2137 1991

Canals, Jordi.
Universal banking: international comparisons and theoretical perspectives / Jordi Canals.
Oxford [England]; New York: Clarendon Press, 1997.
Description: xxii, 359 p.: ill.; 24 cm.
ISBN: 0198775067 0198775059 (pbk.)
Notes: Includes bibliographical references (p. [338]-351) and index.
Subjects: Universal banks. Banks and banking, International.
LC Classification: HG1601 .C26 1997
Dewey Class No.: 332.1 20

Capdevila, Irene.
El caso Graiver / Irene Capdevila.
[Buenos Aires, Argentina?]: Editorial Agora, 1984.
Description: 87 p.; 18 cm.

Notes: Includes bibliographies.
Subjects: Graiver, David, 1940 or 41-1976. Bankers--Argentina. Banks and banking, International.
Series: Temas antiimperialistas; 2
LC Classification: HG1552.G73 C37 1984
Dewey Class No.: 332.1/5/0924 19

Caprara, Giordano.
I regolamenti delle negoziazioni internazionali: valute e problemi valutari.
Varese-Milano [Italy]: Istituto editoriale cisalpino, 1969.
Description: 249 p.; 24 cm.
Notes: Includes bibliographical references.
Subjects: Foreign exchange--Law and legislation. Banks and banking, International.
LC Classification: LAW <Europe Italy 7 Capr 1969>

Capriglione, Francesco,
L'impresa bancaria tra controllo e autonomia: saggi sull'ordinamento del credito / Francesco Capriglione.
Milano: A. Giuffrè, 1983.
Description: 446 p.; 25 cm.
Notes: Includes bibliographical references.
Subjects: Banking law--Italy. Banks and banking--Italy. Banks and banking, International.
LC Classification: LAW
Dewey Class No.: 346.45/082 344.50682 19

Carmody, P.
Neoclassical practice and the collapse of industry in Zimbabwe: The cases of textiles, clothing, and footwear
Economic Geography, 1998, Vol 74, Iss 4, pp 319-343
The World Bank predicted that export-oriented, labor-intensive manufacturing industries, such as textiles, clothing, and footwear, would expand rapidly once Zimbabwe liberalized its economy under structural adjustment. In sharp contrast to these predictions, however, these subsectors have all but collapsed. A large part of the reason for this disjuncture between neoclassical theory and reality relates to a misunderstanding of the way in which markets, particularly those of trade and finance, interact with production in particular contexts. More appropriate alternative approaches to economic development in Africa must take account of how economic and political actions are embedded in a geographic and politico-economic context.

Carosso, Vincent P.
The Morgans: private international bankers, 1854-1913 / Vincent P. Carosso with

the assistance of Rose C. Carosso.
Cambridge, Mass.: Harvard University Press, 1987.
Description: xvi, 888 p., [12] p. of plates: ill.; 25 cm.
ISBN: 0674587294 (alk. paper)
Notes: Includes index. Bibliography: p. 649-653.
Subjects: Morgan, Junius Spencer, 1813-1890. Morgan, J. Pierpont (John Pierpont), 1837-1913. J.P. Morgan & Co.--History. Bankers--Biography. Banks and banking, International--History.
Series: Harvard studies in business history; 38
LC Classification: HG2463.A2 C37 1987
Dewey Class No.: 332.1/5/0922 B 19

Carreau, Dominique.
Le fonds monètaire international.
Paris, Colin [1970]
Description: 270 p. 18 cm.
Notes: Bibliography: p. 257-260.
Subjects: International Monetary Fund.
LC Classification: HG3881 .C316

Carreau, Dominique.
Le systËme monètaire international: aspects uridiques.
Paris, A. Colin [1972]
Description: 397p. 18cm.
Notes: Bibliography: p. 389-391.
Subjects: International Monetary Fund. Foreign exchange--Law and legislation. Balance of payments.
LC Classification: LAW <General Carr>

Carvalho, Soniya.
Implementing projects for the poor: what has been learned? / Soniya Carvalho, Howard White.
Washington, D.C.: World Bank, c1996.
Description: viii, 84 p.: ill.; 23 cm.
ISBN: 0821335316
Notes: Includes bibliographical references (p. 82-84).
Subjects: World Bank--Developing countries. Economic assistance--Developing countries--Evaluation. Economic development projects--Developing countries Evaluation. Poverty--Developing countries.
Series: Directions in development (Washington, D.C.)
LC Classification: HC59.72.P63 C37 1996
Dewey Class No.: 338.9/1/091724 20

Caufield, Catherine.
Masters of illusion: the World Bank and the poverty of nations / Catherine Caufield.
Edition Information: 1st ed.
New York: Henry Holt, 1996.
Description: xii, 432 p.; 24 cm.
ISBN: 0805028757 (alk. paper)
Notes: "A Marian Wood book."
Includes bibliographical references (p. [395]-403) and index.
Subjects: World Bank--Developing countries. Economic assistance--Developing countries. Developing countries--Economic conditions.
LC Classification: HC60 .C345 1996
Dewey Class No.: 332.1/532 20

Cernea, Michael M.
Population Resettlement and Development.
Finance & Development (Intl. Monetary Fund & the World Bank)
Sept. 1994, p46-49

Chalk, Nigel.
What should be done with a fiscal surplus? / prepared by Nigel Chalk and Richard Hemming.
[Washington, D.C.]: International Monetary Fund, 1998.
Description: 19 p.; 28 cm.
Series: IMF paper on policy analysis and assessment; PAA/98/10
LC Classification: IN PROCESS

Chandavarkar, Anand G.
The International Monetary Fund: its financial organization and activities / by Anand G. Chandavarkar.
Washington, D.C.: IMF: Requested from External Relations Dept., IMF, 1984.
Description: vii, 86 p.; 23 cm.
Notes: Includes bibliographical references.
Subjects: International Monetary Fund.
Series: Pamphlet series (International Monetary Fund); no. 2.
LC Classification: HG3881.5.I58 C45 1984
Dewey Class No.: 332.1/52 19

Changes At the World Bank: U.S. Wants More Loans For Businesses, Not Governments - The Associated Press
Newsday June 11, 1991

Chen, Q.
Henan grasps the opportunity to accelerate the pace of popularizing nine years of

compulsory educations - Doing a good job of administering and using the special state funds for education and the World Bank Loan
Chinese Education and Society, 1998, Vol 31, Iss 5, pp 32-34

Cherne, Leo M.,
Bretton Woods, a cornerstone of lasting peace,
New York, Americans united for world organization, inc. [1945]
Description: 1 p. l., 8 p. 24 cm.
Subjects: International monetary fund (Proposed) International bank for reconstruction and development
LC Classification: HG255 .C45

Chin jung yü fa chan.
Edition Information: Chung wen pan.
Pei-ching: Chung-kuo ts`ai cheng ching chi ch`u pan she,
Description: v: ill.; 28 cm.
Assumed the vol. numbering of: Finance & development.
Issues for <1997 nien 6 yüeh-> called also <ti 34 chüan ti 2 ch`i->
[Ti 22 chüan], ti 1 ch`i (1985 nein 3 yüeh hao [Mar. 1985])-
Current Frequency: Quarterly
ISSN: 0256-2561
Notes: Title from cover.
Sponsored by: Kuo chi huo pi chi chin tsu chih and Shih chieh yin hang.
SERBIB/SERLOC merged record
Issued also in Arabic, English, French, German, Spanish and Portuguese editions.
Subjects: International finance--Periodicals. Banks and banking, International--Periodicals. Foreign exchange--Periodicals.
LC Classification: HG3879 .F55
Acquisition Source: International Monetary Fund, 700 19th St., N.W., Washington, DC 20431
Entry: Chin jung yü fa chan. 99-103427

China: power sector regulation in a socialist market economy / edited by Shao Shiwei ... [et al.].
Washington, D.C.: World Bank, c1997.
Editor: Shao, Shiwei.
Description: xxvi, 144 p.: ill.; 28 cm.
ISBN: 0821339133 (alk. paper)
Subjects: World Bank. Electric utilities--Government policy--China. Electric utilities--China--Management. Electric utilities--China--Finance. Electric power systems--China.
Series: World Bank discussion papers; 361.
LC Classification: HD9685.C62 C434 1997

Dewey Class No.: 333.793/2/0951 21

Chossudovsky, Michel

Crime Goes Global: The Criminalisation of the World Economy
Third World Resurgence (Penang, Malaysia) April 1997, p13-20
Nicola Bullard.
Money: Miracle to Meltdown
New Internationalist (Oxford, England) Oct. 1998, p22-24

Chossudovsky, Michel.

The globalisation of poverty: impacts of IMF and World Bank reforms / Michel Chossudovsky.
Penang, Malaysia: Third World Network, c1997.
Description: 280 p.: ill.; 22 cm.
ISBN: 9839747231
Notes: Includes bibliographical references (p. [265]-272) and index.
Subjects: International Monetary Fund. World Bank. Poverty. International finance.
LC Classification: HC79.P6 C48 1997
Dewey Class No.: 332.1/52 21

Chossudovsky, Michel.

The globalisation of poverty: impacts of IMF and World Bank reforms / Michel Chossudovsky.
London; Atlantic Highlands, N.J.: Zed Books; Malaysia: TWN, c1997.
Description: 280 p.; 22 cm.
ISBN: 1856494012 (hardbound) 1856494020 (pbk.)
Notes: Includes bibliographical references (p. [265]-272) and index.
Subjects: International Monetary Fund--Developing countries. International Monetary Fund--Europe, Eastern. World Bank--Developing countries. World Bank--Europe, Eastern. Poverty--Developing countries. Poverty--Europe, Eastern.
LC Classification: HG3881.5.I58 C47 1997
Dewey Class No.: 339.4/6 20

Christensen, Benedicte Vibe.

The Russian Federation in transition: external developments / Benedicte Vibe Christensen.
Washington, D.C.: International Monetary Fund, 1994.
Description: vii, 45 p.: col. ill.; 28 cm.
ISBN: 1557753717 (recycled paper) :
Notes: "February 1994." Includes bibliographical references (p. 43).
Subjects: Russia (Federation)--Foreign economic relations. Soviet Union--Foreign economic relations. Former Soviet republics--Foreign economic

relations. Russia (Federation)--Economic policy--1991- Soviet Union--Economic policy--1986-1991. Former Soviet republics--Economic policy.
Series: Occasional paper (International Monetary Fund); no. 11.
LC Classification: HF1558.2 .C47 1994
Dewey Class No.: 337.47 20

Cities in transition: a strategic view of urban and local government issues.
Washington, D.C.: World Bank, 2000.
Description: p. cm..
ISBN: 0821345915
Notes: Includes bibliographical references
Subjects: World Bank--Developing countries. City planning--Developing countries--Finance. Urbanization--Developing countries--Finance. Urban economics.
LC Classification: HT169.5 .C56 2000
Dewey Class No.: 307.1/2/091724 21

Clairmont, Frederic and others.
50th Anniversary of Bretton Woods
Third World Resurgence (Penang, Malaysia) Sept. 1994, p14-27

Coker, Q. F.
IMF and Nigeria: a selected bibliography, 1960-1985 / Q.F. Coker.
[Lagos]: Nigerian Institute of International Affairs, [1985]
Description: iii, 94 p.; 28 cm.
Notes: Cover title. Includes index.
Subjects: International Monetary Fund--Nigeria--Bibliography. International Monetary Fund--Bibliography. Debts, External--Nigeria--Bibliography. Nigeria--Economic policy--Bibliography.
LC Classification: Z7164.F5 C65 1985 HG3881.5.I58
Dewey Class No.: 016.3321/52 19

Collyns, Charles.
Alternatives to the central bank in the developing world / by Charles Collyns.
Washington, D.C.: International Monetary Fund, 1983]
Description: 23 p.; 28 cm.
Notes: "July 1983." Bibliography: p. 23.
Subjects: Banks and banking, Central--Developing countries. Monetary policy--Developing countries.
Series: Occasional paper (International Monetary Fund); no. 0.
LC Classification: HG3550 .C65 1983

Condliffe, J. B. (John Bell), 1891-1981.
Exchange stabilization, by J.B. Condliffe. [New York] 1945.

United Nations Monetary and Financial Conference, Bretton Woods, N.H., 1944.
Description: 50, [2] p. 23 cm.
Notes: Cover-title. At head of The Committee on international economic policy in cooperation with the Carnegie endowment for international peace. "Bretton Woods agreements Act": p. 47-50. "Select bibliography on international monetary stabilization": p. 41-46.
Subjects: International Monetary Fund. Currency question. Foreign exchange. Commercial policy.
LC Classification: HG255 .C565
Dewey Class No.: 332.45

Convenio constitutivo del Banco Interamericano de Desarrollo: abierto a la firma en la Unión Panamericana el 8 de abril de 1959 / Consejo Interamerican Economico y Social, Comisión Especializada Encargada de la Negociación y Redacción del Instrumento Constitutivo de una Institución Financiera Interamericana.
Washington, D.C.: Unión Panamericana, 1959.
Description: 51 p.; 28 cm.
Notes: Also issued in English.
Subjects: Inter-American Development Bank. Banks and banking, International.
Series: Treaty series (Organization of American States. General Secretariat); no. 14.
LC Classification: JX506 1957 no. 14

Convenio sobre el fondo monetario internacional.
Santiago de Chile. Imprenta universitaria. 1944.
Description: 147 p. 24 cm.
Subjects: International Monetary Fund.
LC Classification: HG3881 .A7818

Convenios sobre el Fondo monetario internacional y el Banco internacional de reconstrucciûn y fomento. Santiago de Chile, Imprenta universitaria, 1946.
Description: 240 p. 24 cm.
Subjects: International Monetary Fund. International Bank for Reconstruction and Development.
LC Classification: HG205.1944 .A14 1946

Coraggio, José Luis.
La educación según el Banco Mundial: un análisis de sus propuestas y métodos / José Luis Coraggio, Rosa María Torres.
Edition Information: 1. ed.
Buenos Aires: Centro de estudios multidisciplinarios : Miño y Dávila editores, 1997.
Description: 161 p.; 20 cm.
ISBN: 950946774X

Notes: Includes bibliographical references.
Subjects: World Bank--History. Educational assistance.
Series: Colección CEM-Educación
LC Classification: HG3881.5.W57 C665 1997

Cottarelli, Carlo.
Limiting central bank credit to the government: theory and practice / Carlo Cottarelli.
Washington, DC: International Monetary Fund, 1993.
Description: v, 57 p.: col. ill.; 28 cm.
ISBN: 155775358X (recycled paper) :
Notes: "December 1993." Includes bibliographical references (p. 54-55).
Subjects: Banks and banking, Central. Credit. Bank loans.
Series: Occasional paper (International Monetary Fund); no. 10.
LC Classification: HG1811 .C67 1993
Dewey Class No.: 332.1/1 20

Country-risk analysis: a handbook / edited by Ronald L. Solberg.
London; New York: Routledge, 1992.
Editor: Solberg, Ronald L., 1953-
Description: xviii, 318 p.; 23 cm.
ISBN: 0415078555
Notes: Simultaneously published in the USA and Canada.
Includes bibliographical references and index.
Subjects: Banks and banking, International. International business enterprises--Finance. Country risk.
LC Classification: HG3881 .C67435 1992
Dewey Class No.: 332.1/5 20

Cross-border electronic banking: challenges and opportunities / edited by Joseph J. Norton, Chris Reed, and Ian Walden.
London; New York: Lloyd's of London Press, 1995.
Editor: Norton, Joseph Jude. Reed, Chris, Walden, Ian.
Queen Mary and Westfield College (University of London). Centre for Commercial Law Studies. Chartered Institute of Bankers.
Description: xxix, 305 p.: ill.; 24 cm.
ISBN: 1850448485
Notes: "Published jointly with the Centre for Commercial Law Studies and the Chartered Institute of Bankers." Includes bibliographical references and index.
Subjects: Banks and banking, International--Automation. Banks and banking, International--Law and legislation. Electronic funds transfers--Law and legislation.
LC Classification: K1088 .C76 1995

Dewey Class No.: 341.7/5110285 21

Curtin, T.R.C. and Nelson, E.A.S.

Economic and health efficiency of education funding policy

Social Science & Medicine, 1999, Vol 48, Iss 11, pp 1599-1611

Public spending programmes to reduce poverty, expand primary education and improve the economic status of women are recommended priorities of aid agencies and are now gradually being reflected in third world governments' policies, in response to aid conditions imposed by the World Bank and OECD countries. However outcomes fall short of aspiration. This paper shows that donors' lending policies, especially those restricting public spending on education to the primary level, (1) perpetuate poverty, (2) minimise socio-economic impact of public health programmes and (3) prevent significant improvement in the economic status of women. These effects are the result of fundamental flaws in donors' education policy model. Evidence is presented to show that health status in developing countries; will be significantly enhanced by increasing the proportion of the population which has at least post-primary education.

Dahl, Hans-Erik.

IMF [i.e. International Monetary Fund]-det internasjonale valutafond.

Oslo, 1966.

Description: iii, 150 l. 30 cm.

Subjects: International Monetary Fund.

LC Classification: HG3881 .D3

Darling, John Ford

A new international currency: the Bank for International Settlements,

London, London general press [1929]

Description: 23 p. 22 cm.

Subjects: Bank for International Settlements. Currency Question.

LC Classification: HG255 .D3

Dauvergne, Alain.

Le Fonds monètaire international: un monde sous influences / Alain Dauvergne.

Paris: A. Moreau, c1988.

Description: 236 p.; 21 cm.

ISBN: 2852090406 :

Notes: Includes index. Bibliography: p. [229]-230.

Subjects: International Monetary Fund.

Series: EnquÍte (Editions Alain Moreau)

LC Classification: HG3881.5.I58 D37 1988

David, Wilfred L.

The IMF policy paradigm: the macroeconomics of stabilization, structural

adjustment, and economic development / Wilfred L. David.
New York: Praeger, 1985.
Description: xiii, 140 p.: ill.; 24 cm.
ISBN: 0030044081 (alk. paper) :
Notes: Includes index. Bibliography: p. 131-137.
Subjects: International Monetary Fund. International finance. Economic stabilization. Economic development. Structural adjustment (Economic policy)
LC Classification: HG3881.5.I58 D38 1985
Dewey Class No.: 332.1/52 19

Davis, Shelton and Partridge, William
Promoting the Development of Indigenous People in Latin America
Finance & Development (Intl. Monetary Fund & the World Bank)
March 1994, p38-40

Dealing with debt, rekindling development: the U.S. stake in the performance of the world's development banks: a report of the Subcommittee on International Development Institutions and Finance of the Committee on Banking, Finance, and Urban Affairs, House of Representatives, Ninety-ninth Congress, first session. Washington: U.S. G.P.O., 1985.
Description: iii, 47 p.: ill.; 24 cm.
Notes: At head of Committee print 99-5. Distributed to some depository libraries in microfiche. Shipping list no.: 85-934-P. "October 1985." Item 1013-A, 1013-B (microfiche) Includes bibliographical references.
Subjects: Banks and banking, International. Development banks. Economic assistance, American--Developing countries.
LC Classification: HG3881 .D341345 1985
Dewey Class No.: 332.1/53 19
Govt. Doc. No.: Y 4.B 22/1:D 35/2

deBeyer, J.A., Preker, A.S. and Feachem, R.G.A.
The role of the World Bank in international health: renewed commitment and partnership
Social Science & Medicine, 2000, Vol 50, Iss 2, pp 169-176
During the course of the past ten years, the World Bank has become the single largest external financier of health activities in low and middle income countries and an important voice in national and international debates on health policy. This article highlights the Bank's new strategic direction in the health sector aimed at: improving health, nutrition, and population outcomes of the poor; enhancing the performance of health care systems; and securing sustainable health care financing. Millions of preventable deaths and treatable illnesses, together with health systems that are inefficient, inequitable and ineffective, have motivated expanded Bank support for the health sector in many of its client countries. The new policy directions and system-wide reforms observed in these

countries are the result of both demand and supply factors.

Decision of the executive directors under Article X of the Articles of Agreement on Questions of Interpretation of the Articles of Agreement / International Development Association.
Washington, D.C.: The Association, [1991]
Description: 2 p.; 23 cm.
ISBN: 0821318470
Subjects: World Bank. International Development Association.
LC Classification: HG3881.5.W57 D43 1991

Deininger, K. and Binswanger H.
The evolution of the World Bank's land policy: Principles, experience, and future challenges
World Bank Research Observer, 1999, Vol 14, Iss 2, pp 247-276
This article examines the evolution of policy recommendations concerning rural land issues since the formulation of the World Bank's "Land Reform Policy Paper" in 1975. That paper set out three guiding principles: the desirability of owner-operated family farms; the need for markets to permit land to be transferred to more productive users; and the importance of an egalitarian asset distribution.

Del Rosso, Joy Miller.
Investing in nutrition with World Bank assistance / Joy Miller Del Rosso.
Washington, D.C.: World Bank, c1992.
Description: iii, 23 p.; 23 cm.
ISBN: 0821322923
Subjects: World Bank--Developing countries. Nutrition policy--Developing countries. Investments, Foreign--Developing countries.
LC Classification: TX360.5 .D45 1992
Dewey Class No.: 363.8/56/091724 20

Der Internationale Whrungsfonds und die unternationale Bank fur Wiederaufbau und Wirtschaftsf rderung.
Wien, Kommissionsverlag: Ringbuchandlung A. exl, 1946.
Description: 160 p. 21 cm.
Subjects: International Monetary Fund. International Bank for Reconstruction and Development.
LC Classification: HG3881 .A785 1946

Dervis, Kemal.
The transition in Central and Eastern Europe and the former Soviet Union / Kemal Dervis, Marcelo Selowsky, and Christine Wallich.
Washington, DC: World Bank, [1994]

Description: 37 p.: maps; 28 cm.
ISBN: 0821330829
Notes: "50th anniversary"--Cover.
Subjects: World Bank--Europe, Eastern. World Bank--Former Soviet republics. Economic assistance, East European. Economic assistance--Former Soviet republics. Europe, Eastern--Economic policy--1989- Former Soviet republics--Economic policy. Europe, Eastern--Social policy. Former Soviet republics--Social policy.
Series: The evolving role of the World Bank
LC Classification: HC244 .D377 1994

Desarrollo, pobreza y medio ambiente: FMI, Banco Mundial, GATT al final del siglo / A. Bilbao ... [et al.]; C. Vaquero, compilador.
Madrid: Talasa Ediciones, c1994.
Editor: Bilbao, Andrés.
Description: 224 p.; 20 cm.
ISBN: 8488119240
Notes: Includes bibliographical references.
Subjects: International Monetary Fund. World Bank. General Agreement on Tariffs and Trade (Organization) Structural adjustment (Economic policy)—Developing countries--Case studies. Economic development--Case studies. Poverty--Developing countries--Case studies. Environmental policy--Developing countries--Case studies. Developing countries--Economic policy--Case studies.
Series: Talasa (Madrid, Spain); 66.
LC Classification: HC59.5 .D368 1994
Dewey Class No.: 338.9/0091724 20

Deschiétère, Raymond.
Les reparations; la protection des obligatoires; la Banque des règlements internationaux.
Paris, Les Presses universitaires de France, 1931.
Description: 240 p. fold. facsim., fold. diagr. 26 cm.
Subjects: Bank for international settlements.
European war, 1914-1918--Reparations.
LC Classification: D648 .D44

Determinación de la eficacia del desarrollo: la evaluación "ex post" en el Banco Mundial y la Corporación Financiera Internacional.
Washington, D.C.: Banco Mundial, 1994.
Description: vi, 41 p.: ill.; 23 cm.
ISBN: 0821328352
Notes: Includes bibliographical references (p. 39-41).
Subjects: World Bank. International Finance Corporation. Economic development projects--Evaluation.

LC Classification: HC79.E44 A8818 1994
Dewey Class No.: 332.1/532 21

Determinar la eficacia de las actividades de desarrollo : la evaluación en el Banco Mundial y la Corporación Financiera Internacional.
Edition Information: 1. ed.
Washington, DC: Banco Mundial, 1999.
Description: p. cm.
ISBN: 0821344552
Notes: English ed. published under Assessing development effectiveness: evaluation in the World Bank and the International Finance Corporation. Includes bibliographical references (p.).
Subjects: World Bank. International Finance Corporation. Economic development projects--Evaluation.
LC Classification: HC79.E44 A8818 1999
Dewey Class No.: 332.1/532 21

Developing countries and the international economy : issues in trade, adjustment, and debt / edited by H. David Evans and David Greenaway.
London; Portland, OR: F. Cass, c1991.
Editor: Evans, H. David (Henry David)
Description: 191 p.: ill.; 23 cm.
ISBN: 0714634336
Notes: "First appeared in a special issue ... of the Journal of development studies, vol. 27, no. 3"--T.p. verso. Includes bibliographical references.
Subjects: World Bank. Debts, External--Developing countries. Developing countries--Foreign economic relations. Developing countries--Commercial policy.
LC Classification: HF1413 .D48 1991
Dewey Class No.: 337/.09172/4 20

Development aid: a guide to national and international agencies / researched and compiled by Eurofi (UK) Limited.
London; Boston: Butterworths; Birmingham [England] ;
New York: Eurofi (UK), 1988, c1987.
Description: 587 p.: ill.; 24 cm.
ISBN: 0408009918 :
Subjects: Banks and banking, International--Directories. Development banks--Directories. Economic assistance--Directories.
Series: IBI international business intelligence
LC Classification: HG3881 .D43 1988
Dewey Class No.: 332.1/53/025 19

Development and global governance: conference proceedings, May 2, 1995, Ottawa, Canada / edited by Roy Culpepper and Caroline Pestieau.
Ottawa: International Development Research Centre ; North-South Institute, c1996.
Editor: Culpeper, Roy,
Description: 147 p.; 23 cm.
ISBN: 0921942974 (North-South Institute) : 0889368058 (IDRC) :
Notes: Papers from a conference organized by the North-South Institute and the International Development Research Centre and held May 2, 1995, in Ottawa, Ont. Includes bibliographical references.
Subjects: International Monetary Fund--Congresses. World Bank--Congresses. International finance--Congresses. Financial institutions, International—Developing countries--Congresses. Economic assistance--Developing countries--Congresses.
LC Classification: HG203 .D475 1996
Dewey Class No.: 332.1/5 21

Development and human rights: the role of the World Bank.
Washington, DC: World Bank, 1998.
Description: p. cm.
ISBN: 0821343408
Subjects: World Bank. Human rights--Developing countries. Economic development.
LC Classification: JC599.D44 W67 1998
Dewey Class No.: 332.1/532 21

Development issues: presentations to the 39th Meeting of the Development Committee, Washington, D.C., September 24, 1990.
Washington, D.C.: Joint Ministerial Committee of the Boards of Governors of the World Bank and the International Monetary Fund on the Transfer of Real Resources to Developing Countries (Development Committee), c1991.
Description: iv, 102 p.: ill.; 28 cm.
ISBN: 0821317601
Subjects: World Bank--Developing countries. International Monetary Fund--Developing countries. Economic development. Debt relief--Developing countries. Poverty. Developing countries--Economic conditions.
Series: Development Committee (Series); no. 26.
LC Classification: HC59.7 .D42 1991

Development theory and practice of the World Bank in Asia.
Ottignies-Louvain-la-Neuve: Centre Tricontinental, [1980]
Description: 29 leaves; 30 cm.
Notes: Includes bibliographical references.
Subjects: World Bank--Asia.

LC Classification: HG3881.5.W57 D48 1980
Dewey Class No.: 332.1/532/095 19

Development: new paradigms and principles for the twenty-first century / edited by Jo Marie Griesgaber and Bernhard G. Gunter.
London; East Haven, Conn.: Pluto Press, c1996.
Editor: Griesgraber, Jo Marie.
Description: p. cm.
ISBN: 0745310486
Notes: Includes bibliographical references (p.) and index.
Subjects: International Monetary Fund. World Bank. International finance--History. Economic development--History. Twenty-first century--Forecasts.
Series: Rethinking Bretton Woods; v. 2
LC Classification: HG3881 .R418 1995 vol. 2 HG3881.5.I58
Dewey Class No.: 332/.042 s 338.9 20

Diabre, Zephirin
Tales of a Frustrated Finance Minister.
World Link (London, England) May/June 1998, p38-44

Die Weltbank: Struktur, Aufgaben und Bedeutung / Thomas U. Koll (Hrsg.).
Berlin: Deutsche Gesellschaft für die VereintenNationen, Landesverband Berlin, c1988.
Editor: Koll, Thomas U.
Description: 187 p.; 21 cm.
ISBN: 3927192007
Notes: One contribution in English. Includes bibliographical references.
Subjects: World Bank.
Series: Schriftenreihe der Deutschen Gesellschaft für die Vereinten Nationen, Landesverband Berlin e.V.; Bd. 1
LC Classification: HG3881.5.W57 W45 1988

Dillinger, William R., 1951-
Better urban services: finding the right incentives.
Washington, D.C.: World Bank, 1995.
Description: xii, 84 p.: ill.; 24 cm.
ISBN: 0821332325
Notes: Includes bibliographical references (p. 81-84).
Subjects: World Bank--Developing countries. Municipal services--Developing countries. Decentralization in government--Developing countries. Intergovernmental fiscal relations--Developing countries.
Series: Development in practice (Washington, D.C.).
LC Classification: HD4431 .D56 1995

Dewey Class No.: 363/.09172/4 20

Directory to World Bank depository libraries.
Washington, D.C., U.S.A.: World Bank, [c1983]
Description: iv, 52 leaves; 28 cm.
ISBN: 0821302949 (unb.)
Subjects: World Bank. Libraries, Depository--Directories. Economic development--Library resources--Directories. Developing countries--Library resources--Directories. Developing countries--Social conditions--Library resources Directories.
LC Classification: Z675.D4 D57 1983
Dewey Class No.: 027/.0025 19

Disbursement handbook.
Edition Information: 2nd ed.
Washington, D.C., U.S.A.: World Bank, 1992.
Editor: World Bank.
Description: viii, 104 p.: ill.; 28 cm.
ISBN: 0821322397
Notes: Includes index.
Subjects: World Bank. Bank loans--Handbooks, manuals, etc.
Loans, Foreign--Developing countries--Handbooks, manuals, etc.
LC Classification: HG3881.5.W57 D57 1992
Dewey Class No.: 332.1/532/0685 20

Disbursement handbook.
Washington, D.C., U.S.A.: World Bank, c1986.
Description: iv, 58 p.: ill.; 28 cm.
ISBN: 0821307460 (pbk.)
Notes: Includes index.
Subjects: World Bank. Bank loans--Handbooks, manuals, etc. Loans, Foreign--Developing countries--Handbooks, manuals, etc.
LC Classification: HG3881.5.W57 D57 1986
Dewey Class No.: 332.1/532/0685 19

Disinvesting in health: the World Bank's prescriptions for health / editor, Mohan Rao.
Thousand Oaks, CA: Sage Publications, 1999.
Editor: Rao, Mohan, 1953-
Description: 238 p.: ill.; 22 cm.
ISBN: 0761993479 (cl.) 0761993487 (pa.)
Notes: Includes bibliographical references and index.
Subjects: World Bank. Medical policy--India--Congresses. Medical care--India--Finance--\Congresses. Medical assistance--India--Congresses.
LC Classification: RA395.I5 D57 1999

Dewey Class No.: 362.1/0954 21

Dixon, John A., 1946-
Dams and the environment: considerations in World Bank projects / John A. Dixon, Lee M. Talbot, and Guy J.-M. Le Moigne.
Washington, D.C.: The Bank, c1989.
Description: viii, 64 p.: ill.; 28 cm.
ISBN: 0821313630
Notes: Report on the key issues and conclusions of a seminar held at the World Bank on June 18, 1987. Includes bibliographical references (p. 51-53).
Subjects: World Bank--Congresses. Dams--Environmental aspects--Congresses. Economic development projects--Environmental aspects Congresses.
Series: World Bank technical paper, 0253-7494; no. 110
LC Classification: TD195.H93 D59 1989
Dewey Class No.: 333.91/14 20

Dutt, Jill and Henry, David STAFF WRITERS
Salomon Loses Major Customer World Bank Suspends Reviews Relationship - Newsday Aug. 22, 1991

Easton, S.T. and Rockerbie, D.W.
Does IMF conditionality benefit lenders?
Weltwirtschaftliches Archiv - Review of World Economics, 1999, Vol 135, Iss 2, pp 347-357

Economía y finanzas: cinco trabajos y comentarios efectuados bajo patrocinio del Instituto de Estudios Bancarios "Guillermo Subercaseaux" y un estudio sobre evolución y papel de la tasa de interés en Chile / realizado por el Depto. de Economía de la Universidad de Chile con la participación de Sergio Baeza P. ... [et al.].
Santiago, Chile: El Instituto, 1980.
Description: 371 p.: ill.; 26 cm.
Notes: Includes bibliographies.
Subjects: Banks and banking, International. Collective labor agreements--Chile. Interest rates--Chile. Chile--Economic conditions--1973-1988.
LC Classification: HC192 .E243 1980
Dewey Class No.: 332/.0983 19

Economic adjustment: policies and problems: papers presented at a seminar held in Wellington, New Zealand, February 17-19, 1986 / edited by Sir Frank Holmes.
[Washington, D.C.]: International Monetary Fund, 1987.
Editor: Holmes, Frank Wakefield, Sir,
Description: x, 281 p.: ill.; 23 cm.
ISBN: 0939934981 (pbk.) :

Notes: Includes bibliographies.
Subjects: Oceania--Economic policy--Congresses. Korea (South)--Economic policy--1960- --Congresses. New Zealand--Economic policy--Congresses.
LC Classification: HC681 .E28 1987
Dewey Class No.: 338.99 19

Economic development and the the private sector.
Washington, D.C. (1818 H St., NW 20433): World Bank, [1991]
Description: 39 p.: ill.; 28 cm.
Notes: Cover title. Includes bibliographical references.
Subjects: World Bank. Economic development--Finance. Free enterprise--Developing countries. Developing countries--Economic policy.
LC Classification: HG3881.5.W57 E23 1991
Dewey Class No.: 338.9 20

Economic development and tribal peoples: human ecologic considerations / World Bank, Office of Environmental Affairs.
Washington, D.C., U.S.A. (1818 H St., N.W., Washington 20433): World Bank, 1981.
Description: iii leaves, 103 p.; 27 cm.
Notes: "July 1981"--Cover. Bibliography: p. 60-103.
Subjects: World Bank. Ethnicity. Acculturation. Human ecology. Rural development.
LC Classification: GN495.6 .E27 1981
Dewey Class No.: 306 19

Economic development of the Arab countries: selected issues / edited by Said El-Naggar.
Washington, D.C.: International Monetary Fund, 1993.
Editor: El-Naggar, Sa`id,
Description: x, 290 p.: ill.; 23 cm.
ISBN: 1557753326
Notes: "Papers presented at a seminar held in Bahrain, February 1-3, 1993." Includes bibliographcal references.
Subjects: Arab countries--Economic conditions--Congresses.
LC Classification: HC498 .E24 1993
Dewey Class No.: 338.9/00917/4927 20

Economic dislocation and recovery in Lebanon / Sena Eken ... [et al.].
Washington, D.C.: International Monetary Fund, 1995.
Description: vii, 64p.: ill.; 29 cm.
ISBN: 1557754594 (recycled paper) :
Notes: "February 1995." Includes bibliographical references (p. 60-62).
Subjects: Industrial promotion--Lebanon. Lebanon--Economic conditions. Lebanon--Economic policy.

Series: Occasional paper (International Monetary Fund); no. 120.
LC Classification: HC415.24 .E26 1995
Dewey Class No.: 330.95692/044 20

Economic policies and unemployment dynamics in Europe / editors, S.G.B. Henry, Dennis J. Snower.
Washington, D.C., U.S.A.: International Monetary Fund, 1996.
Editor: Henry, S. G. B. Snower, Dennis J.
Description: vii, 216 p.: ill.; 23 cm.
ISBN: 1557755787 (recycled paper)
Notes: Includes bibliographical references.
Subjects: Unemployment--Europe. Labor policy--Europe. Labor market--Europe.
LC Classification: HD5764.A6 E27 1996
Dewey Class No.: 331.13/794 21

Economic policies for a new South Africa / edited by Desmond Lachman and Kenneth Bercuson; with a staff team comprising Daudi Ballali ... [et al.].
Washington, DC: International Monetary Fund, c1992.
Editor: Lachman, Desmond. Bercuson, Kenneth.
Description: vii, 41 p.: ill.; 28 cm.
ISBN: 1557751986 :
Notes: "January 1992." Includes bibliographical references (p. 38-39).
Subjects: Poor--South Africa. Blacks--South Africa--Economic conditions. Income distribution--South Africa. Taxation--South Africa. South Africa--Economic policy. South Africa--Politics and government--1989-
Series: Occasional paper (International Monetary Fund); no. 91.
LC Classification: HC905 .E245 1992
Dewey Class No.: 330.968/064 20

Economic policy & equity / editors, Vito Tanzi, Ke-young Chu, Sanjeev Gupta.
Washington, D.C.: International Monetary Fund, c1999.
Editor: Tanzi, Vito.
Description: ix, 293 p.: ill.; 23 cm.
ISBN: 1557757887 (pbk.)
Notes: Includes bibliographical references and index.
Subjects: Income distribution. Economic policy. Social justice. Competition, International.
LC Classification: HC79.I5 E235 1999
Dewey Class No.: 338.9 21

Economic reform in China: a new phase / Wanda Tseng ... [et al.].
Washington, DC: International Monetary Fund, 1994.
Editor: Tseng, Wanda.
Description: viii, 84 p.: col. ill.; 28 cm.

ISBN: 1557754217 (recycled paper) :
Notes: "November 1994." Includes bibliographical references (p. 46).
Subjects: Foreign exchange--China. Monetary policy--China. Fiscal policy--China. China--Economic policy--1976-
Series: Occasional paper (International Monetary Fund); no. 114.
LC Classification: HC427.92 .E3697 1994
Dewey Class No.: 338.951 20

Economic reforms for 1996-1998: the policy framework paper / [prepared by the Government of Kenya in collaboration with the International Monetary Fund and the World Bank].
[Nairobi]: The Government, [1996]
Description: vi, 68 p.; 25 cm.
Notes: "February 16, 1996"--Cover.
Subjects: Economic forecasting--Kenya. Kenya--Economic policy.
LC Classification: HC865 .K46 1996

Economics and finance: index to periodical articles. Second supplement, 1975 1976-1977 / compiled by the staff of the Joint Bank-Fund Library for the International Monetary Fund and the World Bank, Washington, D.C.
Boston, Mass.: G.K. Hall, 1979.
Description: xii, 419 p.; 36 cm.
ISBN: 081610302X
Subjects: Ecoonomics--Periodicals--Indexes. Economic development--Periodicals--Indexes. Economic history--1945- --Periodicals--Indexes. International finance--Periodicals--Indexes.
LC Classification: Z7164.E2 W34 Suppl 2 HB1
Dewey Class No.: 016.33 19

Education and development: views from the World Bank / Aklilu Habte, George Psacharopoulos, and Stephen P. Heyneman.
Washington, D.C.: World Bank, c1983.
Editor: Habte, Aklilu,
Description: 26 p.: ill.; 28 cm.
ISBN: 0821302248 (pbk.)
Notes: Based on articles published in Finance & Development, a publication of the International Monetary Fund and the World Bank. Bibliography: p. 18.
Subjects: World Bank. Education--Developing countries. Education--Economic aspects--Developing countries.
LC Classification: LC2607 .E383 1983
Dewey Class No.: 370/.9172/4 19

Education sector strategy / [the Human Development Network].
Washington, D.C.: World Bank Group, c1999.

Description: xiv, 80 p.: ill., col. maps; 28 cm.
ISBN: 0821345605
Notes: Includes bibliographical references (p. 79-80).
Subjects: World Bank--Developing countries. Education--Developing countries. Economic development--Effect of education on. Educational assistance--Developing countries.
LC Classification: LC2607 .W66 1999
Dewey Class No.: 370/.9172/4 21

Egypt: alleviating poverty during structural adjustment.
Washington, D.C., U.S.A.: World Bank, 1991.
Description: p. cm.
ISBN: 082131873X
Notes: Includes bibliographical references.
Subjects: World Bank. Poor--Egypt. Public welfare--Egypt. Economic assistance--Egypt. Structural adjustment (Economic policy)--Egypt. Egypt--Economic conditions--1952-
Series: A World Bank country study
LC Classification: HC830.Z9 P64 1991
Dewey Class No.: 362.5/8/0962 20

Ehrensperger, Fritz.
Die bedeutung der Bank für internationalen zahlungs-ausgelich;
Zürich, "Züricher port" [1930]
Description: 32 p. fold. tab. 19 cm.
Subjects: Bank for international settlements.
LC Classification: HG1997.I.6 E47

El BID, el Banco Mundial y la sociedad civil: nuevas modalidades de financiamiento internacional / Diana Tussie, compiladora.
Edition Information: 1. ed.
Buenos Aires, Argentina: Oficina de Publicaciones del CBC, Universidad de Buenos Aires: Facultad Latinoamericana de Ciencias Sociales, 1997.
Editor: Tussie, Diana.
Description: 193 p.; 23 cm.
Notes: Includes bibliographical references.
Subjects: Inter-American Development Bank. World Bank. Development banks. International finance. Latin America--Economic conditions--1918-
LC Classification: HG1976.L29 B53 1997

El Fondo Monetario Internacional, el Banco Mundial y la economìa espaòola / coordinaciûn, Manuel Varela Parache.
Madrid: Ediciones Pir·mide, c1994.
Editor: Varela Parache, Manuel.

Description: lxiii, 499, 6 p.: ill.; 24 cm.
ISBN: 8436808487
Notes: Includes bibliographical references.
Subjects: International Monetary Fund--Spain. World Bank--Spain. International finance. Spain--Economic policy.
LC Classification: HG3881.5.I58 F66 1994

El orden económico mundial: (Fondo Monetario Internacional, Banco Mundial y GATT) / coordinador, Jesús de la Iglesia.
Madrid: Editorial Síntesis, c1994.
Editor: Iglesia, Jesús de la.
Description: 260 p.: ill.; 21 cm.
ISBN: 8477382638
Notes: Includes bibliographical references (p. 247-260).
Subjects: International Monetary Fund--History. World Bank--History. General Agreement on Tariffs and Trade (Organization) History. International finance--History.
Series: Economía. Serie Actualidad; 1
LC Classification: HG3881 .O64 1994

EMU and the international monetary system: proceedings of a conference held in Washington DC on March 17-18, 1997, cosponsored by the Fondation Camille Gutt and the IMF / editors, Paul R. Masson, Thomas H. Krueger, and Bart G. Turtelboom.
Washington, D.C., U.S.A.: International Monetary Fund, c1997.
Editor: Masson, Paul R. Krueger, Thomas H. Turtelboom, Bart G.
Description: xii, 563 p.: ill.; 23 cm.
ISBN: 1557756643
Notes: Includes bibliographical references.
Subjects: Monetary unions--European Union countries--Congresses. Foreign exchange--Congresses. Foreign exchange--European Union countries--Congresses. European currency unit--Congresses. International finance--Congresses.
LC Classification: HG3942.8 .E64 1997
Dewey Class No.: 332.4/5/094 21

Environment, growth, and development.
Washington, D.C., U.S.A.: Joint Ministerial Committee of the Boards of Governors of the World Bank and the International Monetary Fund on the Transfer of Real Resources to Developing Countries (Development Committee): Available from the World Bank Sales Unit, [1987]
Description: 33 p.; 22 cm.
ISBN: 0821309269 (pbk.)
Subjects: Environmental policy--Developing countries. Developing countries—

Economic policy.
Series: Development Committee (Series); no. 14.
LC Classification: HC59.72.E5 E58 1987
Dewey Class No.: 363.7/009172/4 19

Environmental impact of World Bank lending: hearing before the Subcommittees on Human Rights and International Organizations, and on International Economic Policy and Trade of the Committee on Foreign Affairs, House of Representatives, One Hundred First Congress, first session ....
Washington: U.S. G.P.O.: For sale by the Supt. of Docs., Congressional Sales Office, U.S. G.P.O., 1989.
Description: 2 v.; 24 cm.
Notes: Distributed to some depository libraries in microfiche. Shipping list no.: 90-023-P (vol. I). Shipping list no.: 90-030-P (vol. II). "September 26, 1989"--Vol. I. "October 4, 1989"--Vol. II. Item 1017-A, 1017-B (MF)
Includes bibliographic references (vol. I, p. 81).
Subjects: World Bank--Developing countries. Economic development projects--Environmental aspects Developing countries. Loans, Foreign--Developing countries. Conservation of natural resources--Developing countries.
LC Classification: KF27 .F645 1989m

Establishing a central bank: issues in Europe and lessons from the US / edited by Matthew B. Canzoneri, Vittorio Grilli, and Paul R. Masson.
Cambridge [England]; New York: Cambridge University Press, 1992.
Editor: Canzoneri, Matthew B. Grilli, Vittorio. Masson, Paul R.
Description: xvii, 307 p.; ill.; 24 cm.
ISBN: 0521420989 (hardback)
Notes: Papers presented at the conference: "Designing a central bank," held May 1-2, 1991 at Georgetown University and sponsored by the Centre for Economic Policy Research, the Center for German and European Studies at Georgetown University, and the International Monetary Fund. Includes index.
Subjects: Banks and banking, Central--European Economic Community countries-Congresses. Banks and banking, Central--United States--Congresses. Fiscal policy European Economic Community countries Congresses.
LC Classification: HG2980.5.A7 E84 1992
Dewey Class No.: 332.1/1/094 20

Estrategia sectorial de educación / Grupo del Banco Mundial, Red sobre Desarrollo Humano.
Washington, D.C.: World Bank, 1999.
Description: p. cm.
ISBN: 0821346334
Subjects: World Bank--Developing countries. Education--Developing countries. Economic development--Effect of education on. Educational assistance--

Developing countries.
Series: Human development network series
LC Classification: LC2607 .W6618 1999
Dewey Class No.: 370/.9172/4 21

Euromoney capital markets directory / PaineWebber.
London: Euromoney Publications PLC in association with PaineWebber, c1998-
Description: v.; 21 cm. 1998-
Current Frequency: Annual
Continues: Paine Webber euromoney directory (DLC) 97651340
Notes: SERBIB/SERLOC merged record
Subjects: Foreign-exchange brokers--Directories. Financial institutions, International--Directories. Banks and banking, International--Directories.
LC Classification: HG3851 .H34
Dewey Class No.: 332.4/5/025 19
Entry: Euromoney capital markets directory. 98-656739

European multinational banking / Greenwich Research Associates.
Greenwich, Conn.: The Associates,
Description: v.; 28 cm.
Current Frequency: Annual
Notes: "Report to participants." Chiefly tables. Description based on: 1982. SERBIB/SERLOC merged record
Subjects: Banks and banking, International--Periodicals. Corporations, European--Periodicals.
LC Classification: HG3879 .E9
Dewey Class No.: 332.1/5/094 19

Evaluation results for ...
Washington, D.C.: Operations Evaluation Dept., World Bank, c1990-
Description: v.; 28 cm. 1988-
Current Frequency: Annual
Continues: Project performance results for ... (DLC) 88650038 (OCoLC)18859544
Continued by: Annual review of development effectiveness (DLC) 98645411 (OCoLC)39113859
ISSN: 1019-4363
Notes: SERBIB/SERLOC merged record. Also issued in a version for official use only, which has Annual review of evaluation results. Annual review of evaluation results (DLC)sn 97036279 (OCoLC)36659282
Subjects: World Bank--Periodicals. Economic development projects--Finance—Evaluation Periodicals. Loans, Foreign--Developing countries—Statistics Periodicals.
Series: A World Bank operations evaluation study

LC Classification: HG3881.5.W57 E93
Dewey Class No.: 332.1/532/05 20
Entry: Evaluation results for ... 90-648363

Exchange arrangements and exchange restrictions.
Washington, D.C.: International Monetary Fund, c1989-c1998.
Description: 10 v.; 28 cm. 1989-1998.
Current Frequency: Annual
Continues: International Monetary Fund. Annual report on exchange arrangements and exchange restrictions 0250-7366 (OCoLC)5248307 (DLC) 79644506
Continued by: Annual report on exchange arrangements and exchange restrictions (Washington, D.C.: 1999) (DLC)sn 99042554 (OCoLC)43020654
ISSN: 0250-7366
Notes: SERBIB/SERLOC merged record
Subjects: Foreign exchange--Law and legislation--Periodicals.
LC Classification: K4440.A13 I57
Dewey Class No.: 341.7/51 20
Entry: Exchange arrangements and exchange restrictions. 89-650948

Exchange rate regimes and policy interdependence / edited by A.W. Hooke.
Washington, D.C.: International Monetary Fund, 1983.
Editor: Hooke, A. W.
Description: x, 222 p.: ill.; 24 cm.
ISBN: 0939934213
Notes: "Proceedings of the National Bureau of Economic Research/International Monetary Fund Conference [held Aug. 31, 1982] reproduced from v. 30, no. 1, the March 1983 issue of Staff papers."
Summaries in English, French, and Spanish. Includes bibliographies.
Subjects: Foreign exchange administration--Congresses. Monetary policy--Congresses. Economic policy--Congresses.
LC Classification: HG205 .E93 1983
Dewey Class No.: 332.4/56 19

Exchange rate regimes in an increasingly integrated world economy / Michael Mussa ... [et al.].
Washington, DC: International Monetary Fund, 2000.
Editor: Mussa, Michael.
Description: p. cm.
ISBN: 1557758921
Notes: Includes bibliographical references.
Subjects: Foreign exchange. Foreign exchange administration. International economic relations.
Series: Occasional paper (International Monetary Fund); no. 193.

LC Classification: HG3851 .E92 2000
Dewey Class No.: 332.4/5 21

Exit strategies: policy options for countries seeking greater exchange rate flexibility /by a staff team led by Barry Eichengreen and Paul Masson with Hugh Bredenkamp ...
Washington, DC: International Monetary Fund, 1998.
Editor: Eichengreen, Barry J. Masson, Paul R. Bredenkamp, Hugh.
Description: v, 50 p.: ill.; 28 cm.
ISBN: 1557757348
Notes: Includes bibliographical references (p. 46-48).
Subjects: Foreign exchange rates--Developing countries. Foreign exchange rates. Monetary policy--Developing countries. Monetary policy. Fiscal policy--Developing countries. Fiscal policy.
Series: Occasional paper (International Monetary Fund); no. 168.
LC Classification: HG3877 .E95 1998
Dewey Class No.: 332.4/56 21

Export credits: developments and prospects / by Eduard Brau ... [et al.].
Washington, D.C.: International Monetary Fund, c1986.
Editor: Brau, Eduard H.
Description: v, 34 p.; 28 cm.
ISBN: 0939934698 (pbk.) :
Notes: "July 1986." Includes bibliographical references.
Subjects: Export credit.
Series: World economic and financial surveys, 0258-7440
LC Classification: HG3753 .E884 1986
Dewey Class No.: 382/.63 19

External evaluation of IMF surveillance: report / by a group of independent experts.
Washington, D.C.: International Monetary Fund, 1999.
Editor: International Monetary Fund.
Description: p. cm.
ISBN: 1557758638 (pbk.)
Notes: Includes bibliographical references.
Subjects: International Monetary Fund. Economic policy--Evaluation.
LC Classification: HG3881.5.I58 E95 1999
Dewey Class No.: 332.1/52 21

External indebtedness of developing countries / by a staff team headed by Bahram Nowzad and Richard C. Williams and consisting of Ulrich Baumgartner...[et al.].
Washington, D.C.: International Monetary Fund, 981.
Editor: Nowzad, Bahram.
Description: vii, 51 p.: ill.; 28 cm.
Notes: Includes bibliographical references.

Subjects: Debts, External--Developing countries.
Series: Occasional paper (International Monetary Fund); no. 3.
LC Classification: HJ8899 .N68 1981
Dewey Class No.: 336.3/435/091724 19

Final report of the Working Party on the Measurement of International Capital Flows.
Washington, D.C.: International Monetary Fund, 1992.
Description: xv, 128 p.: ill.; 28 cm.
ISBN: 1557753075 :
Notes: Cover Report on the measurement of international capital flows. Spine Measurement of international capital flows. "September 1992." Includes bibliographical references.
Subjects: Capital movements--Statistical methods. Capital movements--Statistical services.
LC Classification: HG3891 .R47 1992
Dewey Class No.: 332/.042 20

Final report of the Working Party on the Statistical Discrepancy in World Current Account Balances.
Washington, D.C.: International Monetary Fund, 1987.
Description: xv, 182 p.; 28 cm.
ISBN: 0939934906 (pbk.) :
Notes: Cover Report on the world current account discrepancy. Spine World current account discrepancy. "September 1987." Includes bibliographical references.
Subjects: Balance of payments--Statistical methods.
LC Classification: HG3882 .I57 1987
Dewey Class No.: 382.1/7 19

Financial management and disbursement in World Bank financed projects [computer file]: self-learning program.
Edition Information: Version 1.0.
Washington, DC: World Bank, [2000].
Description: 1 computer optical disc; 4 3/4 in. + 1 user guide.
ISBN: 0821346652
Computer File Info.: Computer data and program.
Summary: Covers the World Bank's project financial management and disbursement policies, guidelines, and requirements. Features graphics and sound.
Notes: Title from cover of user guide.
System requirements: PC; 12MB RAM; Windows 95 or higher; SVGA graphics display (640 x 480 resolution with 256 colors); double-speed CD-ROM drive.
Subjects: World Bank. Economic development projects--Finance.
LC Classification: HG3881.5.W57

Dewey Class No.: 658.15 13

Financial organization and operations of the IMF / Treasurer's Department.
Edition Information: 4th ed.
Washington, D.C.: International Monetary Fund, 1995.
Description: xi, 144 p.; 23 cm.
ISBN: 155775523X
Notes: Includes bibliographical references.
Subjects: International Monetary Fund.
Series: Pamphlet series (International Monetary Fund); no. 45.
LC Classification: HG3881.5.I58 F54 1995
Dewey Class No.: 332.1/52 20

Financial organization and operations of the IMF / Treasurer's Department.
Edition Information: 2nd ed.
Washington, D.C.: International Monetary Fund, 1991.
Description: ix, 115 p.; 23 cm.
Notes: Includs bibliographical references.
Subjects: International Monetary Fund.
Series: Pamphlet series (International Monetary Fund); no. 45.
LC Classification: HG3881.5.I58 F54 1991
Dewey Class No.: 332.1/52 20

Financial policy workshops: the case of Kenya / IMF Institute.
Washington, D.C.: International Monetary Fund, 1981.
Editor: IMF Institute.
Description: xx, 315 p.: ill.; 24 cm.
ISBN: 0939934000 :
Notes: Includes bibliographical references.
Subjects: Finance--Kenya. Money--Kenya. Balance of payments--Kenya. Finance--Developing countries--Case studies. Money--Developing countries--Case studies. Balance of payments--Developing countries--Case studies.
LC Classification: HG187.5.K4 F55 1981
Dewey Class No.: 332/.09676/2 19

Financial programming and policy: the case of Sri Lanka / prepared by a Staff Team in the IMF Institute led by S. Rajcoomar and Michael Bell; with John Karlik, Michael Martin, Charles Sisson.
Washington, D.C.: IMF Institute, International Monetary Fund, 1996.
Editor: Rajcoomar, S. Bell.
Description: ix, 278 p.: ill.; 28 cm.
ISBN: 1557755795
Notes: Includes bibliographical references.
Subjects: Finance--Sri Lanka. Monetary policy--Sri Lanka. Sri Lanka--Economic

policy--1989- Sri Lanka--Economic conditions--Statistics.
LC Classification: HG187.S72 F56 1996

Financial relations among countries of the former Soviet Union / prepared under the direction of John Odling-Smee by an IMF staff team comprising Thomas Wolf et al.
Washington, D.C.: International Monetary Fund, c1994.
Editor: Odling-Smee, J. C. (John C.)
Description: v, 54 p.; 28 cm.
ISBN: 1557753709 (pbk.) :
Notes: "February 1994."
Subjects: Finance--Former Soviet republics. Former Soviet republics--Economic integration.
Series: IMF economic reviews; 1994, 1.
LC Classification: HG186.F6 F55 1994
Dewey Class No.: 332/.042/0947 20

Financial sector crisis and restructuring: lessons from Asia / Carl-Johan Lindgren
Washington, DC: International Monetary Fund, 1999.
Editor: Lindgren, Carl-Johan.
Description: p. cm.
ISBN: 1557758719
Notes: Includes bibliographical references.
Subjects: Finance--Asia--Case studies. Financial crises--Asia--Case studies.
Series: Occasional paper (International Monetary Fund); no. 188.
LC Classification: HG187.A2 F57 1999
Dewey Class No.: 332/.095 21

Financial sector development in Sub-Saharan African countries / Hassanali Mehran
Washington, D.C.: International Monetary Fund, 1998.
Editor: Mehran, Hassanali.
Description: viii, 107 p.; 28 cm.
ISBN: 1557757585
Notes: Includes bibliographical references (p. 105).
Subjects: Financial institutions--Africa, Sub-Saharan.
Series: Occasional paper (International Monetary Fund); no. 171.
LC Classification: HG187.5.A357 F564 1998
Dewey Class No.: 332.1/0967 21

Financial sector operations policy.
[London]: European Bank for Reconstruction and Development, [1992]
Description: 11 leaves; 30 cm.
Notes: "March 1992."
Subjects: European Bank for Reconstruction and Development. Banks and

banking, International. Capital movements.
Series: Document of the European Bank for Reconstruction and Development
LC Classification: HG3881.5.E83 F56 1992

Fiscal policy, economic adjustment, and financial markets / edited by Mario Monti.
Washington, D.C.: International Monetary Fund; Milan: Centro di Economia monetaria e finanziaria 1989.
Editor: Monti, Mario.
Description: x, 283 p.: ill.; 23 cm.
ISBN: 1557751188 :
Notes: "Papers presented at a sminar sponsored by the Internationa Fund and Centro di Economia monetaria e finanziaria, Universite Bocconi, held in Milan on January 28-30, 1988." Includes bibliographical references.
Subjects: Fiscal policy--Congresses. Debts, Public--Congresses. Finance--Congresses.
LC Classification: HJ236 .F556 1989
Dewey Class No.: 336.3 20

Fiscal reforms in low-income countries: experience under IMF-supported programs / by George T. Abed ... [et al.].
Washington, DC: International Monetary Fund, 1998.
Editor: Abed, George T.
Description: vii, 90 p.: ill.; 28 cm.
ISBN: 1557757178
Notes: "February 1998." Includes bibliographical references (p. 87-88).
Subjects: Fiscal policy--Developing countries. Structural adjustment (Economic policy)—Developing countries.
Series: Occasional paper (International Monetary Fund); no. 160.
LC Classification: HJ1620 .F573 1998
Dewey Class No.: 336.3/09172/4 21

Floating exchange rates in developing countries: experience with auction and interbank markets / by Peter J. Quirk ... [et al.].
Washington, D.C.: International Monetary Fund, 1987.
Editor: Quirk, Peter J.
Description: v, 43 p.: col. ill.; 28 cm.
ISBN: 0939934892 (pbk.) :
Subjects: Foreign exchange--Developing countries.
Series: Occasional paper (International Monetary Fund); no. 53.
LC Classification: HG3877 .F58 1987
Dewey Class No.: 332.4/56/091724 19

FMI, Banco Mundial y GATT, 50 años bastan: el libro del foro alternativo: las otras voces del planeta / Antonio Estevan, coordinador.

Madrid: Talasa Ediciones, [1995]
Editor: Estevan, Antonio.
Description: 510 p.; 20 cm.
ISBN: 8488119321
Notes: Includes bibliographical references (p. 261-263).
Subjects: International Monetary Fund. World Bank. General Agreement on Tariffs and Trade (Organization) Economic development. Structural adjustment (Economic policy) Economic assistance. Developing countries--Economic conditions.
Series: Talasa (Madrid, Spain); 71.
LC Classification: HD75 .F63 1995

Fondo monetario international y Banco international de reconstrucciûn y fomento
Buenos Aires, Editorial Losada, s. a., 1945.
Description: 3 p. l., [9]-187 p., 2 l. 23 cm.
Subjects: International Monetary Fund. International bank for Reconstruction and Developement.
Series: Academia de Ciencias Econûmicas, Buenos Aires. Diciones especiales, no. 7.
LC Classification: HG205 1944.A3 A77 1945

Forbes, A.A.
The importance of being local: Villagers, NGOs, and the World Bank in the Arun Valley, Nepal
Global Studies in Culture and Power, 1999, Vol 6, Iss 2-3, pp 319-344
This paper reflects on the ways in which "local" identity became an important basis of legitimacy in the organization of opposition to the Arun dam in Nepal. Large projects such as dams have multiple effects over space and time so that there are many locales that can constitute the proper domain of the "local" voice. Looking only for the most strictly local privileges place over politics and implies that physical boundaries are impermeable. This paper suggests shifting analysis from a search for the legitimate "local" to an understanding of the processes by which different identity claims are employed by various agents to achieve different strategic ends.

Ford, Peter
Enter the Euro.
Christian Science Monitor Dec. 17, 1998, p12-13

Foreign direct investment, the service sector, and international banking / United Nations Centre on Transnational Corporations.
London; Boston: Published in co-operation with the United Nations Centre on Transnational Corporations by Graham & Trotman, 1988.
Description: viii, 71 p.; 30 cm.

ISBN: 1853330485 (pbk.)
Notes: Reprint. Originally published: New York: United Nations, c1987.
Subjects: Investments, Foreign. Service industries. Banks and banking, International. International business enterprises.
Series: UNCTC current studies. Series A.; no. 7
LC Classification: HG4538 .F6194 1988
Dewey Class No.: 332.6/73 19

Foreign exchange issues, capital markets, and international banking in the 1990s / edited by Khosrow Fatemi, Dominick Salvatore.
Washington D.C.: Taylor & Francis, c1993.
Editor: Fatemi, Khosrow. Salvatore, Dominick.
Description: ix, 289 p.: ill.; 24 cm.
ISBN: 0844817376 (cloth) :
Notes: Includes index.
Subjects: Foreign exchange. Capital market. Banks and banking, International.
Series: Series on international business and trade
LC Classification: HG3853 .F67 1993
Dewey Class No.: 332/.042 20

Foreign exchange trading techniques and controls / Donald R. Mandich, editor.
Washington, D.C.: International Bankina Division,
American Bankers Association, c1976.
Editor: Mandich, Donald R.
Description: xii, 203 p.: forms; 24 cm.
Notes: Includes bibliographical references and index.
Subjects: Foreign exchange. Banks and banking, International.
LC Classification: HG3851 .F63
Dewey Class No.: 332.4/5

Forestry: the World Bank's experience.
Washington, D.C.: Operations Evaluation Dept., World Bank, c1991.
Description: xx, 49 p.: ill.; 28 cm.
ISBN: 0821319833
Notes: Text in English with summaries in French and Spanish.
Includes bibliographical references.
Subjects: World Bank. Forestry projects--Developing countries. Forests and forestry--Economic aspects—Developing countries. Forest policy--Developing countries.
Series: A World Bank operations evaluation study, 1011-0984
LC Classification: SD247.5 .F68 1991
Dewey Class No.: 333.75/09172/4 20

Frameworks for monetary stability: policy issues and country experiences: papers presented at the sixth seminar on central banking, Washington, D.C., March 1-10, 1994 / editors, Tom·s J.T. Baliòo, Carlo Cottarelli.
Washington: IMF Institute and Monetary and Exchange Affairs Dept., International Monetary Fund, 1994.
Editor: Baliòo, Tom·s J. T.
Description: xi, 755 p.: ill.; 23 cm.
ISBN: 1557754195
Notes: Includes bibliographical references.
Subjects: Monetary policy--Congresses. Economic stabilization--Congresses. Banks and banking, Central--Congresses.
LC Classification: HG230.3 .F723 1994
Dewey Class No.: 332.5/6 20

Francis, David
New World Order for Finance?.
Christian Science Monitor Sept. 29, 1998, pn.p.

French, Hilary F.
The World Bank: Now Fifty, but How Fit?.
World Watch July/Aug. 1994, p10-18

Friday morning reflections at the World Bank: essays on values and development / David Beckmann ... [et al.] ; foreword by Barber B. Conable.
Washington: Seven Locks Press, c1991.
Editor: Beckmann, David M.
Description: xiii, 80 p.; 23 cm.
ISBN: 093202078X :
Notes: Includes bibliographical references.
Subjects: World Bank--Developing countries. Economic development--Moral and ethical aspects.
LC Classification: HD75 .F75 1991
Dewey Class No.: 332.1/532 20

Friedmann, H.
The globalisation of poverty: Impacts of IMF and World Bank reforms, by M. Chossudovsky
Contemporary Sociology - A Journal of Reviews, 1998, Vol 27, Iss 6, pp 597-598

Fuel for change: World Bank energy policy: rhetoric vs reality / edited by Ian Tellam.
New York: Zed Books, 2000.
Editor: Tellam, lan.
Description: p. cm.
ISBN: 185649781X (cased) 1856497828 (limp)

Notes: Includes bibliographical references and index.
Subjects: World Bank. Energy development--Developing countries--Finance—Case studies. Energy development--Europe, Eastern--Finance—Case studies. Renewable energy sources--Developing countries. Renewable energy sources--Europe, Eastern.
LC Classification: HD9502.D442 F83 2000
Dewey Class No.: 333.79 21

Fujioka, Masao.
Ajia Kaigin S¯osai nikki: Manira e no satogaeri / Fujioka Masao cho.
T¯oky¯o: T¯oy¯o Keizai Shinp¯osha, Sh¯owa 61 [1986]
Description: 185 p.: ill.; 20 cm.
ISBN: 4492650954 :
Subjects: Asian Development Bank. Asia cooperation. Asia--Economic policy.
LC Classification: HG5993 .F84 1986

Functioning of the international monetary system / edited by Jacob A. Frenkel and Morris Goldstein.
Washington, D.C.: International Monetary Fund, c1996.
Editor: Frenkel, Jacob A. Goldstein, Morris,
Description: 2 v.: ill.; 23 cm.
ISBN: 155775554X (set)
Notes: Includes bibliographical references.
Subjects: European Monetary System (Organization) International finance. International economic relations. Monetary policy. Foreign exchange. Money--European Economic Community countries.
LC Classification: HG3881 .F848 1996
Dewey Class No.: 332/.042 20

Fund-supported programs, fiscal policy, and income distribution: a study / by the Fiscal Affairs Department of the International Monetary Fund.
Washington, D.C.: International Monetary Fund, 1986.
Description: v, 58 p.: ill.; 28 cm.
ISBN: 0939934647 (pbk.) :
Notes: Bibliography: p. 54-58.
Subjects: International Monetary Fund. Economic development projects--Developing countries. Fiscal policy--Developing countries. Income distribution--Developing countries. Developing countries--Economic policy.
Series: Occasional paper (International Monetary Fund); no. 46.
LC Classification: HG3881.5.I58 F88 1986
Dewey Class No.: 339.5/09172/4 19

Ganguli, Barin N.
Breakthroughs in forestry development: experience of the Asian Development

Bank / by Barin N. Ganguli.
Manila, Philippines: Asian Development Bank, [1995]
Description: xvii, 269 p.: col. ill., col. maps; 24 cm.
ISBN: 9715610668
Notes: "June 1995." Includes bibliographical references (p. [263]-269).
Subjects: Asian Development Bank. Forestry projects--Asia. Forestry projects--Asia--Finance. Sustainable forestry--Asia--Case studies.
LC Classification: SD387.P74 G35 1995
Dewey Class No.: 333.75/15/095 21

Garuda, Gopal
Lender of Last Resort: Rethinking IMF Conditionality
Harvard International Review Summer 1998, p36-39

Geldschieters van de wereld: de internationale particuliere banken, het Internationale Monetaire Fonds / [tekst, Ludi Boeken en Sarah Bartlett; foto's, Loek Groenendijk et al.].
Den Haag: Novib, 1980.
Editor: Bartlett, Sarah.
Description: 87 p.: ill.; 20 cm.
ISBN: 9021510103 :
Subjects: International Monetary Fund. International finance. Banks and banking, International. Finance--Developing countries--Case studies.
LC Classification: HG3881 .B5625

Gendai kin'y¯u shihon no shoriron: takokuseki kigy¯o to takokuseki gink¯o no taj¯uteki nettow¯aku / Sekishita Minoru hencho.
Edition Information: Shohan.
T¯oky¯o: D¯obunkan, Heisei 1 [1989]
Editor: Sekishita, Minoru,
Description: 9, 230 p.: ill.; 22 cm.
ISBN: 4495423614 :
Notes: Includes bibliographical references.
Subjects: Corporations--Finance. International business enterprises--Finance. Banks and banking, International.
LC Classification: HG4026 .G465 1989

General capital increase for the World Bank: hearing before the Committee on Banking, Finance, and Urban Affairs, House of Representatives, One-hundredth Congress, second session, June 15, 1988.
Washington: U.S. G.P.O.: For sale by the Supt. of Doc., Congressional Sales Office, U.S. G.P.O., 1988.
Description: iii, 63 p.; 24 cm.
Notes: Distributed to some depository libraries in microfiche. Shipping list no.:

88-487-P. "Serial no. 100-72." Item 1013-A, 1013-B (microfiche)
Subjects: World Bank--Developing countries. Economic assistance, American--Developing countries.
LC Classification: KF27 .B5 1988
Dewey Class No.: 332.1/532 19
Govt. Doc. No.: Y 4.B 22/1:100-72

Georgia.
Washington, D.C.: International Monetary Fund,
Description: v.; 28 cm.
ISSN: 1087-3783
Notes: Description based on: 1994. SERBIB/SERLOC merged record
Subjects: Georgia (Republic)--Economic conditions--Periodicals. Georgia (Republic)--Economic policy--Periodicals.
Series: IMF economic reviews, 1020-0576
LC Classification: HC415.19.A1 G46
Dewey Class No.: 330.947/95/005 20
Entry: Georgia (International Monetary Fund) 96-648017

German unification: economic issues / edited by Leslie Lipschitz and Donogh McDonald.
Washington, D.C.: International Monetary Fund, c1990.
Editor: Lipschitz, Leslie.
Description: xv, 171 p.: ill., map; 28 cm.
ISBN: 1557752001 :
Notes: "December 1990." Includes bibliographical references.
Subjects: Germany (West)--Economic policy--1974-1990. Germany (West)--Economic conditions--1974-1990. Germany (East)--Economic policy. Germany (East)--Economic conditions. Germany--History--Unification, 1990.
Series: Occasional paper (International Monetary Fund); no. 75.
LC Classification: HC286.7 .G447 1990
Dewey Class No.: 330.943/0879 20

Getting results: the World Bank's agenda for improving development effectiveness.
Washington, D.C.: World Bank, [1993]
Description: iii, 20 p.: ill.; 23 cm.
ISBN: 0821325949
Subjects: World Bank. Economic development projects--Evaluation.
LC Classification: HC79.E44 G48 1993
Dewey Class No.: 332.1/532/0917124 20

Ghana--adjustment and growth, 1983-91 / Ishan Kapur ... [et al.].
Washington, DC: International Monetary Fund, [1991]
Editor: Kapur, Ishan.
Description: vii, 69 p.: ill.; 28 cm.

ISBN: 155775182X :
Notes: "September 1991." Includes bibliographical references (p. 66-67).
Subjects: Structural adjustment (Economic policy)--Ghana.
Series: Occasional paper (International Monetary Fund); no. 86.
LC Classification: HC1060 .G425 1991
Dewey Class No.: 338.9667/009/048 20

Gibbs, Christopher J. N.
Nongovernmental organizations in World Bank-supported projects: a review / Christopher Gibbs, Claudia Fumo, Thomas Kuby.
Edition Information: 2nd ed.
Washington, D.C.: World Bank, 1999.
Description: xxi, 66 p.; 28 cm.
ISBN: 0821344560
Notes: At head of World Bank Operations Evaluation Department. Includes bibliographical references (p. 65-66). Foreword and summaries also in French and Spanish.
Subjects: World Bank--Developing countries. Non-governmental organizations--Developing countries. Community development--Developing countries. Economic development projects--Developing countries.
Series: OED series (Washington, D.C.)
LC Classification: HC60 .G49 1999
Dewey Class No.: 338.9/009172/4 21

Gink¯oron k¯ogi / Suzuki Yoshinori hencho.
Edition Information: Shohan.
T¯oky¯o: Shinhy¯oron, 1986 (1987 printing)
Editor: Suzuki, Yoshinori,
Description: 224 p.; 22 cm.
Notes: Bibliography: p. 222-224.
Subjects: Banks and banking. Banks and banking--Japan. Banks and banking, International.
LC Classification: HG1697.J3 G56 1986

Gli accordi di Bretton Woods; l'accordo monetario, la banca internazionale per la ricostruzione e lo sviluppo, a cura della Banca commerciale italiana.
[Roma, Tipografia editrice Italia, 1945?]
Editor: Morgenthau, Henry,
Description: 96 p. 21 cm.
Subjects: International Monetary Fund. International Bank for Reconstruction and Development.
LC Classification: HG3881 .A785 1945

Global development fifty years after Bretton Woods: essays in honour of Gerald K. Helleiner / edited by Roy Culpeper, Albert Berry, and Frances Stewart.
New York: St. Martin's Press, 1996.
Editor: Helleiner, Gerald K. Culpeper, Roy, Berry, Albert. Stewart, Frances.
Description: xiii, 381 p.: ill.; 23 cm.
ISBN: 0312162820 (cloth) 0312162839 (pbk.)
Notes: "Gerald K. Helleiner's publications": p. 356-375.
Includes bibliographical references and index.
Subjects: Helleiner, Gerald K. World Bank. International Monetary Fund. International finance. International economic relations.
LC Classification: HG3881 .G5727 1997
Dewey Class No.: 337 20

Global Environment Facility: independent evaluation of the pilot phase / United Nations Development Programme (UNDP), United Nations Environment Programme (UNEP), and the World Bank.
Washington, D.C.: World Bank, c1994.
Description: xxi, 192 p.: ill.; 28 cm.
ISBN: 0821328123
Notes: Includes bibliographical references.
Subjects: United Nations Development Programme. United Nations Environment Programme. World Bank. Global Environment Facility--Evaluation. Environmental policy--Evaluation.
LC Classification: GE170 .G56 1994
Dewey Class No.: 363.7/056 20

Global investment banking strategy: insights from industry leaders / written in co-operation with A.T. Kearney, Inc.
New York, NY: Economist Intelligence Unit, c1998.
Description: vii, 111 p.: ill.; 27 cm.
Notes: Includes index.
Subjects: Investment banking. Banks and banking, International.
Series: Research report (Economist Intelligence Unit (Great Britain))
LC Classification: HG4534 .G55 1998

Global survey of permissible activities for banking organizations in major financial centers outside the U.S.--Canada, France, Germany, Hong Kong, Italy, Japan, The Netherlands, Switzerland, United Kingdom, and a report on financial developments in the European Economic Community / Institute of International Bankers.
[New York, N.Y.] (299 Park Ave., 17th Fl., New York 10171): The Institute, [between 1992 and 1997]
Description: 72 p.; 27 cm.
Notes: Cover title. Includes bibliographical references.

Subjects: Banks and banking, American. Banks and banking, International. Banks and banking--Securities processing. Banks and banking--Insurance business. Bank investments. Banks and banking--European Economic Community countries.
LC Classification: HG2569 .G52 1992

Gonzales, M.C.
The World Bank and African primary education: Policies, practices, and recommendations
Africa Today, 1999, Vol 46, Iss 1, pp 119-134
This paper argues that the World Bank's economic cost-benefit methodology used in assessing primary education projects in Africa is largely ineffective in determining the Likely success and impact of these projects on their host countries. After analyzing the actual methods used, this study argues that to determine the net social value of primary education projects in Africa, the World Bank must reduce its dependence on traditional quantitative measures and incorporate a more pedagogical and sociological methodology combined with specific goals and increased field monitoring and assessment. The analysis ends with recommendations for methodological alterations and suggested means of offsetting additional costs.

Gould Davies, N. and Woods, N.
Russia and the IMF
International Affairs, 1999, Vol 75, Iss 1, pp 1+
Russia's economic crisis in the summer of 1998 has renewed debate as to whether the International Monetary Fund (IMF) has helped, hindered or been irrelevant to economic transition in the core of the former Soviet Union. The examine the relationship between the Fund and Russia over the past ten years, highlighting a mixed record of successes, failures and the limits of the Fund's role. They argue that the institution may well have also inadvertently facilitated the rise of political forces which are today opposed to the second phase of reforms which Russia so desperately needs. In conclusion, the question whether the IMF ought to continue to lead Western attempts to foster stability and growth in Russia.

Green, Reginald Herbold.
Reduction of absolute poverty: a priority structural adjustment / by Reginald Herbold Green.
Brighton, England: Institute of Development Studies, c1991.
Description: 40 p.; 21 cm.
ISBN: 0903715414
Notes: Cover title. "May 1991."
Subjects: World Bank--Africa. Economic assistance, Domestic--Africa. Poor--Africa.
Series: Discussion Paper (University of Sussex. Institute of Development

Studies); 287.
LC Classification: HC800.Z9 P634 1991
Dewey Class No.: 338.96 20

Grossbanken im Weltwirtschaftssystem: Studien- und Bibliothekshilfsmittel / Universität Bremen, Bibliothek, Fachreferat Wirtschaftswissenschaften; Herausgeber, Klaus Jürgen Bönkost --- [et al.].
[Bremen]: Universität Bremen, Bibliothek, Abteilung Jur/Oek., 1981.
Editor: Bönkost, Klaus Jürgen,
Description: ii, 298 p.: ill.; 21 cm.
Notes: Bibliography: p. 290-296.
Subjects: Banks and banking--Directories. Banks and banking, International--Directories.
Series: Veröffentlichungen der Abteilung Jur/Oek; Nr. 8
LC Classification: HG1536 .G76 1981
Dewey Class No.: 332.1/025 19

Growth experience in transition countries, 1990-98 / Oleh Havrylyshyn ... [et al.].
Washington, D.C.: International Monetary Fund, 1999.
Editor: Havrylyshyn, Oli.
Description: p. cm.
ISBN: 1557758034
Notes: Includes bibliographical references (p.).
Subjects: Former Soviet republics--Economic conditions—Econometric models. Europe, Central--Economic conditions--Econometric models. Europe, Eastern--Economic conditions--1989---Econometric models.
Series: Occasional paper (International Monetary Fund); no. 184. Occasional paper (International Monetary Fund). Issues in transition.
LC Classification: HC336.27 .G76 1999
Dewey Class No.: 338.947 21

Growth-oriented adjustment programs / edited by Vittorio Corbo, Morris Goldstein, Mohsin Khan.
Washington, D.C.: International Monetary Fund: World Bank, 1987.
Editor: Corbo, Vittorio.
Description: xiii, 537 p.: ill.; 23 cm.
ISBN: 0939934922 (pbk.)
Notes: "Proceedings of a symposium held in Washington D.C., February 25-27, 1987." Includes bibliographies.
Subjects: Economic policy--Congresses. Industrial policy--Congresses. Economic stabilization--Congresses.
LC Classification: HD73 .G76 1987
Dewey Class No.: 338.9 19

Guide to international business opportunities / World Bank.
Washington, D.C.: The Bank, [1989?-
Description: v.: ill.; 28 cm. [1st ed.]-
Notes: Title from cover. SERBIB/SERLOC merged record
Subjects: World Bank. Investments, Foreign--Developing countries. Economic development projects--Developing countries.
LC Classification: HG3881.5.W57 G85
Entry: Guide; to international business opportunities. 94-649783

Hackenberg, R.A. and Hackenberg, B.H.
You CAN do something! Forming policy from applied projects, then and now
Human Organization, 1999, Vol 58, Iss 1, pp 1-15

Halfway to reform: the World Bank and the Venezuelan justice system / a joint report by the Lawyers Committee for Human Rights and the Venezuelan Program for Human Rights Education and Action.
New York: Lawyers Committee for Human Rights, c1996.
Description: ii, 149 p.; 23 cm.
ISBN: 0934143862
Notes: "August 1996." Includes bibliographical references.
Subjects: World Bank. Justice, Administration of--Venezuela. Law reform--Venezuela. Judicial corruption--Venezuela.
LC Classification: KHW2501 .L38 1996
Dewey Class No.: 347.87 21

Hanchette, John
International Monetary Fund Drawing Increased Congressional Scrutiny.
Gannett News Service Dec. 29, 1999, pn.p.

Handbook on policies, practices and procedures relating to procurement under Asian Development Bank loans / Asian Development Bank.
Manila, Philippines: Asian Development Bank, Central Projects Services Office, 198-?
Description: 90 p.: ill.; 23 cm.
Subjects: Asian Development Bank. Industrial procurement. Government purchasing.
LC Classification: HG3381.5.A75 A84 1980
Dewey Class No.: 332.1/53 19

Hanmer, L.C., Pyatt, G. and White, H.
What do the world bank's poverty assessments teach us about poverty in sub-Saharan Africa?
Development and Change, 1999, Vol 30, Iss 4, pp 795-823

As part of the World Bank's poverty reduction strategy, Poverty Assessments have been carried out for a number of countries which analyse who the poor are, the causes of poverty and poverty reduction policies. This article reviews what can be learnt from the twenty-five Assessments prepared for countries in sub-Saharan Africa up to 1996. Whilst other factors are acknowledged in identifying the poor, the Assessments over-emphasize income-poverty defined against an inevitably arbitrary poverty line.

Harrigan, Susan

Third World Loans Crush Bank Profits -
Newsday Jan. 20, 1988

Herz, Barbara

Bringing Women into the Economic Mainstream.
Finance & Development (Intl. Monetary Fund & the World Bank)
Dec. 1989, p22+

Hoffman, Ellen

One World, One Currency?
Omni June 1991, p51+
Ethan B. Kapstein
Shockproof: The End of the Financial Crisis.
Foreign Affairs Jan./Feb. 1996, p2-8

Hoffman, Jeffrey

Techno Money: As Wall Street Goes High-Tech, Both Benefits
Gazette-Mail (Charleston, WV) May 28, 1995, p1B+

Hook, Walter

Counting on cars, counting out people: a critique of the World Bank's economic assessment procedures for the transport sector and their environmental implications / [Walter Hook].
New York, NY: Institute for Transportation & Development Policy, c1994.
Description: 41 p.; 23 cm.
Subjects: World Bank--Developing countries. Roads--Economic aspects--Developing countries--Evaluation. Roads--Developing countries--Finance. Transportation--Developing countries--Evaluation. Transportation--Developing countries--Finance.
LC Classification: HE368.7 .H66 1994

Housing: enabling markets to work; with technical supplements.

Washington, D.C.: World Bank, c1993.
Description: vii, 159 p.: ill.; 23 cm.
ISBN: 0821324349

Notes: Includes bibliographical references (p. 152-159).
Subjects: World Bank--Developing countries. Housing--Developing countries--Finance. Housing policy--Developing countries.
Series: A World Bank policy paper, 1014-8124
LC Classification: HD7391 .H67 1993
Dewey Class No.: 363.5/09172/4 20

How adjustment programs can help the poor: the World Bank's experience / Helena Ribe ... [et al.].
Washington, D.C.: The Bank, c1990.
Editor: Ribe, Helena,
Description: 49 p.; 28 cm.
ISBN: 0821314343
Notes: Includes bibliographical references (p. 46-49)
Subjects: World Bank--Developing countries. Loans, Foreign--Developing countries. Economic stabilization--Developing countries. Poor--Developing countries. Income distribution--Developing countries. Cost and standard of living--Developing countries.
Series: World Bank discussion papers; 0259-210X; 71
LC Classification: HG3881.5.W57 H68 1990
Dewey Class No.: 332.1/532 20

Huang, Po-Wen.
The Asian Development Bank: diplomacy and development in Asia / by Po-Wen Huang, Jr.
Edition Information: 1st ed.
New York: Vantage Press, c1975.
Description: 210 p.; 22 cm.
ISBN: 0533018641 :
Notes: Includes index. Bibliography: p. 165-204.
Subjects: Asian Development Bank.
LC Classification: HG4517 .H83
Dewey Class No.: 332.1/53

Hurt III, Harry
Do Not Try This at Home.
U.S. News & World Report Dec. 8, 1997,

Husain, Ishrat
The challenge of Africa / Ishrat Husain.
Washington, DC: World Bank, [1994]
Description: 31 p.: ill.; 28 cm.
ISBN: 0821330845
Notes: "50th anniversary"--Cover. Includes bibliographical references (p. 31).

Subjects: World Bank--Africa. Loans, Foreign--Africa. Poverty--Africa. Sustainable development--Africa. Africa--Economic policy.
Series: The evolving role of the World Bank
LC Classification: HG3881.5.W57 H87 1994
Dewey Class No.: 332.1/532/096 20

Huther, Jeff, 1960-
Public expenditure reform under adjustment lending : lessons from World Bank experiences / Jeff Huther, Sandra Roberts, Anwar Shah.
Washington, D.C.: World Bank, c1997.
Description: viii, 55 p.: ill.; 28 cm.
ISBN: 082134160X (pbk.)
Notes: Includes bibliographical references (p. 45-48).
Subjects: World Bank--Developing countries. Expenditures, Public--Developing countries. Government spending policy--Developing countries. Loans, Foreign--Developing countries. Economic assistance--Developing countries.
Series: World Bank discussion papers; 382.
LC Classification: HJ7980 .H88 1997
Dewey Class No.: 336.3/9/091724 21

ICB magazine
London: Reactions Pub. Group,
Description: v.: ill.; 30 cm.
Current Frequency: Bimonthly
Continues: ICB 0953-5632 (DLC)sn 88001460 (OCoLC)17979902
Continued by: CB (London, England: 1995) (DLC)sn 96030044
ISSN: 0968-6118
Notes: Description based on: May/June 1992; title from cover.
SERBIB/SERLOC merged record Indx'd selectively by: Computer & control abstracts 0036-8113 Electrical & electronic abstracts 0036-8105 Physics abstracts 0036-8091
Subjects: Investment banking--Periodicals. Securities industry--Periodicals. Banks and banking--Periodicals. Banks and banking, International--Periodicals.
LC Classification: HG4534 .I27
Dewey Class No.: 332.66/05 20
Entry: ICB magazine. 92-646054

IDA in action 1993-1996: the pursuit of sustained poverty reduction: summary.
Washington, D.C.: World Bank, c1997.
Description: iv, 29 p.: ill., 1 col. map.; 28 cm.
ISBN: 082133963X
Notes: Includes bibliographical references (p. 26).
Subjects: World Bank International Development Association. Economic assistance--Developing countries. Poverty--Developing countries.

LC Classification: HG3881.5.W57 I33 1997
Other System No.: (OCoLC)37152471

Iklé, Max
Die Schweiz als internationaler Bank- und Finanzplatz.
Zürich, Orell Füssli, [1970]
Description: 187 p. 24 cm.
Subjects: Banks and banking—Switzerland Banks and banking, International
LC Classification: HG3204 .I35

Iklé, Max
Switzerland: an international banking and finance center.
Translated from the German by Eric Schiff.
Stroudsburg, Pa., Dowden, Hutchinson & Ross [1972]
Description: 156 p. 24 cm.
ISBN: 0879330023
Notes: Translation of Die Schweiz als internationaler Bank- und Finanzplatz.
Subjects: Banks and banking--Switzerland. Banks and banking, International.
LC Classification: HG3204 .I3513
Dewey Class No.: 332.1/09494

IMF - A retrograde step
Economic and Political Weekly, 1999, Vol 34, Iss 19, pp 1072-1073

IMF and India. Part 1 [microform].
New Delhi: Library of Congress Office; Washington, D.C. : Library of Congress Photoduplication Service, 1998.
Description: 5 microfiches.
Notes: A collection of pamphlets published during 1984-1992. Contents list arranged alphabetically by title. Collected and organized by the Library of Congress Office, New Delhi. Master microform held by: DLC.
Subjects: International Monetary Fund. Economic assistance--India.
Series: South Asia ephemera collection. India; I-CLR-178.1
LC Classification: Microfiche 97/60379 (H)

IMF and the Asian financial crisis / consulting editor, Peter G. Zhang.
Singapore; New Jersey: World Scientific, c1998.
Editor: Zhang, Peter G.
Description: x, 110 p.; 21 cm.
ISBN: 9810236298
Notes: Includes bibliographical references.
Subjects: International Monetary Fund. Financial crises--Asia. Asia--Economic conditions--1945- Asia--Economic policy.
Series: World Scientific Asian economic profiles

LC Classification: HB3808 .I44 1998
Dewey Class No.: 332.1/52 21

IMF conditionality / edited by John Williamson.
Washington, D.C.: Institute for International Economics; Cambridge: Distributed by MIT Press, 1983.
Editor: Williamson, John,
Description: xvi, 679 p.; 24 cm.
ISBN: 0881320064 :
Notes: Based on a conference which was held at Airlie House, Virginia, Mar. 24-26, 1982, sponsored by the Institute. Includes bibliographies and index.
Subjects: International Monetary Fund--Congresses. Loans, Foreign--Congresses. Conditionality (International relations)
LC Classification: HG3881.5.I58 I4 1983
Dewey Class No.: 332.1/52 19

IMF conditionality: experience under stand-by and extended arrangement / Susan Schadler ... [et al.].
Washington, DC: International Monetary Fund, 1995.
Editor: Schadler, Susan.
Description: 2 v.: col. ill.; 28 cm.
ISBN: 1557754926 (pt. 1) 1557755000 (pt. 2)
Contents: pt. 1. Key issues and findings -- pt. 2. Backgroundpapers.
Notes: Includes bibliographical references.
Subjects: International Monetary Fund. International finance. Structural adjustment (Economic policy)—Developing countries. Conditionality (International relations)
Series: Occasional paper (International Monetary Fund); no.128-129.
LC Classification: HG3881.5.I58 I43 1995
Dewey Class No.: 332.1/52 20

IMF economic reviews. 4, Uzbekistan.
Washington, D.C.: International Monetary Fund, c1992-
Description: v. ; 28 cm. 1992-
ISSN: 1020-0576
Notes: SERBIB/SERLOC merged record
Subjects: Uzbekistan--Economic conditions--1991---Periodicals. Uzbekistan--Economic policy--1991---Periodicals.
Series: IMF economic reviews
LC Classification: HC421.7.A1 I47
Entry: IMF economic reviews. 4, Uzbekistan. 96-646649

IMF economic reviews. Press information notices.
Washington, D.C.: International Monetary Fund, 1998.

Description: 1 v.; 28 cm. 1998, no. 1.
Current Frequency: Three issues a year.
Continues in part: International Monetary Fund. Annual report of the executive board for the financial year ended April 30 ... 0250-7498 (DLC) 86647373 (OCoLC)5705422
Continued by: IMF economic reviews. Press/public information notices (DLC)sn 98034805 (OCoLC)40550138
ISSN: 1020-6779
Notes: Press information notices on individual countries available at the IMF web site. Includes Executive Board reviews of member economies previously released in the IMF annual report. SERBIB/SERLOC merged record Continues the monographic series: IMF economic reviews.
Subjects: Economic history--1990---Periodicals. Economic policy--Periodicals.
LC Classification: HC10 .I45
Dewey Class No.: 330.9/005 21
Entry: IMF economic reviews. Press information notices. 98-646708

IMF economic reviews.
Washington, D.C.: International Monetary Fund, c1992-
Description: v.; 28 cm. 1993, 1- Ceased in 1996.
Current Frequency: Irregular
Continues: Economic review (Washington, D.C.)
ISSN: 1020-0576
Notes: Continued in 1998 by the periodical: IMF economic reviews. Press information notices.
Subjects: Former Soviet republics--Economic conditions--1991- Statistics--Periodicals. Former Soviet republics--Economic policy--1991- Periodicals. Europe, Eastern- Economic conditions--1989---Periodicals.
LC Classification: CLASSED SEPARATELY
Dewey Class No.: 332 12

IMF glossary: English, French, Spanish.
Washington, D.C.: International Monetary Fund: Orders to Secretary, International Monetary Fund, 1980.
Description: vii, 162 p.; 28 cm.
Notes: "This revised edition of the IMF glossary has been prepared by the Technical Documentation, Reference, and Interpretation Unit, in cooperation with the translation divisions of the IMF's Bureau of Language Services"--Foreword. "GLO. 1-79/Rev. 1." Includes indexes.
Subjects: International Monetary Fund--Dictionaries--Polyglot. International finance--Dictionaries--Polyglot. Dictionaries, Polyglot.
LC Classification: HG3881.5.I58 I565 1980
Dewey Class No.: 332.1/52 19

IMF glossary: English-French-Spanish.
Edition Information: [3rd ed.].
Washington, D.C.: International Monetary Fund: Address order to Publications Unit, International Monetary Fund, 1986.
Description: vii, 286 p.; 28 cm.
ISBN: 093993471X (pbk.)
Notes: "This third edition of the IMF glossary has been compiled by the Bureau of Language Services' Technical Documentation, Reference, and Terminology Section in cooperation with the Bureau's translation divisions"--Foreword. Includes indexes.
Subjects: International Monetary Fund--Dictionaries--Polyglot. International finance--Dictionaries--Polyglot.
LC Classification: HG3881.5.I58 I565 1986
Dewey Class No.: 332.1/52 19

IMF glossary: English-French-Spanish.
Edition Information: 2nd ed.
Washington, D.C.: International Monetary Fund, 1982.
Description: vii, 292 p.; 28 cm.
ISBN: 0939934043 (pbk.) :
Notes: "This new edition of the IMF glossary has been compiled by the Bureau of Language Services' terminologist in cooperation with the Bureau's translation divisions"--Foreword. "GLO.2-82." Includes indexes.
Subjects: International Monetary Fund--Dictionaries--Polyglot. International finance--Dictionaries--Polyglot. Dictionaries, Polyglot.
LC Classification: HG3881.5.I58 I565 1982
Dewey Class No.: 332.1/52 19

IMF glossary: English-French-Spanish.
Edition Information: 4th rev. ed.
Washington, D.C.: International Monetary Fund, 1992.
Editor: International Monetary Fund.
Description: vii, 341 p.; 28 cm.
ISBN: 1557752672
Notes: "GLO.4-92." Includes indexes.
Subjects: International Monetary Fund--Dictionaries--Polyglot. International finance--Dictionaries--Polyglot.
LC Classification: HG3881.5.I58 I565 1992
Dewey Class No.: 332.1/52 20

IMF glossary: English-French-Spanish.
Edition Information: 5th ed. rev. and enl.
Washington, D.C.: International Monetary Fund, 1997.
Description: vii, 392 p.: ill.; 28 cm.

ISBN: 1557756597
Notes: Prepared by the Bureau of Language Services' Reference, Terminology, and Documentation Section, in collaboration with the Terminology Working Group of the Bureau of Language Services. "Contains a ... selection of terms automatically retrieved from the 'IMF computerized terminology database' by the Reference, Terminology, and Documentation staff--P. v. "GLO.5-97." Includes indexes.
Subjects: International Monetary Fund--Dictionaries--Polyglot. International finance--Dictionaries--Polyglot.
LC Classification: HG3881.5.I58 I565 1997
Dewey Class No.: 332.1/52 21

IMF gold - The euro link
Economic and Political Weekly, 1999, Vol 34, Iss 21, pp 1229

IMF handobukku: kokusai tsuka kikin no soshiki to kino / Ikawa Norimichi hencho.
Edition Information: Shohan.
Tokyo: Nenkin Kenkyujo, 1992.
Editor: Ikawa, Norimichi.
Description: 351 p.: ill.; 21 cm.
Subjects: International Monetary Fund.
LC Classification: HG3881.I58 I44 1992

IMF Han'guk i pakkwinda / Maeil Kyongje Sinmunsa Kukchebu p`yon.
Edition Information: Ch`op`an.
Soul: Maeil Kyongje Sinmunsa, 1998.
Editor: Maeil Kyongje Sinmunsa. Kukchebu.
Description: 327 p.: ill.; 23 cm.
ISBN: 8974421267
Subjects: International monetary fund--Korea (South) Financial crises--Korea (South) Economic stabilization--Korea (South) Korea (South)--Economic conditions--1960-
LC Classification: HG3881.5.I58+

IMF istikrar politikalari ve T‚rkiye / edit^r, Cevdet Erdost; [yazanlar] Korkut Boratov ... [et al.].
Yeni sehir, Ankara: Sava s Yayinlari, 1982.
Editor: Erdost, Cevdet.
Description: xxi, 210 p.; 20 cm.
Subjects: International Monetary Fund--Turkey. Money--Turkey. Loans, Foreign--Turkey.

IMF mit Segye Unhaeng yonch`a pogoso.
1975.

Description: 254 p.: graphs; 22 cm.
Notes: Romanized.
Subjects: International Monetary Fund. International Bank for Reconstruction and Development.
LC Classification: HG3881 .H9

IMF paper on policy analysis and assessment.
[Washington, D.C.?]: International Monetary Fund,
Description: v.; 28 cm. Ceased in 1998?
Current Frequency: Irregular
Continued by: IMF policy discussion paper (DLC) 00238293 (OCoLC)42665000
Notes: Description based on: PPAA/93/1. Additional Form Avail.: Also available in an online version.
Subjects: International Monetary Fund. International finance. International economic relations. Developing countries.
LC Classification: HG3881.5.I58 I566
Electronic File Info.: http://www.imf.org/external/pubs/CAT/ppaa.cfm

IMF policies towards less developed countries (LDCs), with special reference to India / edited by Rama Shankar Singh.
New Delhi: Deep & Deep Publications, c1994.
Editor: Singh, Rama Shankar, 1949-
Description: xii, 237 p.; 22 cm.
ISBN: 8171005144 :
Summary: Contributed articles.
Notes: Includes bibliographical references and index.
Subjects: International Monetary Fund--India. International Monetary Fund--Developing countries.
LC Classification: HG3971 .I44 1994

IMF sat`ae ui wonin kwa kyohun / Nam Tog-u ... [et al.].
Edition Information: Ch`op`an.
Soul-si: Samsong Kyongje Yon'guso, 1998.
Editor: Nam, Tog-u.
Description: 398 p.: ill.; 23 cm.
ISBN: 8976330595
Notes: Includes bibliographical references.
Subjects: International Monetary Fund--Korea (South) Finance--Korea (South)--History. Monetary policy--Korea (South) Korea (South)--Ecnomic policy--1960-
LC Classification: HC467 .I455 1998

IMF to Nihon. 39
[1964]

Description: 7, 277 p.; 19 cm.
Notes: Romanized.
Subjects: International Monetary Fund. International finance. Foreign exchange administration--Japan.
Series: Kanzei shirizu; 1.
LC Classification: HG3881 .I2

IMF wa Han'guk kyongje / Samsong Kyongje Yon'guso p`yon.
Edition Information: Ch`op`an.
Soul: Samsong Kyongje Yon'guso, 1997.
Editor: Samsong Kyongje Yon'guso.
Description: 301 p.: ill.; 23 cm.
ISBN: 8976330463 (pbk.) :
Notes: "Kyongje 97-15-693" -- on cover.
Subjects: International Monetary Fund--Korea (South)--Effect. Debts, External--Korea (South) Foreign economic relations--Korea (South)

IMF working papers and papers on policy analysis and assessment.
Washington, D.C.: International Monetary Fund,
Description: v.; 23 cm. Coverage for each issue begins with Oct. 1986.
Current Frequency: Irregular
ISSN: 1088-8837
Notes: Description based on: Oct. 1986-Mar. 1994.
SERBIB/SERLOC merged record
Subjects: International Monetary Fund--Bibliography--Periodicals. International finance--Bibliography--Periodicals. Policy sciences--Bibliography--Periodicals.
LC Classification: Z7164.E17 I46 HG3881
Dewey Class No.: 332 12
Entry: IMF working papers and papers on policy analysis and assessment.

Imf, World Bank Welcome Russia Los Angeles Times -
Newsday April 28, 1992

IMF-supported programs in Indonesia, Korea, and Thailand: a preliminary assessment / Timothy Lane ... [et al.].
Washington DC: International Monetary Fund, 1999.
Editor: Lane, Timothy D. (Timothy David), 1955-
Description: vii, 82 p.: ill.; 28 cm.
ISBN: 1557757836
Notes: Includes bibliographical references.
Subjects: International Monetary Fund--Economic assistance Indonesia. International Monetary Fund--Economic assistance--Korea. International Monetary Fund--Economic assistance Thailand. Indonesia--Economic policy. Korea--Economic policy. Thailand--Economic policy.

Series: Occasional paper (International Monetary Fund); no. 178.
LC Classification: HC447 .I46 1999
Dewey Class No.: 338.95 21

Implementing the World Bank's strategy to reduce poverty : progress and challenges.
Washington, D.C.: World Bank, c1993.
Description: xiv, 98 p.; 28 cm.
ISBN: 0821323946
Notes: Includes bibliographical references (p. 97-98).
Subjects: World Bank. Economic assistance--Developing countries. Poverty--Developing countries.
LC Classification: HC60 .I415 1993
Dewey Class No.: 338.9/1/091724 20

Improvements needed in system for managing U.S. participation in the Asian Development Bank: Department of the Treasury, Department of State, and other Agencies; report to the Congress, by the Comptroller General of the United States.
[Washington] 1973.
Description: 69 p. 27 cm.
Notes: Cover title. "B-173240."
Subjects: Asian Development Bank. Economic assistance, American.
LC Classification: HG4517 .U56 1973a
Dewey Class No.: 353.007/232

Improving the international monetary system: constraints and possibilities / Michael Mussa ... [et al.].
Washington, DC: International Monetary Fund, c1994.
Editor: Mussa, Michael.
Description: v, 39 p.: ill.; 28 cm.
ISBN: 1557754446
Notes: Includes bibliographical references (p. 35-37).
Subjects: International finance.
Series: Occasional paper (International Monetary Fund); no. 116.
LC Classification: HG3881 .I349 1994
Dewey Class No.: 332.4/566 20

Increasing IMF-World Bank cooperation: joint hearing before the Subcommittee on International Development Institutions and Finance and the Subcommittee on International Finance, Trade, and Monetary Policy of the Committee on Banking, Finance, and Urban Affairs, House of Representatives, Ninety-ninth Congress, first session, July 25, 1985.
Washington: U.S. G.P.O., 1985.
Editor: United States. Congress. House. Committee on Banking, Finance, and

Urban Affairs. Subcommittee on International Finance, Trade, and Monetary Policy.
Description: iii, 89 p.; 24 cm.
Notes: Distributed to some depository libraries in microfiche. Shipping list no.: 85-1030-P. "Serial no. 99-31." Item 1013-A, 1013-B (microfiche) Includes bibliographies.
Subjects: World Bank--Developing countries. International Monetary Fund--Developing countries. Debts, External--Developing countries. Developing countries--Economic conditions.
LC Classification: KF27 .B547 1985k
Govt. Doc. No.: Y 4.B 22/1:99-31

Information technologies for the control of money laundering / Office of Technology Assessment, Congress of the United States.
Washington, D.C.: The Office: For sale by the Supt. Of Docs., U.S. G.P.O., [1995]
Description: xvi, 144 p.: ill.; 28 cm.
ISBN: 0160482941
Notes: "September 1995"--Spine. "OTA-ITC-630"--P. [4] of cover. Includes bibliographical references.
Subjects: Money laundering investigation--Technological innovations. Money laundering--Prevention--Technological innovations. Banks and banking, International--Law and legislation. Information technology.
LC Classification: HV8079.M64 I54 1995

Ingo, Walter
The Market for Financial Secrecy
Financial Times (London, England) Aug. 8, 1991, p10

Intellectual property rights in agriculture: the World Bank's role in assisting borrower and member countries / Uma Lele, William Lesser, Gesa Horstkotte-Wesseler, editors.
Washington, D.C.: World Bank, c2000 (1999 printing)
Editor: Lele, Uma J.
Description: x, 87 p.; 28 cm.
ISBN: 082134496X
Notes: Includes bibliographical references.
Subjects: World Bank. Intellectual property--Developing countries. Agriculture--Research--Law and legislation—Developing countries.
Series: Environmentally and socially sustainable development. Rural development
LC Classification: K1401 .I567 2000
Dewey Class No.: 630/.7/2 21

International Bank and Monetary Fund meeting; report to the Committee on Banking and Currency, United States Senate on the meeting of the Boards of Governors of the International Bank for Reconstruction and Development and the International Monetary Fund at Istanbul, Turkey, with related material. November 17, 1955.
Washington, U.S. Govt. Print. Off., 1955.
Description: v, 128 p. maps. 23 cm.
Notes: At head of 84th Cong. 1st sess. Committee print.
Subjects: International Monetary Fund. World Bank
LC Classification: HG3881 .U575

International Bank for Reconstruction & Development and International Monetary Fund (jointly). Documents issued at annual meeting.
Current Frequency: Annual
Notes: Holdings in 3x5 file.

International Bank for Reconstruction and Development. Amendment to the Articles of agreement of December 27, 1945, between the United States of America and other governments, done at Washington December 16, 1965.
[Washington, For sale by the Supt. of Docs., U.S. Govt. Print. Off., 1966]
Description: 2 p. 23 cm.
Subjects: World Bank.
Series: United States. Treaties, etc. (Treaties and other international acts series); 5929.
LC Classification: JX235.9 .A32 no. 5929 HG388
Dewey Class No.: 341.2/73

International bank insolvencies: a central bank perspective / editors, Mario Giovanoli, Gregor Heinrich.
The Hague; Boston: Kluwer Law International, 1999.
Editor: Giovanoli, Mario.
Description: xlv, 432 p.; 25 cm.
ISBN: 9041197281
Notes: At head of SMU Institute of International Banking and Finance, Dallas, Texas ... [et al.]. Includes bibliographical references and index.
Subjects: Bank failures--Law and legislation. Bankruptcy. Banks and banking, Central. Banks and banking, International--Law and legislation.
Series: International banking, finance, and economic law; v. 12
LC Classification: K1070 .I58 1999
Dewey Class No.: 341.7/511 21

International banker.
New York, NY: *American Banker*, 1998-
Description: v.: ill.; 28 cm v. 10, issue 39 (Oct. 12, 1998)-
Current Frequency: Weekly (except for the last 2 weeks of Aug. and Dec.)

Continues: Thomson's international banking regulator 0958-353X (DLC) 92640550
ISSN: 1522-3124
Notes: "American Banker's publication for cross-border banking." from caption. SERBIB/SERLOC merged record
Subjects: Banks and Banking, International--Law and legislation Periodicals. Banks and banking, International--Periodicals.
LC Classification: K1066.A13 T48
Dewey Class No.: 332.7/51 20
Entry: International banker (New York, N.Y.) sn98-2749

International bankers' directory.
Chester, England: Financial Publishing Group,
Description: v.; 22 x 30 cm.
Notes: Description based on: Fall 1984 ed. SERBIB/SERLOC merged record
Subjects: Banks and banking, International--Directories. Banks and banking--Directories.
LC Classification: HG1536 .I58
Dewey Class No.: 332.1/5/025 19
Entry: International bankers' directory (Chester, Cheshire) Chester, England. 85-643431

International banking developments / Bank for International Settlements, Monetary and Economic Department.
Basle: The Department,
Description: v.; 30 cm.
Current Frequency: Quarterly
Continued by: International banking and financial market developments
Notes: Description based on: 4th quarter 1981; title from caption. SERBIB/SERLOC merged record
Subjects: Banks and banking, International--Periodicals.
LC Classification: HG3879 .I56
Dewey Class No.: 332.1/5/05 19
Entry: International banking developments. Basle. 84-642896

International banking, 1870-1914 / edited by Rondo Cameron and V.I. Bovykin with the assistance of Boris Anan′ich ... [et al.].
New York: Oxford University Press, 1991.
Editor: Cameron, Rondo E.
Description: xiv, 655 p.: ill.; 25 cm.
ISBN: 019506271X (alk. paper)
Notes: Results of a study conceived at the Eighth International Economic History Congress in Budapest, 1982. Includes bibliographical references (p. 539-625) and index.

Subjects: Banks and banking, International--History.
LC Classification: HG3881 .I575124 1991
Dewey Class No.: 332.1/5/09034 20

International banking: government relations status report / prepared by American Bankers Association, International Banking Division.
[Washington, D.C.?]: The Division,
Description: v.; 28 cm.
Current Frequency: Quarterly
Notes: Description based on: Summer/fall 1987.
SERBIB/SERLOC merged record
Subjects: Banking law--United States--Periodicals. Banks and banking, International--Periodicals. Banks and banking--United States--Periodicals.
LC Classification: KF967 .I58
Dewey Class No.: 346.73/082/05 347.3068205 20
Entry: International banking (Washington, D.C.: Quarterly)

International capital markets: developments, prospects, and key policy issues / by a staff team led by Charles Adams ... [et al.].
Washington, DC: International Monetary Fund, c1998.
Editor: Adams, Charles F.,
International Monetary Fund.
Description: xii, 196 p.: col. ill.; 28 cm.
ISBN: 1557757704
Subjects: Capital market. International finance. Banks and banking, International.
Series: World economic and financial surveys, 0258-7440
LC Classification: IN PROCESS

International corporate banking and trade services / Greenwich Associates.
Greenwich, Conn.: The Associates,
Description: v.; 28 cm.
Current Frequency: Annual
Notes: Description based on: 1985.
SERBIB/SERLOC merged record
Subjects: International business enterprises--Finance--Periodicals.
Banks and banking, International--Periodicals.
LC Classification: HG4027.5 .I55
Dewey Class No.: 332.1/5/05 19
Entry: International corporate banking and trade services.

International corporate finance ... report to executives / Greenwich Associates.
Greenwich, Conn.: The Associates,
Description: v.; 28 cm.
Notes: Description based on: 1986. SERBIB/SERLOC merged record

Subjects: International business enterprises--Finance--Periodicals. Banks and banking, International--Periodicals.
LC Classification: HG4027.5 .I56
Dewey Class No.: 338.8/8/05 19
Entry: International corporate finance ... report to executives.

International economic policy review/ International Monetary Fund.
Washington, DC: International Monetary Fund,
Description: v.
ISSN: 1020-7856
Notes: Description based on: Vol. 1, 1999.

International monetary agreements acts; annual report.
Description: 25 cm.
ISSN: 0314-2582
Notes: SERBIB/SERLOC merged record
Subjects: International Monetary Fund. World Bank. International finance--Periodicals.
Series: Parliamentary paper (Australia. Parliament)
LC Classification: J905 .L3 subser
Dewey Class No.: 328.94/01 s 332.4/5/0994
Entry: Australia. Dept. of the Treasury. International monetary agreements acts; annual report. Canberra. 75-645234

International monetary agreements acts; annual report.
Description: 25 cm.
ISSN: 0314-2582
Notes: SERBIB/SERLOC merged record
Subjects: International Monetary Fund. World Bank. International finance--Periodicals.
Series: Parliamentary paper (Australia. Parliament)
LC Classification: J905 .L3 subser
Dewey Class No.: 328.94/01 s 332.4/5/0994
Entry: Australia. Dept. of the Treasury. International monetary agreements acts; annual report. Canberra. 75-645234

International Monetary Fund, International Bank for Reconstruction and Development, Asian Development Bank special funds. Hearing, Ninety-first Congress, second session, on S. 3628 ... and S. 3543 ... May 6, 1970.
Washington, U.S. Govt. Print. Off., 1970.
Description: iii, 88 p. illus. 24 cm.
Subjects: International Monetary Fund. World Bank. Asian Development Bank.
LC Classification: KF26.F6 1970h

Dewey Class No.: 332.1/5

International monetary fund.
[Washington, U. S. Govt. print. off., 1946]
Description: 1 p.l., 43 p. 23 cm.
Subjects: International monetary fund.
LC Classification: JX235.9 .A32 no. 1501 (Rare Bk. Coll.)

International monetary fund.
Wellington, Dept. of external affairs, 1944.
Description: 15, [1] p. 25 cm.
Subjects: Foreign exchange. Currency question. Commercial policy.
LC Classification: DU400 .A33 no. 4

Jacobson, Harold Karan.
China's participation in the IMF, the World Bank, and ATT : toward a global economic order / Harold K. Jacobson and Michel Oksenberg.
Ann Arbor: University of Michigan Press, c1990.
Description: xviii, 199 p.; 24 cm.
ISBN: 0472101773 :
Notes: Includes bibliographical references (p. 185-191).
Subjects: World Bank--China. International Monetary Fund--China. General Agreement on Tariffs and Trade (Organization) China--Foreign economic relations.
LC Classification: HF3836.5 .J33 1990
Dewey Class No.: 337.51 20

Jacobsson, Per
International monetary problems, 1957-1963; elected speeches.
Washington, International Monetary Fund, 1964.
Description: xiii, 368 p. port., col. diagrs. 24 cm.
Notes: "Articles and books, by Mr. Jacobsson 1957-1963": p. 347-355.
Subjects: International Monetary Fund. Foreign exchange.
Series: International Monetary Fund. Monograph series; no. 3.
LC Classification: HG3881 .J23
Dewey Class No.: 332.15

Jagan, Cheddi.
The IMF takes over / by Cheddi Jagan.
Georgetown [Guyana]: People's Progressive arty, [1982]
Description: 36 p.; 20 cm.
Notes: Cover title. Includes bibliographical references.
Subjects: International Monetary Fund.
LC Classification: HG3881.5.I58 J33 1982

Dewey Class No.: 332.1/52 19

James, Harold

International monetary cooperation since Bretton Woods / Harold James.

Washington, D.C.: International Monetary Fund; New York:

Oxford University Press, 1996.

Description: xvi, 742 p.: ill.; 24 cm.

ISBN: 019510448X (hardcover: acid-free paper)0195101138 (hardcover: acid-free paper)

Notes: Includes bibliographical references (p. 689-720) and index.

Subjects: International finance. Monetary policy--International cooperation. Financial institutions, International.

LC Classification: HG3881 .J33 1996

Dewey Class No.: 332/.042 20

Jancauskas, Raymond Casimir.

An evaluation of the International Monetary Fund.

Washington, Catholic University of America Press, 1955.

Description: ix, 29 p. 23 cm.

Subjects: International Monetary Fund.

Series: Catholic University of America. School of Social Science. Studies in economics: abstract series, v. 5, no. 12.

LC Classification: HG3881 .J335

Jayarajah, Carl, 1932-

Social dimension of adjustment: World Bank experience, 1980-93 / Carl Jayarajah, William Branson, and Binayak Sen.

Washington, D.C.: The World Bank, c1996.

Description: xix, 218 p.: ill.; 28 cm.

ISBN: 082133610X

Notes: Includes bibliographical references (p. 197-208).

Subjects: World Bank--Developing countries. Structural adjustment (Economic policy)--Social aspects Developing countries. Economic development. Public welfare--Developing countries. Poverty--Developing countries. Supply-side economics--Social aspects—Developing countries.

Series: A World Bank operations evaluation study, 1011-0984

LC Classification: HC59.7 .J397 1996

Dewey Class No.: 339.5 20

Jayarajah, Carl, 1932-

Structural and sectoral adjustment: World Bank experience, 1980-92 / Carl Jayarajah, William Branson.

Washington, DC: World Bank, c1995.

Description: xvii, 358 p.: ill.; 28 cm.

ISBN: 0821331221
Notes: Includes bibliographical references. Includes bibliographical references.
Subjects: World Bank--Developing countries. Structural adjustment (Economic policy)—Developing countries. Economic assistance--Developing countries.
Series: A World Bank operations evaluation study
LC Classification: HC59.7 .J4 1995
Dewey Class No.: 332.1/532 20

Johns, Richard Anthony.
Finance centres: British Isle offshore development since 1979 / R.A. Johns and C.M. Le Marchant.
London; New York: Pinter Publishers; New York, NY, USA : Distributed exclusively in the USA and Canada by St. Martin's Press, 1993.
Description: xiv, 306 p.: map; 24 cm.
ISBN: 0861877993
Notes: Includes bibliographical references (p. [287]-300) and indcx.
Subjects: Banks and banking, Foreign--Great Britain. Banks and banking, International. Banks and banking--Great Britain. Tax havens.
LC Classification: HG2988 .J64 1993
Dewey Class No.: 332.1/5 20

Johns, Richard Anthony.
Tax havens and offshore finance: a study of transnational economic development / by Richard Anthony Johns.
New York: St. Martin's Press, 1983.
Description: xiv, 259 p.; 24 cm.
ISBN: 0312351801
Notes: Includes index. Bibliography: p. 248-255.
Subjects: Banks and banking, International. Banks and banking, Foreign. Banks and banking--Great Britain. Tax havens.
Series: Studies in international political economy (St. Martin's Press)
LC Classification: HG3881 .J55 1983
Dewey Class No.: 332.1/5 19

Johnson, G. G. (Gilbert Gerald),
Aspects of the international banking safety net / by G.G. Johnson, with Richard K. Abrams.
Washington, D.C.: International Monetary Fund, [1983]
Description: v, 36 p.; 28 cm.
Notes: Bibliography: p. 36.
Subjects: Banks and banking, International. Loans, Foreign.
Series: Occasional paper (International Monetary Fund); no. 17.
LC Classification: HG3881 .J57 1983

Dewey Class No.: 332.1/5 19

Johnson, Hazel J.

Global banking today: the impact, issues, and trends / Hazel J. Johnson.
Chicago, Ill.: Probus Pub. Co.; c1994.
Description: xii, 139 p.: ill.; 23 cm.
ISBN: 1557387109
Notes: Includes bibliographical references and index.
Subjects: Banks and banking, International.
Series: A bankline executive report
LC Classification: HG3881 .J583 1994
Dewey Class No.: 332.1/5 20

Johnson, Hazel J.

Global financial institutions and markets / Hazel J. Johnson.
Malden, MA: Blackwell Publishers, 1999.
Description: p. cm.
ISBN: 1557869928 (alk. paper) 1557869936 (pbk.: alk. paper)
Notes: Includes bibliographical references and index.
Subjects: International finance.Financial institutions, International. Capital market. Banks and banking, International.
LC Classification: HG3881 .J5833 1999
Dewey Class No.: 332.1/5 21

Johnson, Hazel J.

The new global banker: what every U.S. bank must know to compete internationally / Hazel J. Johnson.
Chicago, Ill.: Probus Pub. Co., c1994.
Description: xi, 268 p.: ill.; 24 cm.
ISBN: 1557383588
Notes: Includes bibliographical references (p. 253-263) and index.
Subjects: Banks and banking--United States. Banks and banking, International.
LC Classification: HG2491 .J644 1994
Dewey Class No.: 332.1/5/0973 20

Johnson, J. Keith.

Risk analysis and project selection: a review of practical issues / by J. Keith Johnson.
Manila, Philippines: Asian Development Bank, c1985.
Description: 62 p.; 28 cm.
Notes: Bibliography: p. 59-62.
Subjects: World Bank. Asian Development Bank. Economic development projects--Evaluation. Country risk.
Series: Asian Development Bank economic staff paper; no. 28

LC Classification: HD75.9 .J64 1985
Dewey Class No.: 338.9/0068/4 20

Johnson, Mary Elizabeth.
The International Monetary Fund, 1944-1992: a research guide / by Mary Elizabeth Johnson.
New York: Garland Pub., 1993.
Description: xii, 486 p.; 23 cm.
ISBN: 0815302304 (alk. paper)
Notes: Includes indexes.
Subjects: International Monetary Fund--Bibliography. International finance--Bibliography.
Series: Garland reference library of social science; v. 770 Research and information guides in business, industry, and economic institutions; 9
LC Classification: Z7164.F5 J64 1993 HG3881.5.I58
Dewey Class No.: 016.3321/152 20

Johnston, B. and Turner, T.
The American Anthropological Association, the World Bank Group, and ENDESA SA: Violations of human rights in the Pangue and Ralco Dam projects on the Bio-Bio river, Chile
Global Studies in Culture and Power, 1999, Vol 6, Iss 2-3, pp 387-434

Jones, Geoffrey.
British multinational banking, 1830-1990 / Geoffrey Jones.
Oxford [England]: Clarendon Press; New York: Oxford University Press, 1993.
Description: xiii, 511 p.: ill.; 25 cm.
ISBN: 0198202733 (cloth) :
Notes: Includes bibliographical references (p. [489]-497) and index.
Subjects: Banks and banking, International--History. Banks and banking, British--History.
LC Classification: HG2992 .J66 1993
Dewey Class No.: 332.1/5/0941 20

Jovovic, Dejan, 1947-
Medunarodni monetarni fond: mehanizam, politika, eforma / Dejan Jovovi¥c.
Beograd: Institut ekonomskih nauka, 1992.
Description: 260 p.; 24 cm.
ISBN: 8680315087
Notes: Summary also in English. Includes bibliographical references (p. 242-247).
Subjects: International Monetary Fund.
Series: Ekonomija '90.

LC Classification: HG3881.5.I58 J68 1992

Justice denied!.
Edition Information: 1st ed.
Geneva, Switzerland: Women's International League for Peace and Freedom; Kathmandu, Nepal: International Institute for Human Rights, Environment, and Development, 1994.
Description: iv, 185 p.: ill.; 23 cm.
Subjects: World Bank--Developing countries. International Monetary Fund--Developing countries. Human rights--Developing countries.
LC Classification: JC599.D4 J87 1994

Kafka, Alexandre.
The IMF: the second coming?
Princeton, N.J., International Finance Section, Princeton University, 1972.
Description: 43 p. 23 cm.
Subjects: International Monetary Fund. Monetary policy.
Series: Essays in international finance; no. 94.
LC Classification: HG136 .P7 no. 94 HG3881
Dewey Class No.: 332 s 332.1/52

Kafka, Alexandre.
The International Monetary Fund: reform without reconstruction? / Alexandre Kafka.
Princeton, N.J.: International Finance Section, Dept. of Economics, Princeton University, 1976.
Description: 37 p.; 23 cm.
Subjects: International Monetary Fund.
Series: Essays in international finance; no. 118.
LC Classification: HG136 .P7 no. 118 HG3881
Dewey Class No.: 332 s 332.1/52

Kammert, James L.
International commercial banking management / James L. Kammert.
New York: AMACOM, c1981.
Description: x, 403 p.; 24 cm.
ISBN: 0814456804
Notes: Includes index.
Subjects: Banks and banking, International. Bank management.
LC Classification: HG3881 .K27
Dewey Class No.: 332.1/5/068 19

Kandell, Jonathan
Undamming the World Bank.

Audubon May/June 1993, p106+

Kapstein, Ethan B.

Governing the global economy: international finance and the state / Ethan B. Kapstein.
Cambridge, Mass.: Harvard University Press, 1994.
Description: vii, 224 p.: ill.; 24 cm.
ISBN: 0674357574 (acid-free paper)
Notes: Includes bibliographical references (p. [210]-218) and index.
Subjects: Banks and banking, International. Banks and banking, International--Law and legislation. International business enterprises--Finance. International finance.
LC Classification: HG3881 .K286 1994
Dewey Class No.: 332.1/5 20

Kapstein, Ethan B.

Supervising international banks: origins and implications of the Basle Accord / Ethan B. Kapstein.
Princeton, N.J.: International Finance Section, Dept. of Economics, Princeton University, c1991.
Description: 38 p.; 23 cm.
ISBN: 0881650927 (pbk.) :
Notes: Includes bibliographical references (p. 32-34).
Subjects: Banks and banking, International. International finance.
Series: Essays in international finance, 071-142X; no. 185
LC Classification: HG136 .P7 no. 185 HG3881
Dewey Class No.: 332.1/5 20

Kapur, Devesh

The World Bank: its first half century / Devesh Kapur, John P. Lewis, Richard Webb.
Washington, D.C.: Brookings Institution, c1997.
Editor: Lewis, John Prior.
Webb, Richard Charles, 1937-
Description: 2 v.: ill.; 25 cm.
ISBN: 081575230X (set) 0815752342 (v. 1) 0815752369 (v. 2)
Contents: v. 1. History -- v. 2. Perspectives.
Notes: Includes bibliographical references and indexes.
Subjects: World Bank--History.
LC Classification: HG3881.5.W57 K36 1997
Dewey Class No.: 332.1/532/05 21

Karanikas, Constantin.

La Banque des règlements internationaux.

Paris, Domat-Montchrestian, 1931.
Description: vii, 336 p. 26 cm.
Subjects: Bank for international settlements. European war, 1914-1918--Reparations. Banks and banking.
LC Classification: HG1997.I6 K3

Karsten, Ingo
Internationale Bankkredite an Entwicklungsländer: ökonomische Probleme und Lösungsansätze / Ingo Karsten.
Edition Information: 1. Aufl.
Baden-Baden: Nomos Verlagsgesellschaft, 1984.
Description: 203 p.: ill.; 23 cm.
ISBN: 3789009776
Notes: Bibliography: p. 195-203.
Subjects: Loans, Foreign--Developing countries. Banks and banking, International. International finance. Debts, External--Developing countries.
Series: Schriften zur monetären Ökonomie; Bd. 19
LC Classification: HG3891.5 .K37 1984
Dewey Class No.: 332.1/5/091724 19

Kasten, Hans
Internationale Whrungsreserven und nationale Reservepolitik.
Frankfurt am Main, F. Knapp [1959]
Description: 60 p. tables. 21 cm.
Subjects: International Monetary Fund. Bank reserves.
Banks and banking, International.
Series: Frankfurt am Main. Universit. Institut fur das Kreditwesen. Neue Schriftenfolge.
LC Classification: HG3881 .K3

Katz, Lee Michael
Financial Records Lifting Veil on Bin Laden Network
USA Today Sept. 30, 1998, pn.p.

Kawamoto, Akito, 1950-
Takokuseki gink¯o to kokusai kin'y¯u risuku / Kawamoto Akito cho.
Hiroshima-shi: Hiroshima Sh¯ud¯o Daigaku S¯og¯o Kenky¯ujo, 1990.
Description: vi, 152 p.: ill.; 21 cm.
Notes: Includes bibliographical references.
Subjects: Banks and banking, International. International finance. Risk assessment.
Series: Hiroshima Sh¯ud¯o Daigaku kenky¯u s¯osho; dai 55-g¯o
LC Classification: HG3881 .K363 1990

Keller, Peter, 1946-

Multilateral official debt rescheduling: recent experience / Peter M. Keller, with Nissanke E. Weerasinghe.
Washington, D.C.: International Monetary Fund, 1988.
International Monetary Fund.
Description: v, 22 p.: ill. (some col.); 28 cm.
Notes: "May 1988."
Includes bibliographical references.
Subjects: Paris Club. Debt relief--Developing countries. Debts, External--Developing countries. Loans, Foreign--Developing countries.
Series: World economic and financial surveys, 0258-7440
LC Classification: HJ8899 .K47 1988
Dewey Class No.: 336.3/435/091724 19

Kempner, S. Marshall

Inside Wall Street, 1920-1942, by S. Marshall Kempner.
New York, Hastings House [1973]
Description: 140 p. 21 cm.
ISBN: 0803833865
Subjects: Wall Street. Banks and banking, International.
LC Classification: HG4572 .K45
Dewey Class No.: 332.6/42/0973

Kenen, Peter B., 1932-

Financing, adjustment, and the International Monetary Fund / Peter B. Kenen.
Washington, D.C.: Brookings Institution, c1986.
Description: 89 p.; 23 cm.
ISBN: 0815748833 (pbk.)
Subjects: International Monetary Fund.
Series: Studies in international economics (Washington, D.C.)
LC Classification: HG3881.5.I58 K46 1986
Dewey Class No.: 332.1/52 19

Kenya and the World Bank Group.

[Washington, World Bank] 1973.
Description: 14 p. illus. 23 cm.
Subjects: World Bank. Technical assistance--Kenya. Economic assistance--Kenya.
LC Classification: HC517.K4 K4535
Dewey Class No.: 338.91/676/2

Kern, Tyll-Dietrich.

Der Internationale Whrungsfonds und die ercksichtigung auslndischen Devisenrechts / Tyll-Dietrich Kern.

Baden-Baden: Nomos Verlagsgesellschaft, [1968]
Description: 118 p.; 23 cm.
Notes: Bibliography: p. 109-115.
Subjects: International Monetary Fund. Foreign exchange--Law and legislation.
Series: Schriftenreihe zum Handbuch fur Europische irtschaft ; Bd. 39
LC Classification: LAW <General Law Kern 1968>
Dewey Class No.: 332.1/52

Kessler, J.J. and Van Dorp, M.
Structural adjustment and the environment: the need for an analytical methodology
Ecological Economics, 1998, Vol 27, Iss 3, pp 267-281
This article shows how prevailing World Bank and IMF orthodoxy affects the environment in the South, and offers an analytical methodology for dealing with it. Existing studies and reviews conclude that structural adjustment programmes (SAPs) in developing countries have both negative and positive environmental impacts, and that both types of impacts show great variation. This article summarises the methodological difficulties in environmental impact assessments (EIAs) of SAPs and reports on a study on the environmental impacts of SAPs which took as the entry point of analysis, the three natural resources, soils, water and forests, contrary to other studies on this subject

Key, Sydney J.
International trade in banking services: a conceptual framework / Sydney J. Key, and Hal S. Scott.
Washington, DC (1990 M St., NW, Washington 20036): Group of Thirty, 1991.
Description: v, 54 p.; 23 cm.
Subjects: Banks and banking, International. International trade.
Series: Occasional papers (Group of Thirty); no. 35.
LC Classification: HG3881 .K456 1991
Dewey Class No.: 332.1/5 20

Khambata, Dara, 1948-
The practice of multinational banking: macro-policy issues and key international concepts / Dara Khambata.
Edition Information: 2nd ed.
Westport, Conn.: Quorum Books, 1996.
Description: xii, 303 p.: ill.; 24 cm.
ISBN: 0899309712 (hardcover: alk. paper)
Notes: Includes bibliographical references and index.
Subjects: Banks and banking, International. International finance.
LC Classification: HG3881 .K465 1996
Dewey Class No.: 332.1/5 20

Khambata, Dara, 1948-
The practice of multinational banking: macro-policy issues and key international concepts / Dara M. Khambata.
New York: Quorum Books, 1986.
Description: xii, 269 p.; 25 cm.
ISBN: 0899301398 (lib. bdg.: alk. paper)
Notes: Includes bibliographies and index.
Subjects: Banks and banking, International. International finance.
LC Classification: HG3881 .K265 1986
Dewey Class No.: 332.1/5 19

Khan, Shahrukh Rafi.
Do IMF & World Bank policies work? / by Shahrukh Rafi Khan.
[Islamabad]: SDPI, 1997.
Description: xix, 206 p.; 21 cm.
Notes: Cover title. Includes bibliographical references.
Subjects: International Monetary Fund. World Bank. Banks and banking, International.
Series: SDPI monograph series; # 6
LC Classification: HG3881.5.I58 K53 1997

Khan, Shahrukh Rafi.
Do World Bank and IMF policies work? / Shahrukh Rafi Khan.
New York, N.Y.: St. Martin's Press, 1999.
Description: x, 197 p.; 23 cm.
ISBN: 0312217048 (cloth)
Notes: Includes bibliographical references and index.
Subjects: World Bank. International Monetary Fund. Banks and banking, International.
LC Classification: HG3881.5.W57 K48 1999
Dewey Class No.: 332.1/5 21

Khoury, Sarkis J.
Dynamics of international banking / Sarkis J. Khoury.
New York: Praeger, 1980.
Description: xvi, 261 p.: ill.; 24 cm.
ISBN: 0030532213 :
Notes: Includes bibliographical references and index.
Subjects: Banks and banking, International. Banks and banking, American. Banks and banking, Foreign--United States.
LC Classification: HG3881 .K467
Dewey Class No.: 332.1/5

Khudiakova, Liudmila Semenovna.
Amerikanskie banki na mirovykh rynkakh / L. S. Khudiakova.
Moskva: Nauka, 1979.
Description: 191 p.; 20 cm.
Notes: At head of Akademiia nauk SSSR. Institut mirovoi ekonomiki i mezhdunarodnykh otnoshenii. Bibliography: p. 184-[189]
Subjects: Banks and banking--United States. Banks and banking, International.
LC Classification: HG2481 .K57

Kiljunen, Kimmo.
The World Bank and the world poverty / Kimmo Kiljunen.
Helsinki: University of Helsinki, Institute of Development Studies, 1988.
Description: 1, 15 p.: ill.; 21 cm.
Subjects: World Bank--Developing countries. Poverty--Developing countries. Economic assistance--Developing countries.
Series: Occasional papers (Helsingin yliopisto. Kehitysmaainstituutti); 2.
LC Classification: HC59.69 .O27 no. 2

Killick, Tony.
IMF programmes in developing countries: design and impact / Tony Killick.
London; New York, NY: Routledge, 1995.
Description: p. cm.
ISBN: 0415130409
Notes: Includes bibliographical references and index.
Subjects: International Monetary Fund--Developing countries.
Series: Development policy studies
LC Classification: HG3881.5.I58 K54 1995
Dewey Class No.: 332.1/52 20

Killick, Tony.
The IMF and economic management in Kenya / Tony Killick.
London: Overseas Development Institute, [1981]
Description: 62 p.; 30 cm.
ISBN: 0850030781 (pbk.)
Notes: "July 1981." Bibliography: p. 61-62.
Subjects: International Monetary Fund--Kenya. Kenya--Economic policy.
Series: ODI working paper; no. 4
LC Classification: HC865 .K54 1981
Dewey Class No.: 338.9676/2 19

Kim, Seung Hee.
Competitive structure of the international banking industry / Seung H. Kim, Stephen W. Miller.
Lexington, Mass.: Lexington Books, c1983.

Description: xvi, 234 p.; 24 cm.
Notes: Includes index. Bibliography: p. 219-230.
Subjects: Banks and banking, Foreign--United States. Banks and banking, Foreign--Law and legislation—United States. Banks and banking, American. Banks and banking, International.
LC Classification: HG2491 .K55 1983
Dewey Class No.: 332.1/5/0973 19

Kim, Taeho,
International money and banking / Taeho Kim.
London; New York: Routledge, 1993.
Description: xvii, 416 p.: ill.; 24 cm.
ISBN: 0415059437 0415059445 (pbk.)
Notes: Includes bibliographical references and index.
Subjects: International finance. Banks and banking, International.
LC Classification: HG3851 .K454 1993
Dewey Class No.: 332.1/5 20

King, Kenneth, 1940-
Building capacities in the developing world: a review of experience in the field of education / Kenneth King.
[Edinburgh]: Centre of African Studies, Edinburgh University, 1991.
Description: 55 p.; 21 cm.
Notes: Includes bibliographical references (p. 50-55).
Subjects: World Bank--Developing countries. Educational assistance--Developing countries. Education--Developing countries--Planning. Education--Developing countries--Finance.
Series: Occasional papers (University of Edinburgh. Centre of African Studies); no. 31.
LC Classification: LC2607 .K56 1991
Dewey Class No.: 379.1/54/091724 20

Klausová, Livia
Euromenové trhy--dalsí stupen ve v‡voji mezinárodního úveru / Livia Klausová.
Praha: Ekonomick ústav CSAV, 1986.
Description: 137 p.: ill.; 20 cm.
Notes: Summary in English and Russian. Bibliography: p. 119-122.
Subjects: Euro-dollar market. Banks and banking, International. International finance.
Series: VP; c. 246.
LC Classification: HG3897 .K56 1986

Klipstein, Kurt.
Die Bank für internationalen zahlungsausgleich,

Würzburg, K. Triltsch, 1934.
Description: iv, 147 p. diagrs. 23 cm.
Subjects: Bank for international settlements. European war, 1914-1918--Reparations. Finance--Germany.
LC Classification: HG1997.I6 K55 1934

Kliuchnikov, K. F. (Kirill Fedorovich)
Mezhdunarodnye banki razvitiia: problemy i perspektivy / K.F. Kliuchnikov.
Moskva: Izd-vo "Nauka", Glavnaia red. vostochnoi lit-ry, 1974.
Description: 318 p.; 20 cm.
Notes: At head of Akademiia nauk SSSR. Institut vostokovedeniia. Romanized record.
Subjects: Banks and banking, International.
LC Classification: HG3881 .K55

Klopstock, Fred H.
The Euro-dollar market: some unresolved issues [by] Fred H. Klopstock.
Princeton, N.J., International Finance Section, Princeton University, 1968.
Description: 28 p. 23 cm.
Subjects: Banks and banking, International. International finance.
Series: Essays in international finance; no. 65.
LC Classification: HG136 .P7 no. 65
Dewey Class No.: 332.1/5

Klump, Rainer
Entstehung und Verwendung von Schlüsselwährungen: theoretische Erklärungen, historische Erfahrungen, wirtschaftspolitische Schlussfolgerungen / Rainer Klump.
Hamburg: Verlag Weltarchiv, 1986.
Description: 462 p.: ill.; 24 cm.
ISBN: 3878953100
Notes: Bibliography: p. 435-462.
Subjects: International finance. Money. Banks and banking, International. Foreign exchange.
Series: Veröffentlichungen des HWWA-Institut für Wirtschaftsforschung-Hamburg
LC Classification: HG3881 .K565 1986

Kohli, Kedar N.
Science and technology for development: role of the bank / by K.N. Kohli, Ifzal Ali.
Manila, Philippines: Asian Development Bank, c1986.
Description: 20 leaves; 28 cm.
Notes: "December 1986"--Cover.

Subjects: Asian Development Bank. Technological innovations--Economic aspects—Developing countries. Science--Social aspects--Developing countries.
Series: Asian Development Bank economic staff paper; no. 32
LC Classification: HC59.72.T4 K64 1986
Dewey Class No.: 332.1/53/095 20

Kohn, Meir G.

Money, banking, and financial markets / Meir Kohn.
Chicago: Dryden Press, c1991.
Description: xxxiv, 863, [43] p.: ill.; 25 cm.
ISBN: 0030333342
Notes: Includes bibliographical references and index.
Subjects: Finance. Banks and banking. Money. Monetary policy. Banks and banking, International.
LC Classification: HG173 .K64 1991
Dewey Class No.: 332.1 20

Kolko, G.

Ravaging the poor: The International Monetary Fund indicted by its own data
International Journal of Health Services, 1999, Vol 29, Iss 1, pp 51-57
Recent International Monetary Fund studies on the impact of its structural adjustment programs on the poorest nations reveal that most have stagnated or declined economically. The IMF's requirement that these countries increase exports despite falling world commodity prices has been a principal cause of their economic malaise. Meanwhile, IMF loan conditions demanding lower government expenditures have led to sharp reductions in general social spending, from which the wealthiest quintile of the population receives a disproportionately larger share of outlays for health and education.

Kollner, P.

East Asia: The road to recovery, by the World-Bank
Internationale Politik, 1999, Vol 54, Iss 4, pp 83-84

Kollner, P.

The Asian crisis: Causes, consequences and the role of the International Monetary Fund, by H. Dieter
Internationale Politik, 1999, Vol 54, Iss 4, pp 83-84

Kollner, P.

The east Asian miracle, by World-Bank
Politische Vierteljahresschrift, 1999, Vol 40, Iss 1, pp 135-146
The World Bank and poverty in sub-Saharan Africa: A study of operationalizing policies for poverty reduction, by E.N. Tjonneland, H. Harboe, A.M. Jerve, N. Kanji

Environment and Urbanization, 1999, Vol 11, Iss 1, pp 283-284

Kopits, George.
Transparency in government operations / George Kopits and Jon Craig.
Washington, DC: International Monetary Fund, 998.
Description: v, 42 p.; 28 cm.
ISBN: 155775697X (pbk.)
Notes: "January 1998." Includes bibliographical references (p. 38-40).
Subjects: Finance, Public--Accounting. Fiscal policy.
Series: Occasional paper (International Monetary Fund); no. 58.
LC Classification: HJ9733 .K66 1998
Dewey Class No.: 336.3 21

Krayenbuehl, Thomas E.
Country risk: assessment and monitoring / Thomas Krayenbuehl.
Lexington, Mass.: Lexington Books, 1985.
Description: x, 180 p.; 24 cm.
ISBN: 0669109584
Notes: Includes index. Bibliography: p. 169-172.
Subjects: International Monetary Fund. Loans, Foreign--Evaluation. Debts, External. Country risk.
LC Classification: HG3891.5 .K73 1985
Dewey Class No.: 336.3/435 19

Krishnamurti, R.
ADB--the seeding days / by R. Krishnamurti.
[Manila]: Asian Development Bank, [1977]
Editor: Asian Development Bank.
Description: 153 p.; 23 cm.
Notes: Cover title. Includes bibliographical references.
Subjects: Asian Development Bank.
LC Classification: HG5702 .K74 1977
Dewey Class No.: 332.1/53 19

Krueger, A.O.
Whither the World Bank and the IMF?
Journal of Economic Literature, 1998, Vol 36, Iss 4, pp 1983-2020

Krueger, A.O. and Rajapatirana, S.
The World Bank policies towards trade and trade policy reform
World Economy, 1999, Vol 22, Iss 6, pp 717-740

Krug, Paul.
La Banque des règlements internationaux et son role en matière de crédit.

Paris, Rousseau et cie, 1932.
Description: xvii, 299 p. 26 cm.
Subjects: Bank for international settlements. European war, 1914-1918--Reparations. Credit.
LC Classification: HG1997.I6 K7

Kunimune, K.

Exchange rate stabilization and IMF high interest rate policy: A critical reconsideration using a dynamic model
Developing Economies, 1999, Vol 37, Iss 3, pp 337+
This paper examines whether the IMF high interest rate policy was suitable for crisis-ridden East Asian economies. Using an "overshoot" model similar to that of Dornbusch's (1976), it shows that this sort of policy might cause an unnecessary deflationary adjusting process and have no effect on containing the real depreciation of exchange rates in the long run. The study also demonstrates that Thai economic data coincides quite well with the model presented here. Finally, it points out that the high interest policy itself might provoke high risk-premium, the existence of which, in turn, justifies the policy. This means that the policy has a self-fulfilling property. In conclusion, a "one-size-fits-all" adaptation of high interest rate policy in a currency crisis is very dangerous in general, and was inappropriate for East Asia. The desirable policy would have been to let currencies depreciate and keep interest rates stable.

Kurilin, Nestor Petrovich.

Mezhdunarodnyi valiutnyi fond.
Moskva, Finansy, 1967.
Description: 52 p. 20 cm.
Notes: At head of N. Kurilin.
Bibliographical footnotes.
Subjects: International Monetary Fund.
LC Classification: HG3881 .K83

Kuske, Hans-Martin.

Finanzierung multinationaler Unternehmungen; das Bankgeschäft am internationalen Kapitalmarkt, von Hans-M. Kuske.
Frankfurt am Main, F. Knapp [c1973]
Description: v, 341 p. 21 cm.
Notes: Bibliography: p. 302-341.
Subjects: International business enterprises--Finance. Banks and banking, International. International finance.
Series: Institut für Bankwirtschaft und Bankrecht an der Universität zu Köln. Veröffentlichungen. Wirtschaftswissenschaftliche Reibe; Bd. 25.
LC Classification: HG4026 .K95

Kwak, T`ae-un.
Kukche kumnyung sijang kaeron / Kwak T`ae-un cho.
Soul: Han'guk Kyongje Sinmunsa, 1988.
Description: 243 p.: ill.; 19 cm.
Notes: in English on added t.p.: An introduction to international market places. Bibliography: p. 241-243.
Subjects: International finance. Banks and banking, International.
Series: EM mun'go; 054
LC Classification: HG3881 .K89 1988

La Banca comercial latinoamericana frente a la crisis financiera internacional y el endeudamiento externo.
Bogotá, Colombia: FLB, [1983]
Description: 37 p.; 24 cm.
Contents: Presentación -- Ramón Fernández Rubíes -- Teóphilo de Azeredo Santos -- Javier Vial Castillo – Antonio Carrillo Flórez -- Resúmen y conclusiones – Cuadros anexos.
Subjects: Banks and banking, International. Debts, External--Latin America. International economic relations. Latin America--Foreign economic relations.
Series: Cuadernos de la Biblioteca FELABAN; no. 15.
LC Classification: HG3881 .B2866 1983
Dewey Class No.: 332.1/5/098 19

La función del Banco Mundial en el sector de la electricidad: políticas para efectuar una reforma institucional, regulatoria y financiera eficaz.
Edition Information: 1a ed. en espanol.
Washington, D.C.: Banco Mundial, 1993.
Description: 103 p.: ill.; 22 cm.
ISBN: 0821324519
Notes: Includes bibliographical references (p. 96-103).
Subjects: World Bank. Electric utilities--Government policy—Developing countries.
Electric utilities--Developing countries--Finance.
Series: Documento de política del Banco Mundial, 1014-8124
LC Classification: HD9685.D452 W6718 1993
Dewey Class No.: 333.79/32/091724 20

Lacey, R. M. (Robert M.)
Managing public expenditure: an evolving World Bank perspective / Robert M. Lacey.
Washington, D.C.: World Bank, c1989.
Description: xii, 79 p.; 28 cm.
ISBN: 0821312456
Notes: Includes bibliographical references.

Subjects: World Bank. Expenditures, Public. Budget. Government spending policy--Developing countries. Developing countries--Appropriations and expenditures.
Series: World Bank discussion papers, 0259-210X; 56
LC Classification: HJ7461 .L34 1989
Dewey Class No.: 336.3/9/091724 20

Ladenburg, Hubert
Plan for a postwar world clearing bank / by Hubert Ladenburg.
New York, N.Y.: New School for Social Research, c1942.
Description: p. [510]-529; 23 cm.
Notes: Cover title. "Peace Research Project of The Graduate Faculty of Political and Social Science Organized under the New School for Social Research."
Reprinted from: Social research, November 1942.
Subjects: Banks and banking, International. World War, 1939-1945--Economic aspects. International clearing.
Series: Studies on war and peace; no. 22
LC Classification: HG3881 .L3

Laïdi, Zaki.
Enquête sur la Banque mondiale / Zaki Laïdi.
[Paris]: Fayard, c1989.
Description: 358 p.: ill.; 24 cm.
ISBN: 2213023573 :
Notes: Includes bibliographical references.
Subjects: World Bank.
LC Classification: HG3881.5.W57 L35 1989

Lamola, Malesela John.
The international monetary system and poverty in Africa : a challenge to Christian mission / Malesela John Lamola.
Edition Information: 1st ed.
Bellville: EFSA Institute for Theological & Interdisciplinary Research, 1993.
Description: 20 p.; 21 cm.
ISBN: 1874917051
Notes: Cover title. Includes bibliographical references (p. 17-19).
Subjects: International Monetary Fund--Africa. Poverty--Africa. Economic assistance--Africa--Religious aspects Chrisitianity.
Series: Studies and reports by the EFSA Institute for heological & Interdisciplinary Research Development forum (Bellville, South Africa)
LC Classification: HG3881.I58 L35 1993

Landell-Mills, Joslin.
The Fund's international banking statistics / Joslin Landell-Mills.

Washington, D.C.: International Monetary Fund, 986.
Description: v, 54 p.: ill.; 23 cm.
ISBN: 0939934779 (pbk.) :
Notes: Bibliography: p. 54.
Subjects: Banks and banking, International--Statistical Methods. International financial statistics.
LC Classification: HG3881 .L343 1986
Dewey Class No.: 332.1/5 19

Láng, László.
International regimes and the political economy of East-West relations / Laszlo Lang.
New York: Institute for East-West Security Studies ;
Boulder, Colo.: Distributed by Westview Press, 1989.
Description: ii, 75 p.; 23 cm.
ISBN: 091344913X : 0813379466 (Westview)
Notes: Includes bibliographical references.
Subjects: World Bank--Europe, Eastern. International Monetary Fund--Europe, Eastern. General Agreement on Tariffs and Trade (Organization) East West trade (1945-)
Series: Occasional paper series (Institute for East-West Security Studies); 13.
LC Classification: HF4050 .L36 1989
Dewey Class No.: 337/.09171/7 20

Lange, Hans Dieter.
Die internationalen Banken.
Göttingen [Institut für Völkerrecht der Universität Göttingen] 1963.
Description: xxxiii, 214 p. 21 cm.
Notes: Bibliography: p. vii-xxvii. "Verzeichnis der Abkürzungen und Sammelwerke" p. xxviii-xxxiii.
Subjects: Banks and banking, International.
LC Classification: LAW <General Lang 1963>

Lantz, Edward K.
All banks can provide international services [by] Edward K. Lantz.
Boston, Financial Pub. Co. [c1971]
Description: 160 p. illus. 23 cm.
Notes: "A thesis submitted ... for graduation from the Stonier Graduate School of Banking of the American Bankers Association." Bibliography: p. 157-160.
Subjects: Banks and banking, International.
Series: Publication (Financial Publishing Company); no. 806.
LC Classification: HG3881 .L353
Dewey Class No.: 332.1/5

Larsson, Janerik, 1944-
Världsbanken -- makt i utveckling / Janerik Larsson.
[Göteborg]: Zinderman, [1977]
Description: 108 p.; 21 cm.
ISBN: 9152801950 :
Subjects: World Bank.
LC Classification: HG3881 .L359

Las Instituciones económico-financieras internacionales: participación colombiana y estructura de las mismas.
Bogotá, D.E., Colombia: Banco de la República, c1990.
Description: 2 v. (viii, 738 p.); 24 cm.
ISBN: 9589028632 (set)
Notes: Includes bibliographical references (p. 737-738).
Subjects: Financial institutions, International. Banks and banking, International--Law and legislation. Banking law--Colombia.
Series: Derecho económico Colección bibliográfica (Bogotá, Colombia)
LC Classification: K4451 .I57 1990
Dewey Class No.: 341.7/51 20

Lateef, K. Sarwar.
The first half century: an overview / K. Sarwar Lateef.
Washington, DC: World Bank, [1994]
Description: 36 p.: ill.; 28 cm.
ISBN: 0821330780
Notes: "50th anniversary"--Cover. Includes bibliographical references.
Subjects: World Bank--History. Loans, Foreign--Developing countries. Technical assistance--Developing countries. Economic history--1945-
Series: The evolving role of the World Bank
LC Classification: HG3881.5.W57 L28 1994
Dewey Class No.: 332.1/532 20

Lavalle, Roberto.
La Banque mondiale et ses filiales: aspects juridiques et fonctionnement. Préf. de Wolfgang Friedmann.
Paris, Librairie générale de droit et de jurisprudence, 1972.
Description: 323 p. 26 cm.
Notes: Bibliography: p. [255]-259.
Subjects: World Bank International Monetary Fund.
Series: Bibliothèque de droit international, 65
LC Classification: LAW <General Lava>

Lay, Kenneth G.
Mobilizing private savings for development: IBRD and the capital markets /

Kenneth G. Lay.
Washington, DC: World Bank, [1994]
Description: 22 p.: ill.; 28 cm.
ISBN: 0821330853
Subjects: World Bank. Economic development--Finance. Loans, Foreign. Bonds. Global bonds.
Series: The evolving role of the World Bank
LC Classification: HG3881.5.W57 L39 1994
Dewey Class No.: 332.1/532 20

Le Prestre, Philippe G.
The World Bank and the environmental challenge / Philippe Le Prestre.
Selinsgrove: Susquehanna University Press; London :
Associated University Presses, c1989.
Description: 263 p.: ill.; 24 cm.
ISBN: 0941664988 (alk. paper)
Notes: Includes index. Bibliography: p. [239]-253.
Subjects: World Bank--Developing countries. Development banks--Developing countries. Environmental policy--Developing countries. Economic development projects-Environmental aspects Developing countries.
LC Classification: HG3881.5.W57 L4 1989
Dewey Class No.: 332.1/532 19

Learning from experience: policy and practice in aid to
higher education / editors, Lene Buchert, Kenneth King.
The Hague: Centre for the Study of Education in Developing Countries, c1995.
Editor: Buchert, Lene.
Description: 261 p.: ill.; 24 cm.
ISBN: 9064431701
Notes: Includes bibliographical references.
Subjects: World Bank. Education, Higher--Developing countries--Finance. Educational assistance.
Series: CESO paperback; no. 24
LC Classification: LC2610 .L43 1995
Dewey Class No.: 379.1/54/091724 20

Legal aspects of development financing in the 1980's.
[Washington, D.C.]: The Washington College of Law, The American University, 1982
Description: p. 89-110 p.; 26 cm.
Partial Contents: The role of the International Monetary Fund / Stephen A. Silard -- Prospects of development financing in the 1980's / Ernest Stern.
Notes: "Sponsored by the Washington College of Law in cooperation with the legal department of the World Bank, May 28-29, 1981." "Fall 1982" "Reprinted

from The American University Law Review, Volume 32, Fall 1982, Number 1."
Cover Symposium: Legal aspects of development financing in the 1980's.
Subjects: International Monetary Fund.
World Bank. International finance--Congresses. Economic assistance--Congresses. Finance--Developing countries--Congresses.

Leone, Alfredo M.
Institutional and operational aspects of central bank losses / prepared by Alfredo M. Leone.
[Washington, D.C.]: International Monetary Fund, 1993.
Description: 24 p.; 28 cm.
Subjects: Banks and banking, Central--Developing countries Accounting. Bank loans--Developing countries--Accounting.
Series: IMF paper on policy analysis and assessment; PAA/93/14
LC Classification: HG3881.5.I58 I566 no. 93/14

Lessons from the gender impact of bank assistance : selected proceedings from World Bank workshops / edited by Gita Gopal.
Washington, D.C.: World Bank, 2000.
Editor: Gopal, Gita,
Description: p. cm.
ISBN: 0821346857
Notes: At head of World Bank Operations Evaluation Department.
Subjects: World Bank--Congresses. Women in development--Congresses. Economic assistance--Congresses.
Series: World Bank operations evaluation study
LC Classification: HG3881.5.W57 .L473 2000
Dewey Class No.: 332.1/532/082 21

Letters to the managing director, International Monetary Fund and to the president, World Bank.
Port Louis [Mauritius]: Ministry of Finance, 1983.
Description: ii, 34 p.; 26 cm.
Notes: "September 1983"--Cover.
Subjects: International Monetary Fund--Mauritius. World Bank--Mauritius. Mauritius--Economic policy.
LC Classification: HC597.5 .M393 1983
Dewey Class No.: 338.969/82 19

Levina, L. A.
Pravovoe polozhenie Mezhdunarodnogo valiutnogo onda I Vsemirnogo banka / Levina L.A.
Edition Information: 1. izd.
Moskva: Izd-vo "LEGAT", 1996.

Description: 146 p.; 20 cm.
ISBN: 574950008X
Notes: Includes bibliographical references (p. 138-147).
Subjects: International Monetary Fund. World Bank. Financial institutions, International-Law and legislation. Development banks--Law and legislation.
LC Classification: K4452 .L48 1996

Levitsky, Jacob, 1924-
World Bank lending to small enterprises: a review / Jacob Levitsky.
Washington, D.C., U.S.A.: World Bank, c1986.
Description: viii, 53 p.; 28 cm.
ISBN: 0821308149 (pbk.)
Notes: Includes bibliographical references.
Subjects: World Bank. Small business--Developing countries--Finance. Loans, Foreign--Developing countries.
Series: Industry and finance series, 0256-2235; v. 16
LC Classification: HG3881.5.W57 L48 1986
Dewey Class No.: 332.1/532 19

Levy, Brian.
The design and sequencing of trade and investment policy reform: an institutional analysis / Brian Levy.
[Washington, DC]: Country Economics Dept., World Bank, [1990]
Description: 33 p.; 28 cm.
Notes: Cover title. "May 1990." Includes bibliographical references.
Subjects: World Bank. Foreign trade promotion--Developing countries. Loans, Foreign--Developing countries. Developing countries--Commercial policy. Developing countries--Industrial policy.
Series: Policy, research, and external affairs working papers ; WPS 419
LC Classification: HF1413 .L47 1990

L'Hèriteau, Marie-France.
Le Fonds monètaire international et les pays du Tiers-monde / Marie-France L'Hèriteau.
Edition Information: 1re èd.
Paris: Presses universitaires de France: E.D.E.S., c1986.
Description: 277 p.: ill.; 24 cm.
ISBN: 2130392032 :
Notes: Includes bibliographical references.
Subjects: International Monetary Fund--Developing countries. Finance--Developing countries. Developing countries--Economic policy.
Series: Collection Tiers monde, 0223-5870
LC Classification: HG3881.5.I58 L52 1986

Lichtensztejn, Samuel, 1934-
Capital financiero, deuda externa y politicas conûmicas en Amèrica Latina / Samuel Lichtensztejn.
Montevideo: Ediciones de la Banda Oriental, 1985]
Description: 178 p.; 19 cm.
Notes: Includes bibliographical references.
Subjects: International Monetary Fund--Latin America. Debts, External--Latin America. International finance. Latin America--Economic policy.
Series: Temas del siglo XX; 33
LC Classification: HC125 .L519 1985

Lichtensztejn, Samuel, 1934-
Fondo Monetario Internacional y Banco Mundial : estrategias y politicas del poder financiero / Samuel Lichtensztejn, Mûnica Baer.
Edition Information: 2a ed.
Caracas: Editorial Nueva Sociedad, 1987.
Description: 215 p.: ill.; 20 cm.
Notes: Includes bibliographical references.
Subjects: International Monetary Fund. World Bank.
LC Classification: HG3881.5.I58 L527 1987

Lichtensztejn, Samuel, 1934-
Fondo Monetario Internacional y Banco Mundial : estrategias y polìticas del poder financiero / Samuel Lichtensztejn, Monica Baer.
Edition Information: 1a. ed.
San Josè, Costa Rica: Editorial Nueva Sociedad; uenos Aires, Argentina: Centro de Estudios Transnacionales, 1986.
Description: 215 p.: ill.; 20 cm.
Notes: Includes bibliographical references.
Subjects: International Monetary Fund. World Bank.
LC Classification: HG3881.5.I58 L527 1986

Lichtensztejn, Samuel, 1934-
The IMF and the experience of Latin America's Southern cone / Samuel Lichtensztejn.
Buenos Aires: Centro de Economìa Transnacional, Instituto para Amèrica Latina, [1980]
Description: 18 p.; 28 cm.
Notes: "Junio de 1980." "D/41/i." Bibliography: p. 16-18.
Subjects: International Monetary Fund--Southern Cone of South America. Southern Cone of South America--Economic policy.
LC Classification: HG3881.5.I58 L53 1980
Dewey Class No.: 332.1/52 19

Lim, David.
Export instability and compensatory financing / David im.
London; New York: Routledge, 1991.
Description: xiv, 204 p.: ill.; 23 cm.
ISBN: 0415036453
Notes: Includes bibliographical references (p. 192-200) and index.
Subjects: International Monetary Fund. Exports--Developing countries--Finance. Balance of trade--Developing countries. Compensatory financing--Developing countries. Economic development. Developing countries--Commercial policy.
LC Classification: HF1413 .L54 1990
Dewey Class No.: 382/.17/091724 20

Lindgren, Carl-Johan.
Bank soundness and macroeconomic policy / Carl-Johan Lindgren, Gillian Garcia, and Matthew I. Saal.
Washington, D.C.: International Monetary Fund, 996.
Description: xv, 215 p.: ill.; 24 cm.
ISBN: 155775599X
Notes: Includes bibliographical references (p. 205-215).
Subjects: Banks and banking.
LC Classification: HG1551 .L56 1996
Dewey Class No.: 332.1 20

Lindsey, T.
The IMF and insolvency law reform in Indonesia
Bulletin of Indonesian Economic Studies, 1998, Vol 34, Iss 3, pp 119-124

Lister, Frederick K., 1921-
Decision-making strategies for international organizations : the IMF model / Frederick K. Lister; foreword by Seymour Maxwell Finger.
Denver, Colo.: Graduate School of International studies, University of Denver, c1984.
Description: ix, 142 p.; 21 cm.
ISBN: 0879400757 (pbk.) :
Notes: Bibliography: p. 127-129.
Subjects: International Monetary Fund. International agencies--Decision making--Case studies.
Series: Monograph series in world affairs; v. 20, bk. 4
LC Classification: HG3881.5.I58 L57 1984
Dewey Class No.: 332.1/52 19

Livable cities for the 21st century / World Bank.
Washington, D.C.: World Bank, c1996.
Editor: World Bank.

Description: v, 47 p.: col. ill.; 23 cm.
ISBN: 0821338129
Summary: "As one of the World Bank's contributions to the Habitat II process in Istanbul, this publication first tells the story of nearly a quarter century of the Bank's program of urban assistance for developing countries. It then turns to the future to draw attention to priorities for action"--P. 1.
Notes: Includes bibliographical references (p. 47).
Subjects: World Bank--Developing countries. City planning--Developing countries. Economic assistance--Developing countries.
Series: Directions in development (Washington, D.C.)
LC Classification: HT169.5 .L59 1995

Loan and technical assistance approvals / Asian Development Bank.
[S.l]: The Bank,
Description: v.; 28 cm.
Continued by: Loan, technical assistance, and equity approvals
Notes: Description based on: No. 77/2 (1 Mar. 1977); title from caption. SERBIB/SERLOC merged record
Subjects: Asian Development Bank--Periodicals. Loans, Foreign--Asia--Periodicals. Technical assistance--Asia--Periodicals.
LC Classification: HG3881.5.A75 L6
Dewey Class No.: 332.1/53 19
Entry: Loan and technical assistance approvals. S.1. 84-647291

Loan, technical assistance and private sector operations approvals / Asian Development Bank.
[Manila, Philippines]: The Bank,
Description: v.; 28 cm.
Continues: Loan, technical assistance, and equity approvals (DLC) 87642779
Notes: Description based on: No. 87/2.
Subjects: Asian Development Bank--Periodicals. Loans, Foreign--Asia--Periodicals. Technical assistance--Asia--Periodicals.
LC Classification: HG3881.5.A75 L6
Dewey Class No.: 332.1/53 19

Loan, technical assistance, and equity approvals / Asian Development Bank.
Manila, Philippines: The Bank,
Description: v.; 28 cm.
Continues: Loan and technical assistance approvals (DLC) 84647291 (OCoLC)11242839
Continued by: Loan, technical assistance and private sector operations approvals (DLC) 97946896 (OCoLC)17405784
Notes: Description based on: No. 84/4; title from cover. Prepared by: the Information Office. SERBIB/SERLOC merged record

Subjects: Asian Development Bank--Periodicals. Loans, Foreign--Asia--Periodicals. Technical assistance--Asia--Periodicals.
LC Classification: HG3881.5.A75 L6
Dewey Class No.: 332.1/53 19
Entry: Loan, technical assistance, and equity approvals. 87-642779

Lockheed, Marlaine E.
World Bank lending for education research, 1982-89 / Marlaine E. Lockheed and Alastair G. Rodd.
Washington, DC (1818 H St., NW, Washington 20433) : Population and Human Resources Dept., World Bank, [1991]
Description: ii, 91 p.: ill.; 28 cm. Notes: Cover title. "January 1991." Includes bibliographical references.
Subjects: World Bank. Education--Research--Finance.
Series: Policy, research, and external affairs working papers ; WPS 583
LC Classification: LB1028 .L583 1991

Los Bancos transnacionales, el estado y el endeudamiento externo en Bolivia.
Edition Information: 1a ed.
Santiago de Chile: Naciones Unidas; Nueva York, NY,
Estados Unidos de América: Publicaciones de las Naciones Unidas, Sección Ventas [distributor], 1983.
Description: 282 p.: ill.; 23 cm.
Notes: "E/CEPAL/G.1251, junio de 1983"--T.p. verso.
Bibliography: p. 271-282.
Subjects: Debts, External--Bolivia. Banks and banking, International. Economic development. Bolivia--Economic policy.
Series: Estudios e informes de la CEPAL; 26
LC Classification: HJ8574 .B36 1983
Dewey Class No.: 332.1/5/0984 19

Low U.S. share of World Bank-financed procurement : multiagency report to the Congress / by the Comptroller General of the United States.
[Washington: U.S. General Accounting Office, 1974]
Description: 65 p.; 26 cm. Notes: Cover title. "B-161470." Publication date stamped on cover.
Subjects: World Bank. Economic assistance. Loans, Foreign. United States--Commerce.
LC Classification: HC60.U6 G4 1974
Dewey Class No.: 353/.008/27

Loxley, John.
The IMF and the poorest countries: the performance of the least developed countries under IMF standby arrangements / John Loxley for the North-South

Institute.
Ottawa, Canada: The Institute, c1984.
Description: x, 34 p.; 23 cm.
ISBN: 0920494447 (pbk.)
Notes: Foreword and summary in English and French. Includes bibliographical references.
Subjects: International Monetary Fund. Economic stabilization--Developing countries. Developing countries--Economic conditions.
LC Classification: HG3881.5.I58 L69x 1984

Ludlow, Nicholas H.
The Development Bank highways market, 1987-1991: a practical reference guide / by Nicholas H. Ludlow and Susan Diane Ward.
Washington, D.C., USA (1735 Eye St., NW, Suite 710, Washington 20006): Development Bank Associates, c1987.
Description: 387, 2 p.: ill.; 28 cm.
Notes: Includes index.
Subjects: World Bank. Banks and banking, International Development banks. Road construction--Finance.
LC Classification: HG3881 .L737 1987
Dewey Class No.: 388.1/14 19

Machlup, Fritz, 1902-
Remaking the international monetary system; the Rio agreement and beyond.
Baltimore, Published with the Committee for economic Development by the Johns Hopkins Press [1968]
Description: x, 161 p. 23 cm.
Notes: Appendices (p. 123-155):--A. Outline of a facility based on special drawing rights in the International Monetary Fund.--B. The Articles of agreement of the International Monetary Fund as adopted in 1944 and amended in 968: [list of articles and sections]--C. Proposed modifications of original Articles of agreement.--D. Proposed additions to the Articles of agreement; [a resolution passed by the Fund's Board of Governors at the annual meeting in Rio de Janeiro on Sept. 29,
1967]--E. Impact of hypothetical allocation of SDR's other balances of payments of Fund member countries.
Subjects: International Monetary Fund. Special drawing rights.
LC Classification: HG3881 .M27
Dewey Class No.: 332.1/52

Macro performance under adjustment lending / Riccardo Faini ... [et al.].
Washington, DC (1818 H St. NW, Washington 20433): Country Economics Dept., World Bank, [1989]
Editor: Faini, Riccardo.

Description: 33 p.; 28 cm.
Notes: Cover title. "April 1989." Includes bibliographical references (p. 30-31)
Subjects: World Bank. International Monetary Fund. Loans, Foreign--Developing countries. Economic stabilization--Developing countries. Developing countries--Economic conditions.
Series: Policy, planning, and research working papers; WPS 190
LC Classification: HG3891.5 .M33 1989
Dewey Class No.: 339.5/09172/4 20

Mandle, J.R.
The globalisation of poverty: Impacts of IMF and World Bank reforms, by M. Chossudovsky
Journal of Developing Areas, 1998, Vol 32, Iss 3, pp 415-417

Manzetti, Luigi.
The International Monetary Fund and economic stabilization : the Argentine case / Luigi Manzetti.
New York: Praeger, 1991.
Description: xii, 239 p.; 25 cm.
ISBN: 0275933970 (alk. paper)
Notes: Includes bibliographical references (p. [223]-233) and index.
Subjects: International Monetary Fund--Argentina. Economic stabilization--Argentina. Argentina--Economic policy.
LC Classification: HC175 .M16 1991
Dewey Class No.: 332.1/52 20

Marchesi, S. and Thomas, J.P.
IMF conditionality as a screening device
Economic Journal, 1999, Vol 109, Iss 454, pp C111-C125
A theoretical model is developed in which both buybacks and the adoption of an IMF programme can be used as screening devices which enable a creditor to discriminate between debtor countries which are willing to use debt relief in order to invest and repay and countries which are not. Asymmetric information is assumed. This problem can be solved if the country has sufficient resources to engage in a debt buyback and so gain the debt relief. When the country is credit constrained, an alternative screening mechanism is to undertake an IMF programme in return for debt reduction and possibly an IMF loan.

Marrese, Michael.
An income policy for Russia? / by Michael Marrese.
[Washington, D.C.]: International Monetary Fund, 1994.
Description: ii, 21 p.; 28 cm.
Subjects: Wage policy; Economic policy; Russia
Series: IMF paper on policy analysis and assessment; PAA/94/4

LC Classification: HG3881.5.I58 I566 no. 94/4

Marshall, Tyler
The World Still Loves the Dollar.
Los Angeles Times (Los Angeles, CA) Oct. 9, 1994, pA1+

Masson, Paul R.
The role of the IMF: financing and its interactions with adjustment and surveillance / Paul R. Masson and Michael Mussa.
Washington, D.C.: International Monetary Fund, 995.
Description: v, 41 p.: ill.; 23 cm.
ISBN: 1557755515
Notes: Includes bibliographical references (p. 39-41).
Subjects: International Monetary Fund. International finance. Balance of payments. Economic stabilization. International economic relations.
Series: Pamphlet series (International Monetary Fund); no. 0.
LC Classification: HG3881.5.I58 M37 1995
Dewey Class No.: 332.1/52 20

Matin, K. M.
Bangladesh and the IMF: an exploratory study / K.M. Matin.
Dhaka: Bangladesh Institute of Development studies, 1986.
Description: xii, 143 p.; 23 cm.
Notes: Bibliography: p. 120-122.
Subjects: International Monetary Fund--Bangladesh. Loans, Foreign--Bangladesh. Bangladesh--Economic conditions.
Series: Research monograph (Bangladesh Institute of development Studies); no. 5.
LC Classification: HG3971.6 .M38 1986
Dewey Class No.: 332.1/52 19

McAllister, Bill
Imf, World Bank Back Third World Debt Plan
Newsday April 5, 1989

McAllister, I.
Assessing aid. World Bank Policy Research Report, by D. Dollar, L. Pritchett
Canadian Public Administration - Administration Publique du Canada, 1999, Vol 42, Iss 2, pp 279-282

McCarthy, Patrick A.
Hierarchy and flexibility in world politics: adaptation to shifting power distributions in the United Nations Security Council and the International Monetary Fund / Patrick A. McCarthy.

Aldershot [England]: Brookfield [Vt.] USA: c1998.
Description: ix, 277 p.: ill.; 23 cm.
ISBN: 1840144718
Notes: Includes bibliographical references (p. 245-277).
Subjects: United Nations. Security Council. International Monetary Fund. World politics--1945- Political stability. International relations. International finance.
LC Classification: D843 .M334 1998
Dewey Class No.: 341.23/23 21

McGettigan, Donal.
Current account and external sustainability in the Baltics, Russia, and other countries of the former Soviet Union / Donal McGettigan.
Washington, D.C.: International Monetary Fund,
Description: p. cm.
ISBN: 1557758263
Notes: Includes bibliographical references.
Subjects: Balance of payments--Former Soviet republics. Sustainable development- Former Soviet republics.
Series: Occasional paper (International Monetary Fund); no. 89.
LC Classification: HG3883.F6 M38 2000
Dewey Class No.: 382/.17/0947 21

McLenaghan, John B.
Currency convertibility in the Economic Community of West African States / by John B. McLenaghan, Saleh M. souli, and Klaus-Walter Riechel.
Washington, D.C.: International Monetary Fund, 1982]
Description: v, 46 p.; 28 cm.
Notes: "August 1982." Bibliography: p. 45-46.
Subjects: Economic Community of West African States. Foreign exchange--Africa, West. Currency convertibility--Africa, West.
Series: Occasional paper (International Monetary Fund); no. 3.
LC Classification: HG3986.5 .M34 1982
Dewey Class No.: 332.4/56096 19

McQuillan, Lawrence J., 1961-
The case against the International Monetary Fund / Lawrence J. McQuillan.
Stanford, CA: Hoover Institution on War, evolution and Peace,
Stanford University, 1999.
Description: 29 p.; 23 cm.
ISBN: 0817943323 (alk. paper)
Notes: Includes bibliographical references (p. 25-29).
Subjects: International Monetary Fund.
Series: Essays in public policy; no. 98
LC Classification: HG3881.5.I58 M39 1999

Dewey Class No.: 332.1/52 21

Meeting of the Committee on Banking and Currency, United States Senate, Eighty-third Congress, first session, on a study of the Export-Import Bank and the International Bank for Reconstruction and Development and their relationship to foreign trade, and to organize the Citizens Advisory Committee to the Committee on Banking and Currency, United States Senate.
Washington, U.S. Govt. Print. Off., 1953.
Description: vii, 64 p. tables. 1953.
Notes: At head of 83 Cong., 1st sess. Committee print.
Subjects: Export-Import Bank of Washington. World Bank United States--Commercial policy.
LC Classification: HF1456 1953 .A53
Dewey Class No.: 332.1

Meinecke, Gert.
Fattigdomsorienteret bistand: Verdensbankens overvejelser / Gert Meinecke.
København: Center for udviklingsforskning, 1989.
Description: 54 p.; 21 cm.
Notes: Includes bibliographical references (p. 51-54).
Subjects: World Bank--Developing countries. Economic assistance--Developing countries. Poor--Developing countries.
Series: CUF notat, 0902-9206
LC Classification: HC60 .M372 1989

Mendez, Jose Marìa, 1929-
El Fondo Monetario Internacional: la segunda enmienda Josè Marìa Mendez.
[Madrid, Spain?]: Ministerio de Hacienda, Instituto e Estudios Fiscales, [1978]
Editor: Instituto de Estudios Fiscales (Spain)
Description: 430 p.: ill.; 19 cm.
ISBN: 8471962136
Subjects: International Monetary Fund.
LC Classification: HG3881.5.I58 M45 1978
Dewey Class No.: 332.1/52 19

Message from the President of the United States relative to special borrowing arrangements of the International Monetary Fund. Committee on Banking and Currency, House of Representatives, Eighty-seventh Congress, second session.
Washington, U.S. Govt. Print. Off., 1962.
Description: vii, 24 p. 24 cm.
Notes: At head of Committee print.
Subjects: International Monetary Fund.
LC Classification: HG3881 .U632 1962

Mikesell, Raymond Frech.
The Bretton Woods debates: a memoir / Raymond F. Mikesell.
Princeton, N.J.: International Finance Section, Dept. of
Economics, Princeton University, c1994.
Description: 68 p.; 23 cm.
ISBN: 0881650994 (pbk.) :
Notes: Includes bibliographical references.
Subjects: International Monetary Fund--History. World Bank--History.
United Nations Monetary and Financial Conference (1944: Bretton Woods, N.H.)--History.
Series: Essays in international finance, 0071-142X; no. 192
LC Classification: HG136 .P7 no. 192 HG205
Dewey Class No.: 332.1/52 20

Miller, Morris, 1924-
Coping is not enough!: the international debt crisis and the roles of the World Bank and International Monetary Fund / Morris Miller.
Homewood, Ill.: Dow Jones-Irwin, c1986.
Description: xiii, 268 p.: ill.; 24 cm.
ISBN: 0870949330
Notes: Includes bibliographical references and index.
Subjects: World Bank. International Monetary Fund. Debts, External--Developing countries. International finance.
LC Classification: HJ8899 .M55 1986
Dewey Class No.: 336.3/435/091724 19

Miller, Rich and Belton, Beth
Nations Show Signs of Action on Crisis
USA Today Oct. 6, 1998, pn.p.

Mistry, Percy S.
The present role of the World Bank in Africa / by Percy Mistry.
London: Institute for African Alternatives, [1989]
Description: 28 p.; 30 cm.
ISBN: 1870425162
Notes: At head of Institute for African Alternatives. "Edited lecture delivered at IFAA on Monday, 16th October 1989."
Subjects: World Bank--Africa. Loans, Foreign--Africa. Structural adjustment (Economic policy)--Africa. Africa--Economic conditions--1960-
LC Classification: HG3881.5.W57 M57 1989
Dewey Class No.: 332.1/532/096 20

Mitzakis, Michel.
Les crédits exterieurs;

Paris, Les Éditions internationales, 1939.
Description: 3 p. l., [ix]-xvi, 359 p., 1 l. tables. (part fold.) fold. diagr. 26 cm.
Subjects: Foreign exchange. Credit. Currency question.
Bank for international settlements.
LC Classification: HG255 .M53

Moffet, George D. III and Kaslow, Amy
World Bank Faces New Demands
Christian Science Monitor Aug. 28, 1991, p9

Money: The Facts on Money
New Internationalist (Oxford, England) Oct. 1998, p20-21

Money: The Story of Money
New Internationalist (Oxford, England) Oct. 1998, p14-15

Morgan, Carlyle.
Bretton Woods; clues to a monetary mystery, by Carlyle Morgan ...
Boston, World peace foundation, 1945.
Description: vii p., 1 l., 143 p. 22 cm.
Notes: Bibliography: p. [133]-138.
Subjects: International Monetary Fund. World Bank
United Nations Monetary and Financial Conference (1944 Bretton Woods, N.H.)
LC Classification: HG2051944 .M6
Dewey Class No.: 332.15

Morrell, James.
International institutions and economic sanctions on South Africa / Jim Morrell.
London: Africa Bureau, 1981.
Description: 39 p.; 21 cm.
Notes: Includes bibliographical references.
Subjects: International Monetary Fund. Loans, Foreign--South Africa. Economic sanctions--South Africa.
Series: Economic sanctions against South Africa; 8
LC Classification: HG3881.5.I58 M67 1981
Dewey Class No.: 332.1/52 19

Mortgaging the future: the World Bank and IMF in the Philippines / edited by Vivencio R. Jose.
Quezon City: Foundation for Nationalist Studies, 1982.
Editor: Jose, Vivencio R.
Description: 250 p.; 23 cm.
Notes: Includes bibliographical references.
Subjects: World Bank--Philippines. International Monetary Fund--Philippines.

Philippines--Foreign economic relations.
LC Classification: HG3881.5.W57 M67 1982
Dewey Class No.: 332.1/52 19

Moser, Gary G.
Nigeria: experience with structural adjustment / Gary Moser, Scott Rogers, and Reinhold van Til with Robin Kibuka and Inutu Lukonga.
Washington, D.C.: International Monetary Fund, 997.
Description: viii, 106 p.: ill.; 28 cm.
ISBN: 1557756309
Notes: "March 1997." Includes bibliographical references.
Subjects: Structural adjustment (Economic policy)--Nigeria. Finance, Public--Nigeria. Nigeria--Economic conditions--1970-
Series: Occasional paper (International Monetary Fund); no. 48.
LC Classification: HC1055 .M68 1997
Dewey Class No.: 338.9669 21

Mrabet, Elarbi.
Coopèration internationale multilatèrale et dèveloppement au Maroc / Elarbi Mrabet; prèface de Michel Virally.
Paris: A. Pedone, c1983.
Description: 486 p.: ill.; 24 cm.
ISBN: 2233001192 :
Notes: Bibliography: p. [471]-476.
Subjects: World Bank--Morocco. International Monetary Fund--Morocco. Unesco--Morocco. Morocco--Economic policy.
LC Classification: HC810 .M73 1983
Dewey Class No.: 338.964 19

Mullen, Joseph
Rural poverty alleviation: international development perspectives / by Joseph Mullen.
Aldershot; Brookfield, Vt., USA: Avebury, c1995.
Description: xi, 168 p.: ill.; 23 cm.
ISBN: 1856288641
Notes: "In association with the Institute for Development Policy and Management"—Cover Includes bibliographical references (p. 165-168).
Subjects: World Bank--Developing countries. United Nations Development Programme—Developing countries. Economic assistance--Developing countries. Rural poor--Developing countries.
LC Classification: HC60 .M758 1995
Dewey Class No.: 338.9/1/091724 20

Mulloo, V.
Budgeting, International Monetary Fund, and the World Bank by V. Mulloo.
[Port Louis, Mauritius]: Ministry of Finance, 1988?]
Description: 47 p.; 21 cm.
Notes: Includes bibliographical references.
Subjects: International Monetary Fund. World Bank. Budget.
LC Classification: HJ2005 .M78 1988
Dewey Class No.: 351.72/2 20

Multilateral compensation of international payments in Latin America; study submitted in accordance with the resolution of 24 June 1948 of the first session of the Economic commission for Latin America.
[Lake Success, 1949]
Editor: United Nations. Economic and Social Council. Economic Commission for Latin America.
Description: 75 p. 32 cm.
Subjects: Foreign exchange--Law--Latin America. Latin America—Commerce
Series: United Nations. [Document] E/CN.12.87. 27 May 1949.
LC Classification: JX1977 .A2 E/CN.12/87

Multinationale Konzerne, Weltbank, Internationaler Währungsfonds: ihre Arbeitsweise, ihr Einfluss und die Folgen ihrer Politik / Dietrich Schirmer, Studienleiter Evangelische Akademie Berlin (West); Evangelisches Bildungswerk.
Berlin: Evangelisches Bildungswerk Berlin, Haus der Kirche, [1986]
Editor: Schirmer, Dietrich-
Description: 141 p.: ill.; 30 cm.
Notes: "Seminarreihe der Evangelischen Akademie Berlin (West) im 1. Halbjahr 1986"--Cover.
Includes bibliographical references (p. 134-136). Subjects: World Bank. International Monetary Fund. International business enterprises.
Series: Dokumentation (Ev. Bildungswerk Berlin); 86/54.
LC Classification: HD2755.5 .M836 1986

Muntaner, C. and Lynch, J.
Income inequality, social cohesion, and class relations: A critique of Wilkinson's neo-Durkheimian research program
International Journal of Health Services, 1999, Vol 29, Iss 1, pp 59-81
Wilkinson's "income inequality and social cohesion" model has emerged as a leading research program in social epidemiology. Public health scholars and activists working toward the elimination of social inequalities in health can find several appealing features in Wilkinson's research. In particular, it provides a sociological alternative to former models that emphasize poverty, health behaviors, or the cultural aspects of social relations as determinants of population health. Wilkinson's model calls for social explanations, avoids the subjectivist

legacy of U.S. Functionalist sociology that is evident in "status" approaches to understanding social inequalities in health, and calls for broad policies of income redistribution.

Murphy, Josette.
Gender issues in World Bank lending / Josette L. Murphy.
Washington, D.C.: World Bank, c1995.
Description: xvi, 131 p.: ill.; 28 cm.
ISBN: 0821332139
Notes: "Annex 5: Major World Bank publications on gender issues (by year of publication, 1975-94)": p. 112-118. Includes bibliographical references (p. 119-126).
Subjects: World Bank--Developing countries. Investments, Foreign--Developing countries. Women in development--Developing countries. Economic development projects--Developing countries. Economic assistance--Developing countries. Loans, Foreign--Developing countries.
Series: A World Bank operations evaluation study, ISSN 1011-0984
LC Classification: HG3881.5.W57 M87 1995
Dewey Class No.: 332.1/532/091724 20

Murphy, Josette.
Mainstreaming gender in World Bank lending: an update / Josette Murphy.
Washington, D.C.: World Bank, c1997.
Description: xviii, 64 p.: ill.; 28 cm.
ISBN: 0821339818 (pbk.)
Notes: Includes bibliographical references (p. 55-56).
Subjects: World Bank--Developing countries. Women in development--Developing countries. Investments, Foreign--Developing countries. Economic development projects--Developing countries. Economic assistance--Developing countries. Loans, Foreign--Developing countries.
Series: A World Bank operations evaluation study, 1011-0984
LC Classification: HG3881.5.W57 M873 1997
Dewey Class No.: 332.1/532/091724 21

Nakagawa, K¯oji
Ajia Kaihatsu Gink¯o.
[1979]
Description: 216 p.; 18 cm.
Notes: Romanized.
Subjects: Asian Development Bank.
Series: Jiji mondai kaisetsu; 173.
LC Classification: HG4517 .N3

Nakao, Shigeo, -

En to doru no sonb¯o: kokusai ts¯ukashi kara mita Nichi-Bei no yukue = The fortune of yen and doller / Nakao Shigeo.
Description: 380 p.: ill.; 20 cm.
ISBN: 4895831647
Notes: In Japanese. Includes bibliographical references and indexes.
Subjects: International finance--History. Capital movements--History. Banks and banking, International--History. Japan--Foreign economic relations--United States. United States--Foreign economic relations--Japan.
LC Classification: HG3881 .N292 1996

Nakao, Shigeo,

Sekai man¯e fur¯o: kokusai kin'y¯u shij¯o no rekishi to gendai / Nakao Shigeo cho.
Edition Information: Shohan.
T¯oky¯o: D¯obunkan, Sh¯owa 63 [1988]
Description: v, 280 p.: ill.; 22 cm.
ISBN: 449542131X :
Notes: Includes bibliographical references and indexes.
Subjects: International finance--History. Capital movements--History. Banks and banking, International--History.
LC Classification: HG3881 .N293 1988

Nayyar, Deepak

Globalization: The Past in Our Present.
Third World Economics (Penang, Malaysia) Sept. 1-15, 1997,

Newcomer, Mabel,

Monetary plans for the United nations, a layman's guide to proposals of the Bretton Woods conference, by Mabel Newcomer.
Washington, D.C., American Association of University Women [c1944]
Editor: American Association of University Women.
Description: 1 p. l., 26 p. 23 cm.
Notes: Reproduced from type-written copy. "Suggested readings" included in "Study guide" (p. 21-6)
Subjects: International Monetary Fund. International Bank for Reconstruction and Development. United Nations Monetary and Financial Conference (1944 Bretton Woods, N.H.)
LC Classification: HG205 1944 .U575
Dewey Class No.: 332.15

Noss, Andrew.

Education and adjustment: a review of the literature / Andrew Noss.
Washington, DC (1818 H St. NW, Washington 20433) : Education and

Employment Division, Population and Human Resources Department, World Bank, [1991]
Description: iv, 68 p.; 28 cm.
Notes: Cover title. "July 1991." Includes bibliographical references (p. 61-68).
Subjects: World Bank--Developing countries. Education--Developing countries--Finance. Educational assistance--Developing countries.
Series: Policy, research, and external affairs working papers ; WPS 701
LC Classification: LB2826.6.D44 N67 1991
Dewey Class No.: 370.19/65/091724 20

Nowzad, Bahram
Lessons of the Debt Decade.
Finance & Development (Intl. Monetary Fund & the World Bank)
March 1990, p9-13

Nowzad, Bahram.
The IMF and its critics / Bahram Nowzad.
Princeton, N.J.: International Finance Section, Dept. of Economics, Princeton University, c1982.
Description: 30 p.; 23 cm.
Notes: Includes bibliographical references.
Subjects: International Monetary Fund.
Series: Essays in international finance, 0071-142X; no. 146
LC Classification: HG136 .P7 no. 146 HG3881
Dewey Class No.: 332.1/52 19

O Banco Mundial e as políticas educacionais / Livia De Tommasi, Mirian Jorge Warde, Sérgio Haddad, organizadores.
São Paulo, SP: Cortez Editora: PUC-SP: Ação Educativa, c1996.
Editor: Tommasi, Livia De.
Description: 279 p.: ill.; 23 cm.
ISBN: 8524906200
Notes: Papers presented at the Seminário O Banco Mundial e as Políticas de Educação no Brasil, held at the Pontificia Universidade Católica de São Paulo, June 28-29, 1995. Includes bibliographical references.
Subjects: World Bank--Congresses. Education--Brazil--Finance--Congresses. Politics and education--Brazil--Congresses. Educational assistance--Brazil--Congresses.
LC Classification: LB2826.6.B7 B35 1996

O Brasil e o Banco Mundial: um diagnóstico das relações econômicas, 1949-1989 / Manuel José Forero Gonzalez ... [et al.].
Brasília: IPEA/IPLAN, [1990]
Editor: Gonzalez, Manuel José Forero.

Description: 174 p.; 23 cm.
Notes: Includes bibliographical references (p. 159-161).
Subjects: World Bank--Brazil. Brazil--Economic policy.
LC Classification: HG3881.5.W57 O37 1990

O problema da reforma do sistema monet·rio internacional.
Lisboa, Gabinete de investigaáıes Econûmicas do instituto Superior de Ciíncias e Financeiras, 1967-68.
Description: 2 v. 24 cm.
Subjects: International finance. Currency question.
Series: Lisbon Universidade Tècnica. Instituto Superior de Ciíncias Economicas e Financeiras. Gabinete de Investigaáıes Econûmicas. Textos e documentos. Lisbon. Universidade Tècnica. Instituto Superior de CiÍncias Econûmicas e Financeiras. Gabinete de Investigaáıes Econûmicas. Estudos e documentos.
LC Classification: HG3881 .I6335

OBrien, Caroline P. A.
Bibliography on money, banking, and finance in developing countries / prepared by Caroline P.A. OBrien.
Washington, D.C.: Joint Bank-Fund Library, international Monetary Fund & World Bank, 1981.
Description: [95], 96 p.; 28 cm.
Subjects: Finance--Developing countries--Bibliography. Money--Developing countries--Bibliography. Banks and banking--Developing countries--Bibliography. Developing countries--Bibliography.
Series: Bibliography series (Joint Bank-Fund Library); no. 1.
LC Classification: Z7164.F5 O27 HG195
Dewey Class No.: 016.332/09172/4 19

O'Brien, Patrick
The Economic Effects of the Great War.
History Today (London, England) Dec. 1994, p22-29

O'Callaghan, Gary.
The structure and operation of the world gold market Gary O'Callaghan.
Washington, D.C., U.S.A.: International Monetary Fund, 1993.
Description: v, 39 p.: col. ill.; 28 cm.
ISBN: 1557752818 (recycled paper) :
Notes: "September 1993." Includes bibliographical references (p. 36-37).
Subjects: Gold. Gold--Purchasing.
Series: Occasional paper (International Monetary Fund); no. 05.
LC Classification: HG293 .O28 1993
Dewey Class No.: 338.2/741 20

O'Cleireacain, Seamus.

Third World debt and international public policy / Seamus O'Cleireacain.
New York: Praeger, 1990.
Description: xiv, 244 p.; 24 cm.
ISBN: 027592520X (alk. paper)
Notes: Includes index. Bibliography: p. [231]-238.
Subjects: International Monetary Fund. Debts, External--Developing countries. Debt relief--Developing countries.
LC Classification: HJ8899 .O25 1990
Dewey Class No.: 336.3/435/091724 20

Ofreneo, Rene E.

The employment crisis and the World Bank's adjustment program / [Rene E. Ofreneo, Esther P. Habana].
Diliman, Quezon City: Institute of Industrial Relations, University of the Philippines, c1987.
Description: iii, 186 p.; 23 cm.
Notes: Bibliography: p. 143-157.
Subjects: World Bank--Philippines. Industries--Philippines. Industrial policy--Philippines. Unemployment--Philippines. Labor supply--Philippines.
LC Classification: HC455 .O35 1987
Dewey Class No.: 331.13/79599 19

Ogan, C. A.

Prolegomena to a critical analysis of the stand-by credit arrangements of the International Monetary Fund (IMF) by C.A. Ogan.
Lagos: [Nigerian Society of International Law, 986]
Description: 30 leaves; 30 cm.
Notes: "Paper presented at the annual conference of the Nigerian Society of International Law, Lagos, March 1986." "March 1986."
Bibliography: leaves 26-30.
Subjects: International Monetary Fund--Nigeria--Congresses. Debts, External--Law and legislation--Congresses. Credit--Law and legislation--Congresses. Banks and banking, International--Law and legislation Congresses. Debts, External--Law and legislation--Nigeria--Congresses.
LC Classification: K4450 .A55 1986
Dewey Class No.: 341.7/51 19

Operational information on proposed projects / Asian Development Bank.

Metro Manila, Philippines: The Bank, -1989.
Editor: Asian Development Bank.
Description: v.; 28 cm. -v. 11, no. 3 (Dec. 1988).
Current Frequency: Monthly
Continued by: Proposed projects and contracts awarded

ISSN: 0115-6209
Notes: Description based on: Vol. 5, no. 2 (Nov. 1982).
SERBIB/SERLOC merged record
Subjects: Asian Development Bank--Periodicals. Economic development projects--Asia--Finance--Periodicals. Agricultural development projects--Asia—Finance Periodicals. Rural development projects--Asia--Finance--Periodicals. Loans, Foreign--Asia--Periodicals. Technical assistance--Asia--Periodicals.
LC Classification: HC415.P83 O63
Dewey Class No.: 332.1/53 19
Entry: Operational information on proposed projects. Metro Manila, Philippines. 85-648161

Osunsade, F. L.
IMF assistance to Sub-Saharan Africa / F.L. Osunsade, Paul Gleason.
Washington, D.C.: External Relations Dept., International Monetary Fund, [1992]
Description: 25 p.: ill., map; 23 cm.
ISBN: 1557751811
Subjects: International Monetary Fund--Africa, Sub-Saharan. Economic assistance--Africa, Sub-Saharan.
LC Classification: HC800 .O84 1992

Osunsade, F. L.
IMF support for African adjustment programs: questions and answers / F.L. Osunsade.
Washington, D.C.: External Relations Dept., International Monetary Fund, 1993.
Description: 20 p.; 23 cm.
ISBN: 1557753539
Notes: "September 1993"--T.p. verso.
Subjects: International Monetary Fund--Africa. Structural adjustment (Economic policy)-Africa. Economic assistance--Africa. Africa--Economic conditions--1960-
LC Classification: HC800 .O85 1993
Dewey Class No.: 338.96 20

Oversight of the International Monetary Fund and the World Bank: a meeting of a multinational group of parliamentarians involved in oversight of the IMF and the World Bank: hosted by the Subcommittee on International Development, Finance, Trade, and Monetary Policy of the Committee on Banking, Finance, and Urban Affairs, House of Representatives, One Hundred Third Congress, second session, November 21, 1994.
Washington: U.S. G.P.O.: For sale by the U.S. G.P.O., Supt. of Docs., Congressional Sales Office, 1995.
Description: v, 147 p.; 23 cm.

ISBN: 0160475546
Notes: Distributed to some depository libraries in microfiche. Shipping list no.: 95-0312-P. "Serial no. 103-173." Includes bibliographical references.
Subjects: International Monetary Fund--Congresses. World Bank--Congresses. Development banks--Congresses. Loans, Foreign--Developing countries--Congresses. Economic development--Finance--Congresses.
LC Classification: HG3881.5.I58 O94 1994
Dewey Class No.: 332.15/2 20
GPO Item No.: 1013-A
Report No.: Serial no. 103-173 (United States. Congress. House. Committee on Banking, Finance, and Urban Affairs)

Oversight of the International Monetary Fund and the World Bank: a meeting of a multinational group of parliamentarians involved in oversight of the IMF and the World Bank: hosted by the Subcommittee on International Development, Finance, Trade, and Monetary Policy of the Committee on Banking, Finance, and Urban Affairs, House of Representatives, One Hundred Third Congress, second session, November 21, 1994. Washington: U.S. G.P.O.: For sale by the U.S. G.P.O., Supt. of Docs., Congressional Sales Office, 1995.
Description: v, 147 p.; 23 cm.
ISBN: 0160475546
Notes: Distributed to some depository libraries in microfiche. Shipping list no.: 95-0312-P. "Serial no. 103-173." Includes bibliographical references.
Subjects: International Monetary Fund--Congresses. World Bank—Congresses Development banks--Congresses. Loans, Foreign--Developing countries--Congresses.
Economic development--Finance--Congresses.
LC Classification: HG3881.5.I58 O94 1994
Dewey Class No.: 332.15/2 20
Govt. Doc. No.: Y 4.B 22/1:103-173

Owen, Henry
The World Bank: Is 50 Years Enough? Henry Owen.
Foreign Affairs Sept./Oct. 1994,

Paine Webber euromoney directory.
London: Euromoney Publications PLC in association with Paine Webber, c1997.
Description: 1 v.; 21 cm. 26th ed. (1997).
Current Frequency: Annual
Continues: SBC Warburg euromoney directory (DLC) 97643303 (OCoLC)34523232
Continued by: Euromoney capital markets directory (DLC) 98656739
Notes: SERBIB/SERLOC merged record
Subjects: Foreign-exchange brokers--Directories. Financial institutions,

International--Directories. Banks and banking, International--Directories.
LC Classification: HG3851 .H34
Dewey Class No.: 332.4/5/025 19
Entry: Paine Webber euromoney directory. 97-651340

Pakistan - IMF package: Nothing to celebrate
Economic and Political Weekly, 1999, Vol 34, Iss 8, pp 457-458
The expectation that the resumption of IMF loan will rescue Pakistan's economy is based on fiction, not fact. It will at best provide some breathing space, nothing more.
Pat Wechsler. Newsday Staff Correspondent
Stamps Forty Years For The World Bank - The Washington Post
Newsday Dec. 25, 1988

Pal, Mahendra.
World Bank and the Third World countries of Asia, with special reference to India / Mahendra Pal.
New Delhi, India: National, 1985.
Description: x, 407 p.; 22 cm.
Notes: Includes index. Bibliography: p. [379]-389.
Subjects: World Bank--Asia. Loans, Foreign--Asia. Asia--Economic conditions.
LC Classification: HG3881.5.W57 P35 1985
Dewey Class No.: 332.1/532/095 19

Participation in practice: the experience of the World Bank and other stakeholders / edited by Jennifer Rietbergen-McCracken.
Washington, D.C.: World Bank, c1996.
Editor: Rietbergen-McCracken, Jennifer, 1962-
Description: xi, 97 p.; 28 cm.
ISBN: 0821336843
Notes: Includes bibliographical references.
Subjects: World Bank. Economic development projects--Citizen participation—Case studies.
Series: World Bank discussion papers; 333.
LC Classification: HG3881.5.W57 P363 1996
Dewey Class No.: 332.1/532 20

Participatory development and the World Bank: potential directions for change / edited by Bhuvan Bhatnagar and Aubrey C. Williams.
Washington, D.C.: World Bank, c1992.
Editor: Bhatnagar, Bhuvan.
Description: vi, 195 p.: ill.; 28 cm.
ISBN: 0821322494
Notes: Includes bibliographical references.

Subjects: World Bank. Economic development projects--Citizen participation. International agencies.
Series: World Bank discussion papers, 0259-210X; 183
LC Classification: HG3881.5.W57 P36 1992
Dewey Class No.: 332.1/532/0684 20

Pauly, L.W.
Good governance and bad policy: the perils of international organizational overextension
Review of International Political Economy, 1999, Vol 6, Iss 4, pp 401-424
A significant adaptation has recently occurred in the mandate of the International Monetary Fund. With no alteration to its legal charter, the Fund has effectively become the promoter of a putative consensus among its leading member states on intrusive norms of industrial regulation. At a time when much attention was focused on the need for new tools of global economic governance, such a shift in the role of an organization viewed as emblematic of the post-World War II order potentially had wide implications. Skeptics began to ask whether intergovernmental organizations originally designed to encourage mutually beneficial collaboration among sovereign member states were simply turning into crude instruments for advancing the interests of the strong. This article disputes the historical uniqueness of the turn underway inside post-war international economic organizations; it draws parallels to the work of the League of Nations in the interwar period and to inconclusive multilateral negotiations in the 1940s.

Pavignani, E.
Can the World Bank be an effective leader in international health?
Social Science & Medicine, 2000, Vol 50, Iss 2, pp 181-182

Payment systems, monetary policy, and the role of the central bank / Omotunde E.G. Johnson with Richard K. Abrams ... [et al.].
Washington, D.C.: International Monetary Fund, c1998.
Editor: Johnson, Omotunde E. G.
Description: xviii, 254 p.: ill.; 23 cm.
ISBN: 1557756260
Notes: Includes bibliographical references (p. 249-254).
Subjects: Payment--Case studies. Clearinghouses (Banking)--Case studies. Monetary policy--Case studies. Banks and banking, Central--Case studies.
LC Classification: HG1692 .P388 1998
Dewey Class No.: 332/.0285 21

Perpetuating poverty: the World Bank, the IMF, and the developing world / edited by Doug Bandow and Ian V·squez.
Washington, D.C.: Cato Institute, c1994.
Editor: Bandow, Doug. V·squez, Ian.

Description: ix, 362 p.: ill.; 24 cm.
ISBN: 188257706X (cloth) : 1882577078 (pbk.) :
Notes: Includes bibliographical references and index.
Subjects: International Monetary Fund. World Bank. Economic assistance. Commercial policy. International business enterprises. International finance. Developing countries--Economic conditions.
LC Classification: HG3881.5.I58 P48 1994
Dewey Class No.: 332.1/532 20

Perpetuating poverty: the World Bank, the IMF, and the developing world / edited by Doug Bandow and Ian Vásquez.
Washington, D.C.: Cato Institute, c1994.
Editor: Bandow, Doug.
Description: ix, 362 p.: ill.; 24 cm.
ISBN: 188257706X (cloth) : 1882577078 (pbk.) :
Notes: Includes bibliographical references and index.
Subjects: International Monetary Fund. World Bank. Economic assistance. Commercial policy. International business enterprises. International finance. Developing countries--Economic conditions.
LC Classification: HG3881.5.I58 P48 1994
Dewey Class No.: 332.1/532 20

Pissulla, Petra.
Zur Rolle von IWF, Weltbank und GATT in den Ost-West-Wirtschaftsbeziehungen / Petra Pissulla.
Köln: Bundesinstitut für Ostwissenschaftliche und Internationale Studien, c1991.
Description: vi, 55 p.; 30 cm.
Notes: Cover title. Summary in German and English.
Includes bibliographical references (p. 48-50).
Subjects: International Monetary Fund--Europe, Eastern. World Bank--Europe, Eastern. General Agreement on Tariffs and Trade (Organization) East-West trade (1945-) Europe, Eastern--Foreign economic relations.
Series: Berichte des Bundesinstituts für Ostwissenschaftliche und Internationale Studien; 1991-16. Internationale Studien; 16-1991
LC Classification: HX15 .G468 1991-16 HG3881.5.I58

Plan del F. M. I. para compensar las fluctuaciones de la exportaciûn.
Edition Information: [1. ed.]
Mèxico, 1963.
Editor: Centro de Estudios Monetarios Latino-americanos.
Description: 55 p. 17 cm.
Subjects: Currency question.
LC Classification: HG3881 .I633

Polak, J. J. (Jacques Jacobus), 1914-
The World Bank and the International Monetary Fund: a changing relationship / Jacques J. Polak.
Washington, D.C.: Brookings Institution, c1994.
Description: 59 p.; 23 cm.
ISBN: 0815771495
Notes: Cover The World Bank and the IMF.
Includes bibliographical references (p. 51-59).
Subjects: World Bank--History. International Monetary Fund--History. Economic assistance.
Series: Brookings occasional papers
LC Classification: HG3881.5.W57 P6 1994
Dewey Class No.: 332.1/532 20

Policies for African development: from the 1980s to the 1990s / editor, I.G. Patel; papers presented at a symposium held in Gaborone, Botswana, February 25-27, 1991.
Washington: International Monetary Fund, 1992.
Editor: Patel, I. G. (Indraprasad Gordhanbhai),
Description: xi, 293 p.: ill.; 23 cm.
ISBN: 155775232X :
Notes: Includes bibliographical references.
Subjects: Structural adjustment (Economic policy)—Africa Congresses.
LC Classification: HC800 .P63 1992
Dewey Class No.: 338.96 20

Policy coordination in the European monetary system.
Washington, D.C.: International Monetary Fund: Address orders to External Relations Dept., Publication Services, IMF, c1988.
Editor: Tullio, Giuseppe,
Description: vii, 82 p.: col. ill.; 28 cm.
ISBN: 1557750289
Contents: pt. 1. The European monetary system / by Manuel Guiti·in --pt. 2. Monetary coordination within the European monetary system / by Massimo Russo and Giuseppe Tullio.
Notes: "Addendum" inserted. "September 1988." Includes bibliographies.
Subjects: European Monetary System (Organization) Money--European Economic Community countries.
Series: Occasional paper (International Monetary Fund); no. 61.
LC Classification: HG925 .P64 1988
Dewey Class No.: 332.4/5/094 19

Policy experiences and issues in the Baltics, Russia, and other countries of the former Soviet Union / edited by Daniel A. Citrin and Ashok K. Lahiri, with Jonathan Anderson ... [et al.]

Washington, D.C.: International Monetary Fund, c1995.
Editor: Citrin, Daniel. Lahiri, Ashok.
Description: ix, 126 p.: ill.; 28 cm.
ISBN: 1557755183
Contents: Overview / Daniel A. Citrin -- The decline in output /Jonathan Anderson, Daniel A. Citrin and Ashok K. Lahiri-- The behavior of inflation and velocity / Jonathan Anderson and Daniel A. Citrin -- Interenterprise arrears/ Ashok K. Lahiri and Daniel A. Citrin -- The revenue decline / Richard Hemming, Adrienne Cheasty and Ashok K. Lahiri Stabilization / Jeromin Zettermeyer and Daniel A. Citrin --- External financial assistance Eduard Brau -- Russia and the IMF / Ernesto Hernandez-Cat·.
Notes: "December 1995." Includes bibliographical references.
Subjects: Economic stabilization--Former Soviet republics. Economic stabilization--Europe, Eastern. Former Soviet republics--Economic policy. Europe, Eastern--Economic policy—1989. Former Soviet republics--Economic conditions. Europe, Eastern--Economic conditions--1989-Russia (Federation)--Economic conditions--1991-
Series: Occasional paper (International Monetary Fund); no. 133. LC Classification: HC336.27 .P65 1995

Policy issues in the evolving international monetary system / Morris Goldstein ...
Washington, DC: International Monetary Fund, 1992.
Editor: Goldstein, Morris,
Description: vii, 74 p.: ill.; 28 cm.
ISBN: 1557752346
Notes: Includes bibliographical references (p. 68-72).
Subjects: International finance. Monetary policy. Fiscal policy. Monetary unions.
Series: Occasional paper (International Monetary Fund); no. 96.
LC Classification: HG3881 .P65 1992
Dewey Class No.: 332/.042 20

Policy research working papers.
Washington, D.C.: World Bank, 1991-
Description: v.; 28 cm. WPS 796-
Continues: Policy, research, and external affairs working papers
ISSN: 1020-0525
Subjects: World Bank. Economic development. Developing countries.
LC Classification: HG3881.5.W57 P63
Electronic File Info.:
http://www.worldbank.org/html/dec/Publications/Workpapers/ home.html

Population and development: implications for the World Bank.
Washington, D.C.: World Bank, c1994.
Description: x, 134 p.: ill.; 23 cm.

ISBN: 0821329995
Notes: Includes bibliographical references (p. 128-134).
Subjects: World Bank. Population--Economic aspects. Economic development. Population--Economic aspects--Developing countries.
Series: Development in practice (Washington, D.C.)
LC Classification: HB849.41 .P638 1994
Dewey Class No.: 304.6 20

Population and the World Bank: adapting to change.
Washington, D.C.: World Bank, 1999.
Description: 45 p.: ill., col. map; 28 cm.
ISBN: 0821344404
Notes: Includes bibliographical references.
Subjects: World Bank. Population. Population policy.
Series: Health, nutrition, and population series
LC Classification: HB849.4 .P673 1999
Dewey Class No.: 304.6 21

Post-bubble blues: how Japan responded to asset price collapse / editors, Tamim Bayoumi, Charles Collyns.
Washington, D.C.: International Monetary Fund, 1999.
Editors: Bayoumi, Tamim A. Collyns, Charles.
Description: p. cm.
ISBN: 1557758727
Notes: Includes bibliographical references.
Subjects: Stocks--Prices--Japan. Financial crises--Japan. Monetary policy--Japan. Japan--Economic conditions--1989-
LC Classification: HG5773 .P67 1999
Dewey Class No.: 330.952/049 21

Post-conflict reconstruction: the role of the World Bank.
Washington, D.C.: World Bank, c1998.
Description: x, 69 p.; 23cm.
ISBN: 0821342150
Notes: Includes bibliographical references (p. 69).
Subjects: World Bank. Economic assistance--Developing countries.
LC Classification: HG3881.5.W57 P67 1998
Dewey Class No.: 658.1/532 21

Poverty reduction and the World Bank: progress in fiscal 1994.
Washington, D.C.: World Bank, c1995.
Description: ix, 75 p.; 28 cm.
ISBN: 0821329286
Notes: Includes bibliographical references (p. 75).

Subjects: World Bank. Economic assistance--Developing countries. Poverty--Developing countries.
LC Classification: HC60 .P666 1995

Poverty reduction and the World Bank: progress in fiscal 1993.
Washington, D.C.: World Bank, c1994.
Editor: World Bank.
Description: x, 63 p.; 28 cm.
Notes: "Updates Implementing the World Bank's strategy to reduce poverty: progress and challenges"--p. vii. Includes bibliographical references (p. 63).
Subjects: World Bank. Economic assistance--Developing countries. Poverty--Developing countries.
LC Classification: HC60 .P665 1994

Poverty reduction and the World Bank: progress in fiscal 1996 and 1997.
Washington, D.C.: World Bank, c1997.
Description: x, 182 p.; 28 cm.
ISBN: 0821338013
Notes: Updates the report for fiscal 1995, Poverty reduction and the World Bank: progress and challenges for the 1990s (p. vii).
Includes bibliographical references (p. 182).
Subjects: World Bank. Economic assistance--Developing countries. Poverty--Developing countries.
LC Classification: HC60 .P667 1997

Poverty reduction and the World Bank: progress in fiscal 1998.
Washington, D.C.: World Bank, c1999.
Description: ix, 117 p.: ill.; 28 cm.
ISBN: 082134384X (pbk.)
Notes: Includes bibliographical references (p. 115-117).
Subjects: World Bank. Economic assistance--Developing countries. Poverty--Developing countries.
LC Classification: HC60 .P668 1999
Dewey Class No.: 332.1/532 21

Practical international financial organization, through amendments to Bretton Woods proposals.
[New York] American bankers association, 1945.
Description: 47 p. 23 cm.
Subjects: International Monetary Fund. World Bank United Nations Monetary and Financial Conference (1944 Bretton Woods, N.H.)
LC Classification: HG205 1944 .U546
Dewey Class No.: 332.15

Practical international financial organization, through amendments to Bretton Woods proposals.
[New York?] American bankers association, 1945.
Description: 47 p. 23 cm.
Subjects: International Monetary Fund. World Bank United Nations Monetary and Financial Conference (1944: Bretton Woods, N.H.)
LC Classification: HG205 1944 .U546
Dewey Class No.: 332.15

Prescription for progress?: a commentary on the education policy of the World Bank / edited by Peter Williams.
[London]: University of London Institute of Education ;
Windsor: Distributed by NFER, 1976.
Editor: Williams, Peter R. C.
Description: 98 p.; 22 cm.
ISBN: 085473063X :
Notes: "Papers and a report of proceedings of a seminar held at the University of London Institute of Education in May 1975." Includes bibliographical references.
Subjects: World Bank--Congresses. Education--Developing countries--Congresses. Educational assistance--Developing countries--Congresses.
Series: Studies in education: New series; 3 0458-2101
LC Classification: LC2605 .P75
Dewey Class No.: 370.19/65097124

Preston, Lewis T.
Slowing population growth and accelerating sustainable development: a call to action: an address to the International Conference on Population and Development / Lewis T. Preston.
Washington, D.C.: World Bank, [1994]
Description: 16 p.; 28 cm.
ISBN: 0821330713
Notes: "Cairo, Egypt, September 6, 1994"--Cover. English, French, Spanish, and Arabic.
Subjects: World Bank--Developing countries. Population--Economic aspects. Sustainable development--Developing countries.
Developing countries--Population.
LC Classification: HB884 .P74 1994

Presyong di kayang abutin, pisong walang mabili.
[Manila Philippines]: Church-Based Consumers' Movement, [1989]
Description: 20 p.: ill.; 22 cm.
Notes: In Tagalog. Cover title. "April 1989"--P. [4] of cover. Includes bibliographical references (p. 19).
Subjects: International Monetary Fund--Cariacatures and cartoons. Cost and

standard of living--Philippines--Caricatures and cartoons. Loans, Foreign--Philippines--Caricatures and cartoons. Philippines--Economic policy--Caricatures and cartoons.
LC Classification: HD7056 .P74 1989

Primary commodities: market developments and outlook / by the Commodities Division of the Research Department, International Monetary Fund.
Washington, D.C.: The Division, 1986-
Description: v.: ill.; 28 cm. May 1986- Ceased in 1990?
Current Frequency: Annual
ISSN: 1010-2736
Notes: SERBIB/SERLOC merged record
Subjects: Commodity exchanges--Periodicals. Primary commodities--Periodicals. Produce trade--Periodicals. Commercial products--Periodicals.
Series: World economic and financial surveys, 0258-7440
LC Classification: HG6046 .P74
Dewey Class No.: 332.64/4/05 20
Entry: Primary commodities. 89-646516

Private market financing for developing countries / by a staff team from the Exchange and Trade Relations Department.
Washington, DC: International Monetary Fund, 1991-
Description: v.; 28 cm.
Notes: Vols. for 1992-<1995> "Prepared in the IMF's Policy Development and Review Department." SERBIB/SERLOC merged record
Subjects: Debt equity conversion--Developing countries--Periodicals. Debt equity conversion--Developing countries—Statistics Periodicals.
Series: World economic and financial surveys 0258-7440
LC Classification: HJ8899 .P74
Dewey Class No.: 336.3/435/09172405 21
Entry: Private market financing for developing countries.

Problems and issues in structural adjustment: papers / prepared by the staffs of the World Bank and the International Monetary Fund for the Development Committee.
Washington, D.C., U.S.A.: Joint Ministerial Committee of the Boards of Governors of the World Bank and the International Monetary Fund on the Transfer of Real Resources to Developing Countries (Development Committee), [1990]
Description: vii, 97 p.: ill.; 22 cm.
ISBN: 082131436X
Notes: Includes bibliographical references.
Subjects: World Bank--Developing countries. Economic stabilization--Developing countries. Loans, Foreign--Developing countries. Structural adjustment (Economic policy)—Developing countries.

Series: Development Committee (Series); no. 23.
LC Classification: HG3881.5.W57 P74 1990
Dewey Class No.: 332.1/52 20

Problems of international money, 1972-85 / edited by Michael Posner.
Washington D.C.: International Monetary Fund; London : Overseas Development Institute, 1986.
Editor: Posner, Michael,
Description: ix, 191 p.: ill.; 24 cm.
ISBN: 0939934582 (pbk.)
Notes: "Papers presented at a seminar organized by the International Monetary Fund and the Overseas Development Institute in London in March 1985."
Includes bibliographies.
Subjects: International finance.
LC Classification: HG3881 .P77 1986
Dewey Class No.: 332/.042 19

Proceedings: annual meeting of the Board of Governors / International Bank for Reconstruction and Development.
Washington, D.C.: The Bank, 1947-1949.
Description: 3 v.; 28 cm. 2nd (Sept. 11-17, 1947)-4th (Sept. 13-16, 1949).
Current Frequency: Annual
Continues: World Bank. Board of Governors. Proceedings and related documents Continued by: World Bank. Board of Governors. Summary proceedings
Subjects: World Bank--Congresses. International Finance Corporation--Congresses. International Development Association--Congresses. Multilateral Investment Guarantee Agency--Congresses.
LC Classification: HG3881 .I553
Dewey Class No.: 332.1/532/05 20
Entry: World Bank. Summary proceedings [of the] annual meeting of the Board of Governors.

Procurement of works.
Washington, DC: World Bank, 1999.
Description: xiii, 74 p.: ill.; 28 cm.
ISBN: 0821346016
Notes: "September 1999".
Subjects: World Bank. Requests for proposals (Public contracts)—Developing countries. Letting of contracts--Developing countries. Economic assistance--Developing countries. Public works--Developing countries--Finance. Economic development projects--Developing countries Finance.
LC Classification: HG3881.5.W57 P7483 1999

Dewey Class No.: 352.7/7253/091724 21

Procurement of works: major equipment and industrial installations: standard prequalification documents.
Washington, D.C.: World Bank, [1993]
Description: vii, 53 p.; 28 cm.
Notes: "April 1993."
Subjects: World Bank. International Development Association. Industrial procurement. Loans, Foreign. Credit.
LC Classification: HG3881.5.W57 P75 1993

Procurement of works: smaller contracts.
Washington, D.C. (1818 H St., N.W., Washington 20433): World Bank, [1995]
Description: viii, 98 p.; 28 cm.
ISBN: 0821333615
Notes: "January 1995." Includes index.
Subjects: World Bank. International Development Association. Industrial procurement. Letting of contracts--Forms. Contracts for work and labor--Forms.
LC Classification: HG3881.5.W57 P753 1995
Dewey Class No.: 332.1/532/0687 20

Procurement of works: smaller contracts.
Washington, D.C. (1818 H St., N.W., Washington 20433) :
World Bank, [1993]
Description: 94 p.; 28 cm.
Notes: "Edition test, May 1993." Includes index.
Subjects: World Bank. International Development Association. Industrial procurement. Letting of contracts--Forms. Contracts for work and labor--Forms.
LC Classification: HG3881.5.W57 P753 1993
Dewey Class No.: 332.1/532/0687 20

Procurement under IBRD loans and IDA credits: guidelines.
Washington, D.C.: World Bank,
Description: v.; 10 x 23 cm.
Current Frequency: Irregular
Notes: At head of Guidelines. Description based on: 3rd ed. (May 1985).
SERBIB/SERLOC merged record
Subjects: World Bank. International Development Association. Industrial procurement. Loans, Foreign.
LC Classification: HG3881.5.W57 P76
Entry: Procurement under IBRD loans and IDA credits. 95-642389

Producciûn agropecuaria y FMI / panel organizado por Coloquio Agropecuario; panelistas, Carlos Ascuasiati ... [et al.]; comentarios, Ramûn Alm·nzar.

Santo Domingo, Republica Dominicana: Ediciones CEPAE, 1991.
Editor: Ascuasiati, Carlos.)
Description: 58 p.: ill.; 21 cm.
Subjects: International Monetary Fund--Dominican Republic Congresses. Agriculture--Economic aspects--Dominican Republic Congresses. Dominican Republic--Economic policy--Congresses.
LC Classification: HD1844.Z8 P764 1991

Professional luncheon meeting [sound recording]: Dr. Alfred Schaefer: '68, 3/20. 1968.
Description: 2 sound tape reels: analog, 7 1/2 ips, full track, mono.; 7 in.
Summary: Mr. Schaefer, chairman of the Union Bank of Switzerland, speaks on the Swiss banking system. His talk focuses on confidential Swiss bank accounts, the gold exchange standard, and the importance of foreign business.
Includes question-and-answer session.
Notes: An address to the Foreign Correspondents Club of Japan, Mar. 20, 1968.
Subjects: Banks and banking--Switzerland. Banks and banking, International. Gold standard.
LC Classification: LWO 5746, reel 166-167

Progress of initiatives to benefit Sub-Saharan Africa / prepared by the staffs of the World Bank and the International Monetary Fund for the Development Committee.
Washington, D.C., U.S.A.: Joint Ministerial Committee of the Boards of Governors of the World Bank and the International Monetary Fund on the Transfer of Real Resources to Developing Countries (Development Committee), [1990]
Description: 75 p.: ill.; 22 cm.
ISBN: 0821313452
Notes: Includes bibliographical references (p. 41-44).
Subjects: Economic assistance--Africa, Sub-Saharan. Africa, Sub-Saharan--Economic policy.
Series: Development Committee (Series); no. 21.
LC Classification: HC800 .P78 1990

Progress report on the implementation of portfolio management: next steps, a program of actions.
Washington, D.C.: World Bank, c1994.
Description: 44, 25 p.; 28 cm.
ISBN: 0821331485
Subjects: World Bank. Loans, Foreign. Economic development projects--Finance.
LC Classification: HG3881.5.W57 P764 1994

Project notes: a publication of the World Bank's Mozambique Resident Mission.
[Maputo, Mozambique]: The Mission,

Description: v.: ill.; 30 cm.
Current Frequency: Quarterly
Notes: Description based on: Vol. 2, no. 1 (Mar. quarter 1995); title from caption. SERBIB/SERLOC merged record
Subjects: World Bank--Periodicals. Economic development projects--Mozambique--Periodicals. Mozambique--Economic conditions--1975---Periodicals.
LC Classification: HC890.Z9 E447
Dewey Class No.: 338.9679/005 21
Entry: Project notes (Maputo, Mozambique) 96-983340

Proposed third amendment of the Articles of Agreement of the International Monetary Fund: report / of the Executive Board to the Board of Governors.
Washington, D.C.: International Monetary Fund, 1990.
Description: 14 p.; 23 cm.
ISBN: 1557752036
Subjects: International Monetary Fund--Rules and practice. Banks and banking, International.
LC Classification: HG3881.5.I58 P76 1990

Protecting the poor during periods of adjustment.
Washington, D.C., U.S.A.: Joint Ministerial Committee of the Boards of Governors of the World Bank and the International Monetary Fund on the Transfer of Real Resources to Developing Countries (Development Committee): Copies from World Bank Publications Sale Unit, [1987]
Description: 53 p.; 22 cm.
ISBN: 0821309250 (pbk.)
Subjects: World Bank--Developing countries. Economic assistance, Domestic--Developing countries. Poor--Developing countries.
Series: Development Committee (Series); no. 13.
LC Classification: HC59.72.P63 P76 1987
Dewey Class No.: 362.5/09172/4 19

Protocol regarding the immunities of the Bank for International Settlements. Brussels, July 30, 1936.
London, H. M. Stationery off., 1937.
Description: 9 p. 25 cm.
Subjects: Bank for International Settlements.
LC Classification: JX636 1892 1937, no. 25

Protocol regarding the immunities of the Bank of International Settlements.
London, H. M. Stationery off., 1937.
Description: 8 p. 25 cm.
Subjects: Bank for International Settlements.

LC Classification: HG1997.I6 P7

Protocol regarding the immunities of the Bank of International Settlements, Brussels, 30th July 1936.
Dublin, Stationery Office [1956]
Description: 8 p. 25 cm.
Subjects: Bank for International Settlements.
Series: [Ireland (Eire) Treaties, etc.] Treaty series, 1954. no. 20.
LC Classification: JX640.I7 A3 1954, no. 20

Protocol regarding the immunities of the Bank of International Settlements.
London, H. M. Stationery off., 1937.
Description: 8 p. 25 cm.
Subjects: Bank for International Settlements.
LC Classification: HG1997.I6 P7

Providing for additional U.S. contributions to the Asian Development Bank and the International Development Association. Hearings, Ninety-third Congress, first session ...
Washington, U.S. Govt. Print. Off., 1973.
Description: iii, 356 p. 24 cm.
Notes: Hearings held Nov. 14-Dec. 6, 1973 on H.R. 11354, 11355, and 11666. "Printed for the use of the Committee on Banking and Currency."
Subjects: Asian Development Bank. International Development Association.
LC Classification: KF27 .B346 1973b
Dewey Class No.: 341.7/51

Psacharopoulos, George and Patrinos, Harry A.
Indigenous People and Poverty in Latin America
Finance & Development (Intl. Monetary Fund & the World Bank)
March 1994, p41-43

Questions & answers: bidding for contracts in World Bank financed projects.
Washington, D.C., U.S.A.: World Bank, [1991]
Description: 31 p.; 28 cm.
Subjects: World Bank. Letting of contracts. Economic development projects.
LC Classification: HD2365 .Q47 1991
Dewey Class No.: 332.1/523 20

Questions & answers: bidding for contracts in World Bank financed projects.
Washington, D.C., U.S.A: World Bank, 1988.
Description: 18 p.; 23 cm.
Subjects: World Bank. Letting of contracts. Economic development projects.
LC Classification: HD2365 .Q47 1988

Dewey Class No.: 332.1/532 19

Ramstetter, E.D.
Private capital flows to developing countries: The road to financial integration, by World-Bank
Journal of Developing Areas, 1998, Vol 32, Iss 4, pp 547-549

Razavi, Hossein
Financing Oil and Gas Projects in Developing Countries
Finance & Development (Intl. Monetary Fund & the World Bank)
June 1996, p. 2-5.

Recent developments in external debt restructuring / by K. Burke Dillon ... [et al.].
Washington, D.C.: International Monetary Fund, c1985.
Editor: Dillon, K. Burke.
Description: vii, 68 p.: col. ill.; 29 cm.
ISBN: 0939934523 (pbk.) :
Notes: "October 1985." Includes bibliographical references.
Subjects: Loans, Foreign. Debts, External. Debt relief.
Series: Occasional paper (International Monetary Fund); no. 40.
LC Classification: HG3891.5 .R43 1985
Dewey Class No.: 336.3/435 19

Recent World Bank activities in energy / Industry and Energy Department.
Washington, DC (1818 H St. NW, Washington DC 20433) :
Industry and Energy Dept., World Bank, [1989]
Description: 60 p.; 28 cm.
Notes: Cover title. "February 1989."
Subjects: World Bank. Energy development--Developing countries. Loans, Foreign--Developing countries.
Series: Policy, planning, and research working papers; WPS 111
LC Classification: HD9502.D442 R43 1989
Dewey Class No.: 333.79/323 20

Recolonization or liberation: the bonds of structural adjustment and struggles for emancipation / by the Ecumenical Coalition for Economic Justice.
Toronto, Ont.: The Coalition, c1990.
Description: 96 p.: ill.; 22 cm.
ISBN: 0969233426
Notes: Includes bibliographical references.
Subjects: World Bank--Developing countries. Structural adjustment (Economic policy)—Developing countries. Debts, External--Developing countries. Structural adjustment (Economic policy)--Canada. Structural adjustment (Economic policy)—Political aspects.

LC Classification: HC59.7 .R345 1990

Recovery in the developing world: the London Symposium on the World Bank's Role.
Washington, D.C., U.S.A.: World Bank, c1986.
Description: vi, 122 p.: ill.; 23 cm.
ISBN: 0821307762 (pbk.)
Notes: Sponsored by the World Bank. Bibliography: p. 121-122.
Subjects: World Bank--Congresses.
LC Classification: HG3881.5.W57 L66 1985
Dewey Class No.: 332.1/532 19

Redwood, John, III.
World Bank approaches to the environment in Brazil: a review of selected projects / John Redwood III.
Washington, D.C.: World Bank, c1993.
Description: xviii, 92 p.; 28 cm.
ISBN: 0821325116
Notes: Includes bibliographical references (p. 91-92).
Subjects: World Bank--Brazil. Environmental policy--Brazil. Economic development projects--Environmental aspects Brazil.
Series: A World Bank operations evaluation study, 1011-0984
LC Classification: HG3881.5.W57 R43 1993
Dewey Class No.: 332.1/532/0981 20

Reform of the international monetary system: a report / by the executive directors to the Board of Governors.
Washington: International Monetary Fund, 1972.
Description: vii, 78 p.; 23 cm.
Subjects: International finance. Balance of payments. Developing countries--Finance.
LC Classification: HG3881 .I6363 1972
Dewey Class No.: 332.1/52

Reinvigorating growth in developing countries: lessons from adjustment policies in eight economies / David Goldsbrough ... [et al.].
Washington, DC: International Monetary Fund, 1996.
Editor: Goldsbrough, David John.
Description: vii, 113 p.: ill.; 28 cm.
ISBN: 1557755590 :
Notes: "Bangladesh, Chile, Ghana, India, Mexico, Morocco, Senegal, and Thailand during 1970-93"-Pref. Includes bibliographical references (p. 107-111).
Subjects: Structural adjustment (Economic policy)--Developing countries--Case studies. Economic development--Case studies. Developing countries--Economic policy--Case studies.

Series: Occasional paper (International Monetary Fund); no. 139.
LC Classification: HC59.7 .R424 1996
Dewey Class No.: 338.9/009172/4 21

Renewable resource management in agriculture / Operations Evaluation Department.
Washington, D.C.: World Bank, c1989.
Description: xxi, 189 p.: ill.; 28 cm.
ISBN: 0821313738
Subjects: World Bank. Agricultural resources--Developing countries--Management. Agricultural development projects--Developing countries Management. Forestry projects--Developing countries--Management. Agricultural resources--Management--Environmental aspects Developing countries. Agricultural development projects--Environmental aspects Developing countries. Forestry projects--Environmental aspects—Developing countries.
Series: A World Bank operations evaluation study, 1011-0984
LC Classification: S604.64.D44 R46 1989
Dewey Class No.: 333.76/15/091724 20

Report on audit.
Washington. [n.d.]
Description: v. 28 cm.
LC Classification: HG3881 .I635

Reports and summary proceedings of the international
Monetary Fund, 1946-1974 [microform].
Arlington, Va.: University Publications of America, [197-]
Description: 6 microfilm reels; 35 mm.
LC Classification: Microfilm 88/185 (H)

Research activities of the International Monetary Fund prepared by the Interdepartmental Working Group on Fund Policy Advice.
Washington, D.C., U.S.A.: International Monetary Fund, 1994-
Description: v.; 23 cm. Jan. 1991-Dec. 1993-
Notes: SERBIB/SERLOC merged record Additional Form Avail.: Also available via the Internet.
Subjects: International Monetary Fund--Research--Periodicals.
LC Classification: HG3881.5.I58 I568b
Dewey Class No.: 332.1/52 20
Entry: Research activities of the International Monetary Fund. 95-640331

Research bulletin: economic research and policy analysis / Asian Development Bank.
Manila, Philippines: Economics and Development Resource Center, [1993-
Description: v.; 28 cm. Vol. 1, no. 1 (Jan.-Apr. 1993)-
Current Frequency: Semiannual, Jan.-June 1994-

Former Frequency: Three times a year, Jan.-Apr. 1993-<May-Aug. 1993->
ISSN: 0117-6064
Notes: from caption. SERBIB/SERLOC merged record
Subjects: Asian Development Bank--Periodicals. Asia--Economic policy--Periodicals. Asia--Economic conditions--1945---Periodicals.
LC Classification: HC411.A1 A79a
Entry: Research bulletin (Asian Development Bank) 97-942197

Reshaping regional institutions: APEC and the IMF in East Asia
Pacific Review, 1999, Vol 12, Iss 1, pp 1-24
One of the most striking aspects of attempts to manage the crisis in East Asia has been the very different roles played by APEC and the IMF, Although both organizations have similar market-centred reform agendas, APEC has been conspicuous by its absence in the wake of the crisis. This paper considers the actions of both organizations and their very different approaches to institutional reform. It is suggested that the crisis in general and the actions of these two organizations in particular provides a timely opportunity to review the more influential varieties of institutional theory to see whether they provide either useful tools for understanding the roles and activities of APEC and the IMF, or plausible models of reform for policy-makers.

Restructuring economies in distress: policy reform and the World Bank / edited by Vinod Thomas ... [et al.].
Oxford, England; New York: Published for the World Bank [by] Oxford University Press, c1991.
Editor: Thomas, Vinod, 1949-
Description: xiv, 566 p.: ill.; 24 cm.
ISBN: 0195208706
Notes: Includes bibliographical references and index.
Subjects: World Bank--Developing countries. Balance of payments--Developing countries. Economic stabilization--Developing countries. Developing countries--Economic policy.
LC Classification: HG3881.5.W57 R47 1991
Dewey Class No.: 339.5/09172/4 20

Rethinking Bretton Woods / series editors, Jo Marie Griesgraber and Bernhard G. Gunter.
London; East Haven, Conn.: Pluto Press, with Center of Concern, Washington, DC, 1995-
Editor: Griesgraber, Jo Marie.
Description: v. <1, 3 >; 22 cm.
Notes: Includes bibliographical references and index.
Subjects: World Bank. International finance--History. International Monetary Fund. Economic development--History. Twenty-first century--Forecasts.
LC Classification: HG3881 .R418 1995

Dewey Class No.: 332/.042 20

Review of bank operations in the irrigation sector, 1966-1985.
Manila, Philippines: Asian Development Bank, [1986]
Description: vii, 92 p.: ill.; 23 cm.
Notes: "March 1986." Includes bibliographical references.
Subjects: Asian Development Bank. Irrigation--Economic aspects--Asia. Irrigation--Asia-Finance.
Series: Staff working paper (Manila, Philippines)
LC Classification: HD1741.A78 R48 1986
Dewey Class No.: 332.1/53/095 20

Ribe, Helena, 1949-
World Bank treatment of the social impact of adjustment programs / Helena Ribe and Soniya Carvalho.
Washington, DC (1818 H St., NW. Washington 20433): World Bank, [1990]
Description: 58 p.; 28 cm.
Notes: At head of Review and analysis, Policy and Review Department, World Bank. Cover title. "October 1990."
Subjects: World Bank--Developing countries. Structural adjustment (Economic policy)—Developing countries--Finance. Developing countries--Social conditions.
Series: Policy, research, and external affairs; WPS 521
LC Classification: HC59.7 .R485 1990

Rich, Bruce
Ideas Nations to World Bank
Newsday Aug. 1, 1993

Rich, Bruce.
Mortgaging the earth: the World Bank, environmental impoverishment, and the crisis of development / Bruce Rich.
Boston: Beacon Press, c1994.
Description: xiv, 376 p.; 24 cm.
ISBN: 080704704X :
Notes: Includes bibliographical references and index.
Subjects: World Bank--Developing countries. Environmental policy--Developing countries. Economic assistance--Developing countries.
LC Classification: HG3881.5.W57 R53 1994
Dewey Class No.: 332.1/532/091724 20

Robertson, James
Money: Our Money

New Internationalist (Oxford, England) Oct. 1998, p25-27

Roett, Riordan and Crandall, Russell
Confining Conditions
Harvard International Review. Summer 1999, p64-67

Role For World Bank News Dispatches
Newsday- Oct. 16, 1991

Root, Hilton
Self-Inflicted Wounds
National Interest No. 58 Winter 1999-2000, p105-108

Rosenbaum, Tibor, 1923-
Ein Weg zu einer Internationalen Bankorganisation, IBO. Eine Internationale Bankorganisation zur Verbesserung der internationalen zwischenbanklichen Zusammenarbeit.
Genf. Paris, München, Nagel, [1968]
Description: 119 p. 19 cm.
Subjects: Banks and banking, International.
LC Classification: HG3881 .R67

Rosenbaum, Tibor, 1923-
Towards a new International Banking Organisation. An International Banking Organisation for the improvement of international cooperation among banks, IBO.
Geneva, Paris, Munich, Nagel, (1968)
Description: 111 p. 19 cm.
Notes: Translation of Ein Weg zu einer Internationalen Bankorganisation, IBO. "Questionnaire": 1 leaf inserted.
Subjects: Banks and banking, International.
LC Classification: HG3881 .R673
Dewey Class No.: 332.1/5

RP-Japan relations and ADB: in search of a new horizon / edited by Mamoru Tsuda & Leo A. Deocadiz.
Metro Manila, Philippines: National Book Store, 1986.
Editor: Tsuda, Mamoru,
Description: x, 137 p.: ill.; 26 cm.
ISBN: 9710831569 (pbk.)
Notes: "A Business day book"--Cover. Bibliography: p. 18-20.
Subjects: Asian Development Bank. Philippines--Foreign economic relations--Japan. Japan--Foreign economic relations--Philippines.
LC Classification: HF1600.15.J3 R68 1986

Dewey Class No.: 337.520599 19

RP-US relations and IMF, World Bank: in search of a new horizon / edited by Mamoru Tsuda and Leo A. Deocadiz.
Metro Manila, Philippines: National Book Store, 1986.
Editor: Tsuda, Mamoru, Deocadiz, Leo A.
Description: xiii, 246 p.: ill., ports.; 26 cm.
ISBN: 9710831550 (pbk.)
Notes: "A Business day book"--Cover. Articles reprinted from issues of the newspaper Business day for Jan.-Apr. 1986.
Subjects: International Monetary Fund--Philippines. World Bank--Philippines. United States--Foreign relations--Philippines. Philippines--Foreign relations--United States. United States--Foreign relations--1981-1989. Philippines--Foreign relations--1946-1986.
LC Classification: E183.8.P6 R6 1986
Dewey Class No.: 327.730599 19

Ruffini, Pierre-Bruno, 1949-
Les banques multinationales: de la multinationalisation des banques au système bancaire transnational / Pierre-Bruno Ruffini.
Paris: Presses universitaires de France, c1983.
Description: 299 p.: ill.; 22 cm.
ISBN: 2130376274 :
Notes: A revision of the author's thesis (doctoral--Université de Paris X, 1979) Bibliography: p. [277]-292.
Subjects: Banks and banking, International. International finance.
Series: Publications de l'Université de Rouen Collection Perspective multinationale.
LC Classification: HG3881 .R79 1983
Dewey Class No.: 332.1/5 19

Rural energy and development: improving energy supplies for two billion people.
Washington, D.C.: World Bank, c1996.
Description: xii, 118 p.: ill.; 23 cm.
ISBN: 0821338064
Contents: 1. Introduction -- 2. The rural energy situation -- 3. Emerging practices and policies -- 4. Options for rural electrification -- 5. Innovations in renewable energy -- 6. Cooking fuels: toward more sustainable supply and use -- 7. The role of the World Bank Group -- Appendix. World Bank lending to rural and renewable energy projects, fiscal 1980-95.
Notes: "This report was prepared by Douglas Barnes, Dennis Anderson, and Karl Jechoutek, under the direction of Richard Stern"-P. xi. Includes bibliographical references (p. 110-118).
Subjects: World Bank. Energy development--Developing countries. Rural

development--Developing countries.
Series: Development in practice (Washington, D.C.)
LC Classification: HD9502.D442 R87 1996

Rutigliano, Michele.
La concorrenza nell'attività bancaria internazionale / Michele Rutigliano.
[Milano]: Giuffrè, 1980.
Description: 148 p.; 24 cm.
Notes: Bibliography: p. [137]-141.
Subjects: Banks and banking, International. Competition.
Series: Università "L. Bocconi," Dipartimento di economia aziendale (Series); 17.
LC Classification: HG3881 .R84

Sacks, Paul M.
New products, new risks: how bankers are adapting to the new international marketplace / Paul M. Sacks, Samuel H. Crawford.
[New York, NY]: HarperBusiness, c1991.
Description: xviii, 158 p.; 24 cm.
ISBN: 0887304990 :
Notes: Includes bibliographical references (p. 147-149) and index.
Subjects: Banks and banking, International. Financial services industry. Risk assessment. Banks and banking--United States. Banks and banking--Great Britain. Banks and banking--Canada. Bankers--Attitudes.
LC Classification: HG3881 .S152 1991
Dewey Class No.: 332.1 20

Salvatore, D.
International monetary and financial arrangements: Present and future
Open Economies Review, 1998, Vol 9, Suppl. 1, pp 375-415
The paper deals with a broad range of topics under the rubric of the international monetary system: exchange rate agreements, International Monetary Fund structure, history and functioning of the European Monetary Union, monetary and fiscal policies adopted in recent years by different countries, with a special emphasis on central bank independence and inflation control, capital flows and cross-border assets growth and their influence on financial stability, and policy proposals to enhance financial stability.

Sampson, Anthony.
The money lenders / Anthony Sampson.
London: Hodder and Stoughton, 1981.
Description: 336 p.; 24 cm.
ISBN: 0340257199 :
Notes: Includes index.

Subjects: Banks and banking, International.
LC Classification: HG3881 .S1827 1981
Dewey Class No.: 332.1/5 19

Sampson, Anthony.
The money lenders / by Anthony Sampson.
Harmondsworth, Middlesex; New York, N.Y.: Penguin Books, 1983, c1981.
Description: 428 p.; 20 cm.
ISBN: 0140064850 (pbk.)
Notes: Includes bibliographical references and index.
Subjects: Banks and banking, International. Bankers. Banks and banking--Developing countries.
LC Classification: HG3881 .S1827 1983
Dewey Class No.: 332.1/5 19

Sampson, Anthony.
The money lenders: bankers and a world in turmoil / Anthony Sampson.
New York: Viking Press, 1982, c1981.
Description: 336 p.; 25 cm.
ISBN: 0670211060
Notes: Includes bibliographical references and index.
Subjects: Banks and banking, International. Bankers. Banks and banking--Developing countries.
LC Classification: HG3881 .S1827 1982
Dewey Class No.: 332.1/5 19

Sanford, Jonathan E.
U.S. policy and the multilateral banks: politicization and effectiveness: staff report to the Subcommittee on Foreign Assistance of the Committee on Foreign Relations, United States Senate.
Washington: U.S. G.P.O., 1977.
Description: v, 33 p.; 23 cm.
Notes: At head of 95th Congress, 1st session. Committee print. "May 1977." Includes bibliographical references.
Subjects: Economic assistance, American. Banks and banking, International. United States--Foreign relations--1945-1989.
LC Classification: HC60 .S157
Dewey Class No.: 332.1/53 19

Sarchev, A. M. (Aleksandr Mikhailovich)
Vedushchie kommercheskie banki v mirovoi ekonomike / A.M. Sarchev.
Moskva: "Finansy i statistika", 1992.
Description: 174 p.; 20 cm.
ISBN: 5279008052

Notes: "Nauchnoe izdanie"--Colophon. Includes bibliographical references (p. 171-174).
Subjects: Banks and banking, International.
LC Classification: HG3881 .S1895 1992

Sau, R.

An open letter to the IMF
Economic and Political Weekly, 1998, Vol 33, Iss 50, pp 3191-3193
The world needs international flows of capital. But the present arrangements are structurally flawed. And the IMF's contemplated 'new chapter' to the Bretton Woods agreements offers more of the same.

Savings banks foreign business directory.

Geneva: International Savings Banks Institute,
Description: v.; 21 cm.
Notes: Description based on: '89. SERBIB/SERLOC merged record
Subjects: Savings banks--Directories. Banks and banking, International--Directories. Bankers--Directories.
LC Classification: HG1881 .S27
Dewey Class No.: 332.1/5/025 20
Entry: Saving banks foreign business directory. 89-659205

SBC Warburg euromoney directory.

London: Euromoney Publications PLC in association with SBC Warburg, c1996.
Editor: SBC Warburg (Firm)
Description: 1 v.; 21 cm.
Vol. for 1996 called also 25th ed. 1996.
Current Frequency: Annual
Continues: Cedel euromoney directory (DLC)sn 93017397 (OCoLC)27743742
Notes: SERBIB/SERLOC merged record Split into: Euromoney directory (London, England: 1997), and: Paine Webber euromoney directory.
Subjects: Foreign-exchange brokers--Directories. Financial institutions, International--Directories. Banks and banking, International--Directories.
LC Classification: HG3851 .H34
HG3881 .C4
Dewey Class No.: 332.4/5/025 19
Entry: SBC Warburg euromoney directory. 97-643303

Schedule of par values.

Washington. [n.d.]
Description: v. 23 cm.
Current Frequency: Unknown
Notes: Serial. PREMARC/SERLOC merged record
Subjects: Money--Tables, etc.

LC Classification: HG3863 .I5
Entry: International Monetary Fund. Schedule of par values.
48-17763

Scheer, Harold.
The multinational bank: an application of the theory of the multinational enterprise / par Harold Scheer.
Genève: Institut universitaire de hautes études internationales, 1987.
Description: 131, [6] p.: ill.; 30 cm.
Notes: "Mémmoire présenté en vue de l'obtention du diplôme."
Bibliography: p. [133]-[137]
Subjects: Banks and banking, International. International finance.
LC Classification: HG3881 .S338 1987
Dewey Class No.: 332.1/5 19

Schiltknecht, Beatrice M., 1967-
Eigenkapitalbeschaffung auf internationalen Märkten / Beatrice M. Schiltknecht.
Bern; New York: P. Lang, c1995.
Description: 260 p.: ill.; 21 cm.
ISBN: 3906755452
Notes: Originally presented as the author's thesis (doctoral--Universität Basel, 1995) under the Möglichkeiten der Eigenmittelbeschaffung schweizerischer Gesellschaften auf ausländischen Kapitalmärkten.
Includes bibliographical references (p. 253-260).
Subjects: Investments, Foreign. Banks and banking, International. Capital market--Switzerland. Corporations--Finance. Securities--Switzerland.
LC Classification: HG4538 .S32 1995

Schmidt-Wilke, Hans-Jürgen.
Risikoproblematik und Risikopolitik im internationalen Bankgeschäft.
Frankfurt am Main, F. Knapp [1970]
Description: 250 p. 23 cm.
Notes: Bibliography: p. 233-250.
Subjects: Banks and banking, International. International clearing. Risk.
LC Classification: HG3881 .S36

Schneider, Jerome.
The complete guide to offshore money havens: how to make millions, protect your privacy, and legally avoid taxes / Jerome Schneider.
Edition Information: Rev. and updated 3rd ed.
Rocklin, Calif.: Prima Pub., c2000.
Description: xx, 442 p.; 23 cm.
ISBN: 0761520104
Notes: Includes index.

Subjects: Banks and banking, International. Tax havens. Investments, American.
LC Classification: HG3881 .S3714 2000
Dewey Class No.: 332.1/5 21

Schneider, Jerome.
The complete guide to offshore money havens: how to make millions, protect your privacy, and legally avoid taxes--whether your net worth is $100 or $100 million / Jerome Schneider.
Edition Information: Rev. and updated [ed.]
Rocklin, CA: Prima Pub., c1997.
Description: xiii, 352 p.: forms; 23 cm.
ISBN: 0761509968
Notes: Includes index.
Subjects: Banks and banking, International. Tax havens. Investments, American.
LC Classification: HG3881 .S3714 1997
Dewey Class No.: 332.1/5 21

Schwartzman, Stephan.
Bankrolling disasters: international development banks and the global environment: a citizens' environmental guide to the World Bank and the regional multilateral development banks / [author, Stephan Schwartzman].
[San Francisco?]: Sierra Club; San Francisco, CA, USA :
Copies available from Sierra Club, Public Affairs, c1986.
Description: 32 p.: ill. (some col.); 28 cm.
Notes: Bibliography: p. 32.
Subjects: World Bank--Developing countries. Environmental policy--Developing countries. Economic assistance--Developing countries. Development banks--Developing countries.
LC Classification: HC59.72.E5 S39 1986
Dewey Class No.: 332.1/53/091724 19

Second special report to the President and to the Congress on the operations and policies of the International Monetary Fund and the International Bank for Reconstruction and Development.
[Washington] 1950.
Description: 37 l. 27 cm.
Notes: Cover title.
Subjects: International Monetary Fund. World Bank.
LC Classification: HG3881 .N297 1950
Dewey Class No.: 332.1/5

Sector paper on development finance institutions.
Manila, Philippines: Asian Development Bank, [1978]
Description: 68 p.; 22 cm.

Notes: "April 1978."
Subjects: Asian Development Bank. Development banks--Asia. Development credit corporations--Asia.
LC Classification: HG3252 .A84 1978
Dewey Class No.: 332.1/53 19

Sector paper on forestry and forest industries.
Manila, Philippines: Asian Development Bank, [1978]
Description: 78 p.; 22 cm.
Subjects: Asian Development Bank. Forests and forestry--Economic aspects--Asia. Forests and forestry--Economic aspects--Australasia. Forest products industry--Asia. Forest products industry--Australasia.
Series: A Bank staff working paper
LC Classification: SD219 .S43 1978
Dewey Class No.: 338.1/749 19

Selected decisions of the International Monetary Fund and selected documents.
Washington, D.C., International Monetary Fund.
Description: 13 v. 23 cm. 6th- 1972-
Current Frequency: Biennial, <1976-1985>
Continues: International Monetary Fund. Selected decisions of the executive directors and selected documents
Continued by: International Monetary Fund. Selected decisions and selected documents of the International Monetary Fund
ISSN: 0094-1735
Notes: SERBIB/SERLOC merged record Also published in translation in French as: International Monetary Fund. Recueil de dècisions du Fonds monètaire international et annexe; and in Spanish as: International Monetary Fund. Recopilaciûn seleccionada de decisiones del Fondo Monetario Internacional y otros documentos.
Subjects: International Monetary Fund--Periodicals. International finance--Periodicals.
LC Classification: HG3881 .I6358a
Dewey Class No.: 332.1/52
Entry: International Monetary Fund. Selected decisions of the International Monetary Fund and selected documents. Washington, D.C. 74-644496

Selected documents, Board of governors inaugural meeting, Savannah, Ga., March 8 to 18, 1946.
Washington, D.C., International monetary fund, 1946.
Description: 60 p. 23 cm.
Notes: "By-laws of the International monetary fund": p. 8-16.
Subjects: International Monetary Fund.

LC Classification: HG3881 .I636

Sharma, Yojana
IMF Says More Needed for Highly Indebted Countries
Inter Press Service Sept. 26, 1997, pn.p.

Shaw, J.
A World Bank intervention in the Sri Lankan welfare sector: The National Development Trust Fund
World Development, 1999, Vol 27, Iss 5, pp 825-838
In 1991 the World Bank moved to streamline the Sri Lankan welfare sector by funding a poverty alleviation project which promoted the role of non-government organization (NGOs) and decentralized government agencies and replaced traditional consumption-oriented transfers with an emphasis on household self-reliance through productive activity. The project's design was based on a model which depends for its success on key conditions-guaranteed political independence and a well-developed NGO sector-which did not exist in Sri Lanka in the early 1990s. Additional problems included management deficiencies and failure to provide key supports for production-related poverty reduction.

Shih chieh yin hang hsiang mu kuan li = The World Bank project management / "Shih chieh yin hang hsiang mu kuan li" pien hsieh tsu.
Edition Information: Ti 1 pan.
Pei-ching: Chung-kuo ts`ai cheng ching chi ch`u pan she : Hsin hua shu tien Pei-ching fa hsing so fa hsing, 1983.
Description: 363 p., [1] folded leaf of plates: ill.; 21 cm.
Notes: In Chinese, with table of contents also in English. Includes bibliographical references.
Subjects: World Bank. Economic development projects--Evaluation. Economic development projects--Management.
Series: Shih chieh yin hang p`ei hsün chiao ts`ai
LC Classification: HD47.4 .S55 1983
Dewey Class No.: 338.91/0068 19

Shih chien yin hang: hsün ch`iy fa chan chih lu / chu pien Chin Li-ch`ün; chuan kao jen Tsou Chia-i ... [et al.].
Edition Information: Ti 1 pan.
[Peking]: Pei-ching kung yeh ta hsüeh ch`u pan she, 1994.
Editor: Chin, Li-ch`ün.
Description: 3, 278 p.; 19 cm.
ISBN: 7563903399
Notes: Includes bibliographical references.
Subjects: World Bank.
Series: Shih ch`ang ching chi yü kuo chi shih ch`ang chih shih ts`ung shu

LC Classification: HG3881.5.W57 S476 1994

Shihata, I.F.I.
The creative role of the lawyer - Example: The office of the World Bank's General Counsel
Catholic University Law Review, 1999, Vol 48, Iss 4, pp 1041-1053

Sklar, Leonard
Drowning in Aid: The World Bank's Bangladesh Flood Action Plan
Multinational Monitor April 1993, p8-13

Sobhan, Rehman.
Rethinking the role of the state in development: Asian perspectives / Rehman Sobhan.
Dhaka, Bangladesh: University Press, 1993.
Description: 323 p.; 22 cm.
ISBN: 9840512099 :
Notes: Includes bibliographical references (p. 310-311) and index.
Subjects: World Bank--Asia. State, The. Structural adjustment (Economic policy)--Asia. Developing countries--Economic policy. Developing countries--Social policy.
LC Classification: HC59.7 .S564 1993
Dewey Class No.: 338.95 20

Social action programs and social funds: a review of design and implementation in Sub-Saharan Africa / Alexandre Marc ... [et al.].
Washington, D.C.: World Bank, c1995.
Editor: Marc, Alexandre
Description: xv, 155 p.; 28 cm.
ISBN: 0821331671
Notes: Includes bibliographical references (p. 149-155).
Subjects: World Bank--Africa, Sub-Saharan. Economic assistance, Domestic--Africa, Sub-Saharan. Poor--Africa, Sub-Saharan. Social action--Africa, Sub-Saharan. Community development--Africa, Sub-Saharan.
Series: World Bank Discussion papers; 274 World Bank Discussion papers. Africa Technical Department series
LC Classification: HC800.Z9 P637 1995
Dewey Class No.: 338.967 20

Social funds and reaching the poor: experiences and future directions: proceedings from an international workshop organized by the World Bank ... [et al.] / edited by Anthony G. Bigio.
Washington, D.C.: World Bank, c1998.
Editor: Bigio, Anthony G.

Description: vii, 247 p.; 28 cm.
ISBN: 0821342096
Notes: Papers presented at the International Workshop on Social Funds, May 27-30, 1997, Washington, D.C.
Subjects: World Bank. Economic development projects--Citizen participation Congresses. Community development--Congresses. Social funds.
Series: EDI learning resources series
LC Classification: HD75.8 .S66 1998
Dewey Class No.: 338.9/22 21

Social issues in IMF-supported programs / Sanjeev Gupta ... [et al.].
Washington, DC: International Monetary Fund, 2000.
Editor: Gupta, Sanjeev.
Description: vi, 33 p.: col. ill.; 28 cm.
ISBN: 1557758735
Notes: Includes bibliographical references.
Subjects: International Monetary Fund. Social policy. Expenditures, Public.
Series: Occasional paper (International Monetary Fund); no. 191.
LC Classification: HG3881.5.I58 S664 2000
Dewey Class No.: 332.1/52 21

Son, Johanna
Leaders Vow to Cure Crisis, Fix Financial System.
Inter Press Service Nov. 18, 1998, pn.p.

Special report of the National Advisory Council on increases in the resources of the International Monetary Fund and of the International Bank for Reconstruction and Development, Message from the President of the United States relative to a special report of the National Advisory Council ... Washington, U.S. Govt. Print. Off., 1959.
Description: ix, 40 p. 24 cm.
Subjects: International Bank for Reconstruction and Development International Monetary Fund.
Series: United States. Congress. House. (86th, 1st session : 1959). Document; no. 77.
LC Classification: HG3881 .U632

Special report on increases in the resources of the International Monetary Fund and the International Bank for Reconstruction and Development; letter transmitting a draft of proposed legislation to authorize an increase in the resources of the International Monetary Fund and the International Bank for Reconstruction and Development, and for other purposes; together with a report of the National Advisory Council on International Monetary and Financial Policies. Washington, U.S. Govt. Print. Off., 1970.

Description: x, 47 p. 24 cm.
Subjects: International Monetary Fund. World Bank.
Series: House document (United States. Congress. House); 1st Congress, 2nd session, no. 281.
LC Classification: LAW
Dewey Class No.: 346.73/082152 347.30682152 19

Special report on the proposed U.S. contribution to the Consolidated Special Funds of the Asian Development Bank; communication from the Secretary of the Treasury.
Washington, U.S. Govt. Print. Off., 1970.
Description: 53 p. 24 cm.
Subjects: Asian Development Bank. Economic assistance, American.
Series: House document (United States. Congress. House);
91st Congress, 2nd session, no. 261.
LC Classification: HG4517 .N34 1970
Dewey Class No.: 332.1/53

Special report to the President and to the Congress on special borrowing arrangements of the International Monetary Fund.
[Washington, D.C.?]: The Council, [1962]
Editor: International Monetary Fund.
Description: 16, 7, [16] p.; 29 cm.
LC Classification: MLCM 94/2906 (H)

Special report to the President and to the Congress on the proposed establishment of a facility based on special drawing rights in the International Monetary Fund and modifications in the rules and practices of the Fund.
[Washington] 1968.
Description: 41, vi, 80 p. illus. 27 cm.
Subjects: International Monetary Fund.
LC Classification: LAW
Dewey Class No.: 346.73/082152 347.30682152 19

Staff papers - International Monetary Fund.
Washington, International Monetary Fund.
Description: 45 v. tables, diagrs. 23 cm. v. 1-45; Feb. 1950-Dec. 1998.
Current Frequency: Four no. a year, 1978-1998 Former Frequency: Three no. a year, 1950-1977 Continued by: IMF staff papers 1020-7635
ISSN: 0020-8027
Notes: Text in English with summaries in English, French, and Spanish. SERBIB/SERLOC merged record Indexed entirely by: Business periodicals index 0007-6961 Social sciences index 0094-4920 Indx'd selectively by: America, history and life 0002-7065 1963-1969 Historical abstracts. Part A. Modern history abstracts 0363-2717 1963-1969 Historical abstracts. Part B.

Twentieth century bstracts 0363-2725 1963-1969 Index of economic articles in journals and collective volumes 0536-647X
Public Affairs Information Service bulletin 0033-3409 Recently published articles 0145-5311
Indexes: Vols. 1-10, 1950-63. 1 v.; v. 1-16, 1950-69. 1 v.; v. 1-27, 1950-80. 1 v.
Subjects: Foreign exchange--Periodicals. Commerce--Periodicals. Currency question--Periodicals.
LC Classification: HG3810 .I5
Dewey Class No.: 332.082
Entry: International monetary fund. Staff papers. Washington, D.C.)

Staines, Verdon S.
A health sector strategy for the Europe and Central Asia region / Verdon S. Staines.
Washington, D.C.: World Bank, c1999.
Description: 85 p.; 28 cm.
ISBN: 0821344811
Notes: At head of Human Development Network. Includes bibliographical references.
Subjects: World Bank--Former Soviet republics. World Bank--Europe, Eastern. Medical policy--Former Soviet republics. Medical policy--Europe, Eastern. Health planning--Former Soviet republics. Health planning--Europe, Eastern.
Series: Health, nutrition, and population series
LC Classification: RA395.F6 S73 1999

Stauffer, Robert B.
The Manila-Washington connection: continuities in the transnational political economy of Philippine development / Robert B. Stauffer.
[Sydney]: Transnational Corporations Research Project, c1983.
Description: 40 p.; 30 cm.
ISBN: 0908470312 (pbk.)
Notes: "September 1983." Bibliography: p. 29-40.
Subjects: International Monetary Fund--Philippines. World Bank--Philippines. Investments, American--Philippines. Philippines--Investment policy. Philippines--Foreign economic relations--United States. United States--Foreign economic relations--Philippines.
Series: Research monograph (Transnational Corporations Research Project (University of Sydney)); no. 17.
LC Classification: HC455 .S78 1983
Dewey Class No.: 338.8/8973/0599 19

Stewart, Frances, 1940-
Adjustment and poverty: options and choices / Frances Stewart.
London; New York: Routledge, 1995.

Description: x, 243 p.: ill.; 24 cm.
ISBN: 0415091349 0415124360 (pbk.)
Notes: Includes bibliographical references (p. [217]-231) and index.
Subjects: World Bank--Developing countries. International Monetary Fund--Developing countries. Structural adjustment (Economic policy)—Developing countries. Poverty--Developing countries.
Series: Priorities for development economics
LC Classification: HC59.7 .S824 1995
Dewey Class No.: 338.9/0091722 20

Strategy for forest sector development in Asia / Land Resources Unit, Asia Technical Department.
Washington, D.C.: World Bank, 1992.
Description: 41 p.; 28 cm.
ISBN: 0821322052
Notes: Includes bibliographical references (p. 40-41).
Subjects: World Bank. Forests and forestry--Asia. Forests and forestry--Economic aspects--Asia. Forest policy--Asia.
Series: World Bank technical paper; no. 182. World Bank technical paper. Asia Technical Department series. Technical Department series
LC Classification: SD219 .S77 1992
Dewey Class No.: 333.75/095 20

Strengthening efforts to reduce poverty / prepared by the staffs of the World Bank and the International Monetary Fund for the Development Committee.
Washington, D.C., U.S.A.: Joint Ministerial Committee of the Boards of Governors of the World Bank and the International Monetary Fund on the Transfer of Real Resources to Developing Countries (Development Committee): Available from World Bank Publications Sales Unit, [1989]
Description: 39 p.; 22 cm.
ISBN: 0821312030
Notes: Includes bibliographical references.
Subjects: World Bank. International Monetary Fund. Poor--Developing countries.
Series: Development Committee (Series); no. 19.
LC Classification: HG3881.5.W57 S77 1989
Dewey Class No.: 362.5/526 20

Structural adjustment and macroeconomic policy issues : papers presented at a seminar held in Lahore, Pakistan, October 26-28, 1991 / moderator, V.A. Jafarey.
Washington: International Monetary Fund; [Lahore] : Pakistan Administrative Staff College, 1992.
Description: x, 137 p.: ill.; 23 cm.
ISBN: 1557753024 (paper)

Notes: Includes bibliographical references.
Subjects: Economic policy--Congresses. Structural adjustment (Economic policy)--Congresses.
LC Classification: HD73 .S77 1992
Dewey Class No.: 338.9 20

Structural Adjustment in Haiti.
Monthly Review Jan. 1997, p25-39

Structural adjustment in the world economy and East-West-South economic cooperation / edited by Karl Wohlmuth.
Bremen: Institute for World Economics and International Management, University of Bremen, 1989.
Editor: Wohlmuth, Karl.
Description: 546 p.; 25 cm.
ISBN: 3887222016
Notes: "Based on an international seminar which took place in Dubrovnik at the Inter-University Centre of Postgraduate Studies from February 17-March 2, 1985"--P. 5. Includes bibliographical references.
Subjects: International Monetary Fund--Developing countries Congresses. World Bank--Developing countries--Congresses. Structural adjustment (Economic policy)--Developing countries--Congresses. International economic relations--Congresses. Debts, External--Developing countries--Congresses. Developing countries--Foreign economic relations Congresses.
LC Classification: HC59.7 .S87363 1989

Structural change in Japan: macroeconomic impact and policy challenges / [edited by] Bijan B. Aghevli, Tamim Bayoumi, Guy Meredith.
Washington, D.C.: International Monetary Fund, c1998.
Editors: Aghevli, Bijan B. Bayoumi, Tamim A. Meredith, Guy.
Description: v, 244 p.: ill.; 23 cm.
ISBN: 1557756961 (pbk.)
Partial Contents: Introduction / Stanley Fischer -- The yen: summary of staff views / Bijan B. Aghevli -- The yen: past movements and future prospects / Guy Meredith -- External sector: summary of staff views / Bijan B. Aghevli -- Japanese foreign direct investment and regional trade / Tamim Bayoumi and Gabrielle Lipworth -- Monetary policy: summary of staff views / Guy Meredith -- Structural change and information content of financial variables for monetary policy / Christopher Towe -- Background paper: a reexamination of indicators of monetary and financial conditions / Gabrielle Lipworth and Guy Meredith -- Fiscal policy: summary of staff views / Guy Meredith -- The Japanese fiscal system and fiscal transparency / Tamim Bayoumi -- Background paper: Japan's medium- and long-term fiscal challenges / Kenji Okamura -- Concluding remarks.

Notes: "This volume is based on a seminar on structural change in Japan held in early 1997 and chaired by the IMF's First Deputy Managing Director, Stanley Fischer"--P. 4 of cover. Includes bibliographical references.
Subjects: Structural adjustment (Economic policy)--Japan Congresses. Foreign exchange rates--Japan--Congresses. Balance of payments--Japan--Congresses. Monetary policy--Japan--Congresses. Fiscal policy--Japan--Congresses. Japan--Economic policy--1989---Congresses.
LC Classification: HC462.95 .S77 1998
Dewey Class No.: 338.952 21

Strukturanpassungspolitik der Weltbank: will die Weltbank mehr als Wirtschaftswachstum in Entwicklungsländern? / Michael v. Hauff, Heinecke Werner (Hrsg.).
Ludwigsburg: Verlag Wissenschaft & Praxis, c1992.
Editor: Hauff, Michael von.
Description: 154 p.: ill.; 21 cm.
ISBN: 3928238183 :
Notes: Includes bibliographical references.
Subjects: World Bank--Developing countries. Structural adjustment (Economic policy)—Developing countries. Economic stabilization--Developing countries. Developing countries--Economic policy.
Series: AGEG-Forum (Series); 2.
LC Classification: HC59.7 .S8745 1992

Study of Export-Import Bank and World Bank. Hearings before the Committee on Banking and Currency, United States Senate, Eighty-third Congress, second session, on S. Res. 25, a resolution to authorize and direct a thorough study of the operations of the Export-Import Bank and the International Bank for Reconstruction and Development and their relationship to expansion of international trade ...
Washington, U.S. Govt. Print. Off., 1954.
Description: 2 pts. (vi, 1301 p.) illus., maps. 24 cm.
Notes: Homer E. Capehart, chairman. Hearings held Jan. 25-June 14, 1954. Pt. 2, hearings on S. Res. 25 and S. Res. 183.
Subjects: Export-Import Bank of Washington. World Bank.
LC Classification: HG2613.W34 E834
Govt. Doc. No.: Y4.B22/3:Ex7/10/pt.-

Study of Latin American countries; interim report. A study of the operations in Latin American countries of the Export-Import Bank and the International Bank and their relationship to the expansion of international trade, pursuant to S. Res. 25, 83d Congress, 1st session.
Washington, U.S. Govt. Print. Off., 1954.
Description: vi, 648 p. illus., maps. 23 cm.

Notes: At head of Confidential committee print.
Subjects: Export-Import Bank of Washington. World Bank. Investments, American--Latin America. Latin America--Commerce--United States. United States--Commerce--Latin America. Latin America--Economic conditions--1918-
Series: United States. 83d Cong., 2d sess., 1954. Senate. Report; no. 1082.
LC Classification: HF3376 .U485
Dewey Class No.: 330.98

Summary of poverty reduction and the World Bank: progress and challenges in the 1990s = Résumé de la réduction de la pauvreté et la Banque mondiale: les années 90 : progrès réalisés et défis de l'avenir.
Washington, D.C.: World Bank, c1996
Description: 23, [7] p.; 27 cm.
ISBN: 0821332945
Notes: English, French, Spanish and Arabic.
Subjects: World Bank--Developing countries. Economic assistance--Developing countries. Economic development projects--Developing countries Finance. Poverty--Developing countries.
LC Classification: HC60 .S887 1996

Summary of Poverty reduction and the World Bank: progress in fiscal 1993.
Washington, D.C.: World Bank, c1994.
Description: 14 p.; 28 cm.
ISBN: 0821328522
Subjects: World Bank. Economic assistance--Developing countries. Poverty--Developing countries.

Summary of proceedings: ... annual meeting of the Board of Governors / Asian Development Bank.
[S.l.: The Board?], 1968-
Description: v.; 23-29 cm. First issue preceeded by a summary of the proceedings of the inaugual meeting, Tokyo, 24-26 Nov. 1966. 1st (1968)-
Current Frequency: Annual
Notes: Title from cover.
Subjects: Asian Development Bank--Periodicals. Banks and banking--Asia--Congresses.
LC Classification: WMLC L 82/84 HG3881.5.A75 B63

Summary proceedings: annual meeting of the Board of Governors / International Bank for Reconstruction and Development.
Washington, D.C.: The Bank, 1950-1987.
Description: 38 v.; 26 cm. Vols. for 1958-1987 lack numerical designation. 5th (Sept. 6-14, 1950)-1987.
Current Frequency: Annual

Continues: World Bank. Board of Governors. Proceedings
Absorbed: International Finance Corporation. Board of Governors.
Summary proceedings, annual meeting of the Board of Governors Continued by: World Bank Group. Summary proceedings
Notes: varies slightly.
Vols. for 1961-1964 include the summary proceedings of the International Development Association; 1965-1981 include also the summary proceedings of the International Finance Corporation. SERBIB/SERLOC merged record.
Subjects: World Bank--Congresses. International Finance Corporation--Congresses. International Development Association--Congresses. Banks and banking, International--Periodicals. Banks and banking, International--Congresses.
LC Classification: HG3881 .I553
Dewey Class No.: 332.1/532/05 20
Entry: World Bank. Summary proceedings [of the] annual meeting of the board of governors. Washington, D.C. 1946- . 56-22310

Summers, Lawrence H.
The Challenges of Development
Finance & Development (Intl. Monetary Fund & the World Bank)
March 1992, p. 6-9

Supplement on international liquidity.
Washington, D.C., U.S.A.: International Monetary Fund, c1988.
Description: xiii, 174 p.; 28 cm.
Series: International financial statistics. Supplement series, 0252-3027; no. 14
LC Classification: IN PROCESS

Surveys of African economies.
Washington, 1968-
Description: v. illus., maps (part col.) 24 cm.
Incomplete Contents: v. l. Cameroon, Central African Republic, Chad, Congo (Brazzaville), and Gabon.--v. 2. Kenya, Tanzania, Uganda, and Somalia.--v. 3. Dahomey, Ivory Coast, Mauritania, Niger, Senegal, Togo, and Upper Volta.--v. 4. Democratic Republic of Congo, Malagasy Republic, Malawi, Mauritius, and Zambia.--v. 5. Botswana, esotho, Swaziland, Burundi, Equatorial Guinea, and Rwanda.--v. 6. The Gambia, Ghana, Liberia, Nigeria, and Sierra Leone.--v. 7. Algeria, Mali, Morocco, and Tunisia.
Notes: Includes bibliographical references.
Subjects: Africa--Economic conditions--1960-
LC Classification: HC502 .I57
Dewey Class No.: 330.96

Surveys of exchange controls and restrictions in Argentina, Burma, Federal Republic of Germany, Hashemite Kingdom of the Jordan, Indonesia, Japan, New Zealand, Portugal, Spain, Sweden, Switzerland. Prepared by the Exchange Restrictions Dept. Washington, 1951.
Description: v, 24 p. 24 cm.
Subjects: Foreign exchange--Law and legislation.
LC Classification: LAW <General IMF 1951>

Taking action to reduce poverty in Sub-Saharan Africa.
Washington, D.C.: World Bank, c1997.
Description: xvi, 151 p.: ill., map; 23 cm.
ISBN: 0821336983
Notes: Includes bibliographical references (p. 143-151).
Subjects: World Bank--Africa, Sub-Saharan. Poverty--Africa, Sub-Saharan. Economic assistance--Africa, Sub-Saharan.
Series: Development in practice (Washington, D.C.)
LC Classification: HC800.Z9 P628 1997
Dewey Class No.: 362.5/8/0967 20

Tarullo, Daniel K.
Rethinking the G7.
International Economy Jan./Feb. 1999, p37-39

Tatlow, Didi Kirsten
Strong Debut for European Currency.
Sun Herald (Biloxi, MS) Jan. 4, 1999, pn.p.

Tavlas, George S.
International Currencies: The Rise of the Deutsche
Finance & Development (Intl. Monetary Fund & the World Bank) Sept. 1990,

Technical assistance activities / Asian Development Bank. Manila, Philippines: Information Office, Asian Development Bank,
Editor: Asian Development Bank. Information Office.
Description: v.: ill.; 22 cm.
Notes: Description based on: 1980. SERBIB/SERLOC merged record
Subjects: Asian Development Bank. Economic assistance--Asia.
LC Classification: HG3254.A74 T43
Dewey Class No.: 332.1/53 19
Entry: Technical assistance activities. Manila, Phillippines.
86-647245

Technical assistance and training services of the International Monetary Fund.
Washington, D.C.: The Fund, 1985.

Description: iii, 31 p.: ill.; 23 cm.
Subjects: International Monetary Fund. Technical assistance--Developing countries. Finance--Study and teaching--Developing countries.
Series: Pamphlet series (International Monetary Fund); no. 3.
LC Classification: HG3881.5.I58 I568 1985
Dewey Class No.: 332.1/52 19

Technical assistance services of the International Monetary Fund.
Washington, D.C.: The Fund, 1979.
Description: v, 25 p.: ill.; 23 cm.
Subjects: International Monetary Fund. Technical assistance.
Series: Pamphlet series (International Monetary Fund); no. 0.
LC Classification: HG3881 .I5766 1979
Dewey Class No.: 332.1/52

Technology and science in World Bank operations.
Washington, D.C.: World Bank, [c1982]
Editor: Shapiro, Paul S.,
Description: 208 p. in various pagings; 28 cm.
ISBN: 082130058X (pbk.) :
Notes: "Prepared by Paul S. Shapiro"--7th prelim. p.
Subjects: World Bank. Technical assistance--Developing countries. Technology--Developing countries.
LC Classification: HG3881 .T38 1982
Dewey Class No.: 332.1/532 19

Technology, finance, and development: an analysis of the World Bank as a technological institution / edited by Charles Weiss, Nicolas Jéquier.
Lexington, Mass.: LexingtonBooks, 1984.
Editor: Weiss, Charles.
Description: vi, 342 p., [4] p. of plates: ill. (some col.); 24 cm.
ISBN: 0669077623
Notes: Includes bibliographies and index.
Subjects: World Bank. Technical assistance. Technology transfer--Developing countries.
LC Classification: HG3881.5.W57 T42 1984
Dewey Class No.: 338.91 19

Telecommunications: World Bank experience and strategy /
Bjorn Wellenius and others.
Washington, D.C.: The Bank, c1993.
Editor: Wellenius, Bjorn.
Description: v, 29 p.; 28 cm.
ISBN: 0821323911

Notes: Includes bibliographical references (p. 21-25).
Subjects: World Bank--Developing countries. Telecommunication policy--Developing countries.
Series: World Bank discussion papers, 0259-210X; 192
LC Classification: HE8635 .T45 1993
Dewey Class No.: 384/.68 20

The ... guide to offshore financial centres.
London: Euromoney Publications, c1992-
Description: v.: ill.; 30 cm. 1992-
Current Frequency: Annual
Notes: SERBIB/SERLOC merged record
Subjects: Banks and banking, International--Periodicals. Banks and banking, Foreign--Periodicals. International finance--Periodicals.
Series: Euromoney research guides
LC Classification: HG3881 .G777
Entry: Guide to; offshore financial centres. 97-651321

The African response: adjustment or transformation / introduction by Bade Onimode; [edited by Mary Turok]
London, U.K.: Institute for African Alternatives, 1992.
Editor: Onimode, Bade.
Description: viii, 164 p.; 21 cm.
ISBN: 1870425324
Notes: "Proceedings of the IFAA workshop to review: The World Bank report; Sub-Saharan Africa: from Crisis to Sustainable Growth-A Long-term Perspective Study; The Uruguay Round of GATT; The Fraser Report on Africa's Commodity Problems, held January 1991 at the United Nations Economic Commission for Africa (ECA), Addis Ababa, Ethiopia." Includes bibliographical references.
Subjects: World Bank--Africa--Congresses. Structural adjustment (Economic policy)—Africa Congresses. Sustainable development--Africa.--Congresses. Commercial products--Africa--Congresses. Africa--Foreign economic relations--Congresses.
LC Classification: HC800 .A5687 1992

The Asian Development Bank and trade liberalization.
New York, 1965.
Description: 137 p. 28 cm.
Notes: United Nations. [Document] E/CN.11/707. "United Nations publication. Sales no. 65.II.F.15." Includes the reports of the Working Group of Experts on the Asian Development Bank and the Working Group of Experts on Trade Liberalization. Bibliographical footnotes.
Subjects: Asian Development Bank. Asia--Commerce.
Series: United Nations. Economic Commission for Asia and the Far East.

Regional economic co-operation series, no. 2. United Nations. Document; E/CN.11/707.
LC Classification: JX1977 .A2 E/CN.11/171
Dewey Class No.: 332.153095

The Bankers' almanac world ranking.
East Grinstead, West Sussex: Thomas Skinner Directories, c1985-
Description: v.; 24 cm. 1st ed.-
Current Frequency: Annual
Notes: SERBIB/SERLOC merged record Extracted from the pages of: Bankers almanac and yearbook. Bankers almanac and yearbook (OCoLC)7114550
Subjects: Banks and banking--Rankings--Periodicals. Banks and banking--Statistics--Periodicals. Banks and banking, International--Directories. Banks and banking, International--Statistics--Periodicals.
LC Classification: HG1503 .B18
Dewey Class No.: 332.1/05 19
Entry: Bankers' almanac world ranking. 87-644659

The Bankers' almanac.
West Sussex, England: Reed Information Services,
Description: v.; 26 cm. Vols. for <July 1993-Jan. 1994> issued in parts.
Began in Jan. 1993.
Current Frequency: Semiannual
Continues: Bankers' almanac and year book (DLC)sn 90040407
Notes: Description based on: 148th (July 1993). "A directory of some 4,000 major international banks and their 165,000 branches worldwide."
SERBIB/SERLOC merged record
Subjects: Banks and banking--Directories. Banks and banking, International--Directories.
LC Classification: HG2984 .B3
Entry: Bankers' almanac (West Sussex, England) 94-647899

The bank's operational program, 1986-1988 / Asian Development Bank.
[Manila]: Country Dept., [1986]
Description: 196 p.; 28 cm. Notes: Cover title. "20 February 1986."
Subjects: Asian Development Bank.
LC Classification: HG3881.5.A75 A84 1986

The Bretton Woods agreement -- and why it is necessary.
New York, N.Y., Citizens Conference on international Union [1944]
Editor: Alfred, Helen L., ed.
Description: 50 p., 1 l. 22 cm.
Notes: "Digest of the ... agreement, and report of speeches delivered at a public meeting, held under the auspices of the Citizens Conference on International

Economic Union at Washington. Edited by Helen Alfred."-- p. 3.
Subjects: International Monetary Fund. International Bank for Reconstruction and Development. United Nations Monetary and Financial Conference, Bretton Woods, N.H., 1944. Commercial policy.
LC Classification: HG205 1944 .U555
Dewey Class No.: 332.15

The Bretton Woods-GATT system: retrospect and prospect after fifty years / Orin Kirshner, editor ; contributors, Edward M. Bernstein ... [et al.].
Armonk, NY: M. E. Sharpe, c1996.
Editor: Kirshner, Orin
Description: xiii, 321 p.; 24 cm.
ISBN: 1563246295 (alk. paper) 1563246309 (pbk.: alk. paper)
Notes: Consists of over twenty papers produced for the Bretton Woods revisited conference, which was convened by the Institute for Agriculture and Trade Policy held in Bretton Woods, N.H., October 15-17, 1994. Includes bibliographical references and index.
Subjects: General Agreement on Tariffs and Trade (Organization) International Monetary Fund. World Bank. United Nations Monetary and Financial Conference (1944: Bretton Woods, N.H.) International finance. Free trade.
LC Classification: HG205 .B74 1996
Dewey Class No.: 332/.042 20

The complementary financing scheme of the Asian Development Bank: with model of complementary loan agreements and participation agreements.
[Manila, Philippines]: The Bank, 1984.
Description: 130 p.: ill.; 28 cm.
Subjects: Asian Development Bank. Development banks--Law and legislation—Developing countries. Bank loans--Developing countries.
LC Classification: HG3881.5.A75 A84 1984
Dewey Class No.: 332.1/53/095 20

The dividends of learning: World Bank support for education.
Washington D.C.: The Bank, c1990.
Description: 39 p.: ill.; 23 cm.
ISBN: 0821314602
Notes: "This booklet was prepared by the Population and Human Resources Department, Education and Employment Division, of the World Bank"--Verso t.p.
Subjects: World Bank--Developing countries. Education--Developing countries--Finance. Education--Developing countries--Finance--Statistics.
LC Classification: LB2826.6.D44 I58 1990
Dewey Class No.: 379.1/2/091724 20

The economics of involuntary resettlement: questions and challenges / edited by Michael M. Cernea.
Washington, D.C.: World Bank, c1999.
Editor: Cernea, Michael M.
Description: xii, 259 p.: ill.; 23 cm.
ISBN: 082133798X
Notes: Includes bibliographical references.
Subjects: World Bank--Developing countries. Economic development projects--Developing countries. Forced migration--Economic aspects--Developing countries. Developing countries--Economic policy.
Series: Directions in development (Washington, D.C.)
LC Classification: HC59.72.E44 E285 1999
Dewey Class No.: 333.3/1/091724 21

The economy of the former U.S.S.R. in 1991 / prepared under the direction of John Odling-Smee, by an IMF staff team comprising Thomas Wolf ... [et al.].
Washington, D.C.: International Monetary Fund, c1992.
Description: 103 p.; 28 cm.
ISBN: 1557752591 :
Notes: "April 1992." Includes bibliographical references.
Subjects: Soviet Union--Economic conditions--1985-1991.
Series: Economic review (Washington, D.C.)
LC Classification: HC336.26 .E278 1992

The economy of the West Bank and Gaza Strip: recent experience, prospects, and challenges to private sector development / Steven Barnett ... [et al.].
Washington, DC: International Monetary Fund, 1998.
Editor: Barnett, Steven.
Description: v, 58 p.: ill.; 28 cm.
ISBN: 1557757259 (pbk.)
Notes: Includes bibliographical references.
Subjects: West Bank--Economic conditions. Gaza Strip--Economic conditions. West Bank--Economic policy. Gaza Strip--Economic policy.
LC Classification: HC415.254 .E26 1998
Dewey Class No.: 338.95694 21

The European monetary system: developments and perspectives / by Horst Ungerer ... [et al.].
Washington, D.C.: International Monetary Fund, 1990.
Editor: Ungerer, Horst.
Description: vi, 99 p.: ill.; 28 cm.
ISBN: 1557751722
Notes: Includes bibliographical references (p. 96-99).
Subjects: Money--European Economic Community countries. Monetary policy-

European Economic Community countries.
Series: Occasional paper (International Monetary Fund); no. 73.
LC Classification: HG930.5 .E86855 1990
Dewey Class No.: 332.4/94 20

The European monetary system: recent developments / by Horst Ungerer ... [et al.].
Washington, D.C.: International Monetary Fund, c1986.
Editor: Ungerer, Horst.
Description: vii, 75 p.: col. ill.; 28 cm.
ISBN: 0939934795 (pbk.) :
Notes: "December 1986." Bibliography: p. 74-75.
Subjects: Money--European Economic Community countries.
Series: Occasional paper (International Monetary Fund); no. 48.
LC Classification: HG930.5 .E86863 1986
Dewey Class No.: 332.4/5/094 19

The evolving role of the World Bank: helping meet the challenge of development / editor, K. Sarwar Lateef.
Washington, DC: World Bank, c1995.
Editor: Lateef, K. Sarwar.
Description: vii, 230 p.: ill.; 28 cm.
ISBN: 0821332341
Contents: The first half century: an overview / K. Sarwar Lateef -- From reconstruction to development in Europe and Japan / Caroline Doggart -- The food crisis in South Asia: the case of India / Uma Lele and Balu Bumb -- The Latin American debt crisis / Sebastian Edwards – The transition in Central and Eastern Europe and the former Soviet Union / Kemal Dervis, Marcelo Selowsky, and Christine Wallich -- The East Asian economic miracle / Vinod Thomas and Peter Stephens -- The challenge of Africa / Ishrat Husain -- Mobilizing private savings for development: IBRD and the capital markets / Kenneth G. Lay.
Notes: Includes bibliographical references.
Subjects: World Bank. Economic assistance. Economic development. Economic history--1945-
LC Classification: HG3881.5.W57 E964 1995
Dewey Class No.: 332.1/532 20

The Forest sector.
Washington, D.C.: World Bank, c1991.
Description: 98 p.: ill.; 23 cm.
ISBN: 0821319175
Notes: Includes bibliographical references (p. 96-98).
Subjects: World Bank. Forests and forestry--Developing countries. Forest policy--Developing countries. Forests and forestry--Economic aspects—Developing countries. Deforestation--Control--Developing countries. Forest products

industry--Developing countries.
Series: A World Bank policy paper, 1014-8124
LC Classification: SD247.5 .F67 1991
Dewey Class No.: 333.75/09172/4 20

The Fund and bank review; finance and development. Washington.
Description: v. illus. 25 cm.
Subjects: International finance. Underdeveloped areas--Finance. Economic assistance.
LC Classification: HG3881 .F85

The Fund and China in the international monetary system: papers presented at a colloquium held in Beijing, China, October 20-28, 1982 / edited by A.W. Hooke. [Washington, D.C.]: International Monetary Fund, 1983.
Editor: Hooke, A. W.
Description: x, 187 p.; 23 cm.
ISBN: 093993423X (pbk.) 0939934221 (hard)
Notes: "Jointly sponsored by the People's Bank of China and the International Monetary Fund"--P. v. Includes bibliographies.
Subjects: International Monetary Fund--Congresses. International finance--Congresses. Economic history--1971-1990--Congresses. China--Economic conditions--1976- --Congresses.
LC Classification: HG3881.5.I58 F86 1983
Dewey Class No.: 332.4/5/0951 19

The future role of the World Bank: addresses / by Robert S. McNamara ... [et al.] presented at a conference at the Brookings Institution on January 7, 1982; edited by Edward R. Fried and Henry D. Owen.
Washington, D.C.: Brookings Institution, c1982.
Editor: McNamara, Robert S.,
Description: ix, 91 p.: ill.; 28 cm.
ISBN: 0815729294 (pbk.)
Subjects: World Bank--Congresses.
Series: Brookings dialogues on public policy
LC Classification: HG3881 .F88 1982
Dewey Class No.: 332.1/532 19

The global monetary system after the fall of the Soviet Empire: in memoriam Robert Triffin 1911-1993 / edited by M. Szabó-Pels´oczi; foreword by Bernard Snoy.
Aldershot, Hants, England; Brookfield, Vt., USA: Avebury, c1995.
Editor: Szabó-Pels´oczi, Miklós,
Description: xiii, 268 p.: ill.; 22 cm.
ISBN: 1859720161 :
Notes: Includes bibliographical references.

Subjects: International finance. Banks and banking, International. International economic relations.
LC Classification: HG3881 .G576 1995
Dewey Class No.: 332.1 20

The IMF and Ghana: the confidential record / Eboe Hutchful.
London: Institute for African Alternatives; New Jersey : Zed Books, c1987.
Editor: Hutchful, Eboe.
Description: 298 p.; 23 cm.
ISBN: 086232615X (pbk.)
Notes: Includes bibliographical references.
Subjects: International Monetary Fund. World Bank. Debts, External--Ghana. Ghana--Economic conditions. Ghana--Economic policy. Ghana--Foreign economic relations.
LC Classification: HG3881.5.I58 I38 1987
Dewey Class No.: 332.1/52 20

The IMF and stabilization: developing country experiences / directed and edited by Tony Killick; contributors, Graham Bird ... [et al.].
New York: St. Martin's Press, 1984.
Editor: Killick, Tony. Bird, Graham R.
Description: viii, 216 p.: ill.; 23 cm.
ISBN: 0312402295 :
Contents: 1. Introduction and summary of companion volume / Mary Sutton -- 2. Structuralism / Mary Sutton -- Indonesia, 1966-70 / Mary Sutton -- Jamaica, 1972-80 / Jennifer Sharpley -- Kenya, 1975-81 / Tony Killick.
Notes: Companion vol.: The Quest for economic stabilization. 1984. Includes bibliographies.
Subjects: International Monetary Fund. Economic stabilization--Developing countries. Balance of payments--Developing countries. Developing countries--Economic policy.
LC Classification: HG3881.5.I58 I39 1984
Dewey Class No.: 332.1/52 19

The IMF and Tanzania: the dynamics of liberalisation / edited by Horace Campbell and Howard Stein.
Edition Information: 1st ed.
Harare, Zimbabwe: Southern Africa Political Economy Series (SAPES) Trust, 1991.
Editor: Campbell, Horace.,
Description: vi, 271 p.: map; 21 cm.
ISBN: 0797409572
Notes: Includes bibliographical references (p. 247-264) and index.
Subjects: International Monetary Fund--Tanzania. Free enterprise--Tanzania.

Tanzania--Economic policy.
Series: Debt and structural adjustment series; no.1
LC Classification: HC885 .I44 1991
Dewey Class No.: 338.9678 20

The IMF and the debt crisis: a guide to the Third World's dilemma / Peter K^rner ... [et al.]; translated from the German by Paul Knight.
London; Atlantic Highlands, N.J., USA: Zed Books; Atlantic Highlands, N.J.: Distributed in the U.S.A. and Canada by Humanities Press, 1986.
Editor: K^rner, Peter.
Description: 226 p.: ill.; 23 cm.
ISBN: 0862324874 0862324882 (pbk.)
Notes: Translation of: Im Teufelskreis der Verschuldung. Includes index.
Bibliography: p. 210-219.
Subjects: International Monetary Fund. Debts, External--Developing countries.
LC Classification: HG3881.5.I58 I3713 1986
Dewey Class No.: 336.3/435 19

The IMF and the poor / Fiscal Affairs Department; prepared by Sanjeev Gupta ... [et al.].
Washington, D.C.: International Monetary Fund, 1998.
Editor: Gupta, Sanjeev.
Description: v, 25 p.: ill.; 23 cm.
ISBN: 1557757453
Notes: Includes bibliographical references (p. 22-25).
Subjects: International Monetary Fund. Poverty--Developing countries. Fiscal policy--Developing countries. Structural adjustment (Economic policy)—Developing countries.
Series: Pamphlet series (International Monetary Fund); no. 52.
LC Classification: HG3881.5.I58 I394 1998

The IMF and the south: the social impact of crisis and adjustment / edited by Dharam Ghai.
London; Atlantic Hig[h]lands, N.J., USA: Zed Books Ltd. on behalf of UNRISD, Geneva [and] ISER/UWI, Kingston, 1991.
Editor: Ghai, Dharam P.
Description: xi, 273 p.; 23 cm.
ISBN: 0862329507 (hb.) 0862329515 (pbk.)
Notes: Includes bibliographical references and index.
Subjects: International Monetary fund. Economic assistance. Economic development--Social aspects. Debt relief--Developing countries. Deficit financing--Developing countries.
LC Classification: HG3881.5.I58 I395 1991
Dewey Class No.: 332.1/52 20

The IMF and the World Bank in Africa: conditionality, impact, and alternatives / edited by Kjell J. Havnevik.
Uppsala: Scandinavian Institute of African Studies; Stockholm, Sweden: Distributed by Almquist & Wiksell International, 1987.
Editor: Havnevik, Kjell J.
Description: 177 p.; 23 cm.
ISBN: 9171062645
Notes: Includes bibliographies.
Subjects: International Monetary Fund--Africa--Congresses. World Bank--Africa--Congresses. Conditionality (International relations)
Series: Seminar proceedings from the Scandinavian Institute of African Studies; 18.
LC Classification: HG3881.5.I58 I56 1987
Dewey Class No.: 332.1/5/096 19

The IMF and the World Bank in Africa: conditionality, impact, and alternatives / edited by Kjell J. Havnevik.
Uppsala: Scandinavian Institute of African Studies ;
Stockholm, Sweden: Distributed by Almquist & Wiksell International, 1987.
Editor: Havnevik, Kjell J.
Description: 177 p.; 23 cm.
ISBN: 9171062645
Notes: Includes bibliographies.
Subjects: International Monetary Fund--Africa--Congresses. World Bank--Africa--Congresses. Conditionality (International relations)
Series: Seminar proceedings from the Scandinavian Institute of African Studies; 18.
LC Classification: HG3881.5.I58 I56 1987
Dewey Class No.: 332.1/5/096 19

The IMF loan: facts and issues.
Calcutta: Govt. of West Bengal, [1981]
Description: 107 p.; 23 cm.
Notes: "November, 1981."
Subjects: International Monetary Fund. Loans, Foreign--India.
LC Classification: HG3971 .I4 1981
Dewey Class No.: 338.91/0954 19

The IMF memorandum.
[Calcutta]: Communist Party of India (Marxist), [1981]
Description: 58 p.; 28 cm.
Subjects: International Monetary Fund. Loans, Foreign--India. India--Economic policy--
LC Classification: HJ8086.I4 I47 1981

Dewey Class No.: 332.1/52 19

The IMF, the World Bank, and the African debt / edited by Bade Onimode.
London; Atlantic Highlands, N.J., USA: Zed Books, 1989.
Editor: Onimode, Bade.
Description: 2 v.: ill.; 23 cm.
ISBN: 0862328284 (v. 1) : 0862328292 (pbk.: v. 1) :
0862328306 (v. 2) : 0862328314 (pbk.: v. 2) :
Contents: v. 1. The economic impact -- v. 2. The social and political impact.
Notes: Papers presented at a conference in London in October 1987. Co-published with the Institute for African Alternatives. Includes bibliographies and index.
Subjects: International Monetary Fund--Africa. World Bank--Africa. Debts, External--Africa. Loans, Foreign--Africa.
LC Classification: HJ8826 .I54 1989
Dewey Class No.: 336.3/435/090 20

The IMF's statistical systems in context of revision of the United Nations' A system of national accounts / Statistics Department; edited by Vicente Galbis.
Washington, D.C.: International Monetary Fund, 1991.
Editor: Galbis, Vicente,
Description: xxvii, 599 p.: ill.; 23 cm.
ISBN: 1557751595 :
Notes: "A selection of papers presented at three expert group meetings sponsored by the Fund in 1987-88"--Foreword. Includes bibliographical references.
Subjects: National income--Accounting.
LC Classification: HC79.I5 I44 1991
Dewey Class No.: 339.3/2/015195 20

The impact of environmental assessment: a review of World Bank experience / Environment Department.
Washington, D.C.: World Bank, c1997.
Description: xxiii, 146 p.: ill.; 28 cm.
ISBN: 0821339230
Notes: Includes bibliographical references (p. 99-100).
Subjects: World Bank--Developing countries. Economic development projects--Developing countries. Environmental impact analysis--Developing countries.
Series: World Bank technical paper, 0253-7494; no. 363
LC Classification: HC59.72.E44 I454 1997
Dewey Class No.: 363.7/062/091724 21

The international monetary and financial system : developing-country perspectives / edited by G.K. Helleiner.
Houndmills, Basingstoke, Hampshire: Macmillan Press; New

York: St. Martin's Press, 1996.
Editor: Helleiner, Gerald K.
Description: xviii, 499 p.; 23 cm.
ISBN: 0333642473 (cloth) 0312129742 (cloth)
Notes: "This volume contains the main contributions to a conference, sponsored by the Intergovernmental Group of Twenty-four on International Monetary Affairs (G-24) on April 18-20, 1994, in Cartagena de Indias, Colombia"--Pref. Includes bibliographical references and indexes.
Subjects: World Bank--Congresses. International Monetary Fund--Congresses. International finance--Developing countries--Congresses. Monetary policy -- Developing countries--Congresses. Development banks--Congresses.
LC Classification: HG3881 .I608 1996
Dewey Class No.: 332/.042 20

The International Monetary Fund, 1944-1949 [by] Raymond F. Mikesell.
New York, Carnegie Endowment for International Peace [1949]
Description: 787-874 p. 20 cm.
Notes: Cover title. Bibliographical footnotes.
Subjects: World Bank
Series: International conciliation, no. 455
LC Classification: JX1907 .A8 no. 455

The international monetary system, progress and prospects / The Atlantic Council Working Group on the International Monetary System; Robert Solomon, rapporteur; William McChesney Martin, Jr., and Frank . Southard, Jr., co-chairmen.
Boulder, Colo.: Westview Press, c1977.
Editor: Solomon, Robert.
Description: xvii, 86 p.: graph; 23 cm.
ISBN: 0891582355
Notes: "An Atlantic Council policy paperback." Includes bibliographical references.
Subjects: International Monetary Fund. International finance. Foreign exchange.
Series: Atlantic Council of the United States. Atlantic Council policy series.
LC Classification: HG3881 .A84 1977
Dewey Class No.: 332.4/5

The international monetary system: its institutions and its future / Hans Genberg
Berlin; New York: Springer, c1995
Editor: Genberg, Hans.
Description: 215 p.: ill.; 24 cm.
ISBN: 3540591303 (Berlin: acid-free paper)
Notes: Papers originally presented at a conference sponsored by the International Center for Monetary and Banking Studies and held in Geneva on Sept. 2-4, 1993.

Includes bibliographical references.
Subjects: International Monetary Fund--Congresses. World Bank--Congresses. International finance--Congresses.
LC Classification: HG205 .I5577 1995
Dewey Class No.: 332.4/566 20

The Merrill Lynch euromoney directory.
London: Euromoney Publications PLC in association with Merrill Lynch, c1987-c1992.
Description: 6 v.: ill.; 21 cm. 1987-1992.
Current Frequency: Annual
Continues: Hambro euromoney directory 0306-3933 (DLC) 75644094
Continued by: Cedel euromoney directory (DLC)sn 93017397 (OCoLC)27743742
Notes: SERBIB/SERLOC merged record
Subjects: Foreign-exchange brokers--Directories. Financial institutions, International--Directories. Banks and banking, International--Directories.
LC Classification: HG3851 .H34
Dewey Class No.: 332.4/5/025 19
Entry: Merrill Lynch euromoney directory. 88-646274

The multilateral development banks.
Boulder, Colo.: L. Rienner, 1995-1997.
Description: 5 v.; 24 cm.
ISBN: 1555874673 (alk. paper: v. 1) 1555874932 (pbk.: alk. paper: v. 1) 1555874681 (alk. paper: v. 2) : 1555874940 (pbk.: alk. paper: v. 2) : 155587469X (alk. paper: v. 3) : 1555874959 (pbk.: alk. paper: v. 3) :
Incomplete Contents: v. 1. The African Development Bank / E. Philip English, Harris M. Mule -- v. 2. The Asian Development Bank / Nihal Kappagoda -- v. 3. The Caribbean Development Bank / by Chandra Hardy -- v. 4. Inter-American Development Bank / Diana Tussie -- v. 5. Titans or behemoths? / Roy Culpeper.
Notes: Includes bibliographical references and indexes.
Subjects: Asian Development Bank. Caribbean Development Bank. African Development Bank. Inter-American Development Bank. Development banks.
LC Classification: HG1975 .M848 1995
Dewey Class No.: 332.2 20

The new international monetary system / Robert A. Mundell and Jacques J. Polak, editors.
New York: Columbia University Press, 1977.
Editor: Mundell, Robert A.
Description: x, 244 p.: graphs; 24 cm.
ISBN: 0231043686
Notes: Conference sponsored by the International Monetary Fund and Columbia

University as a memorial to J. Marcus Fleming. Includes bibliographical references.
Subjects: International finance--Congresses.
Foreign exchange rates--Congresses. International liquidity--Congresses.
LC Classification: HG3881 .C663 1976
Dewey Class No.: 332.4/5

The Philippines, aspects of the financial sector: a joint World Bank/IMF study.
Washington, D.C., U.S.A.: East Asia and Pacific Regional Office, World Bank, c1980.
Description: ix, 99 p.; 28 cm.
Notes: "May 1980"--Cover.
Subjects: Finance--Philippines.
Series: A World Bank country study
LC Classification: HG187.P6 P59 1980
Dewey Class No.: 332/.09599 19

The political economy of South Africa's relations with the International Monetary Fund and the World Bank: papers presented at a workshop / organised by the Centre for International and Comparative Politics, University of Stellenbosch and sponsored by the Konrad-Adenauer-Foundation, held at Strand Pavilion, during November 1993; edited by Anthony Leysens.
Stellenbosch, South Africa: University of Stellenbosch: Konrad-Adenauer-Stiftung, c1994.
Editor: Leysens, Anthony.
Description: v, 152 p.; 25 cm.
ISBN: 0797205136
Notes: Includes bibliographical references.
Subjects: International Monetary Fund--South Africa--Congresses. World Bank--South Africa--Congresses. South Africa--Economic policy--Congresses.
LC Classification: HG3881.5.I58 P648 1994

The Political morality of the International Monetary Fund / edited by Robert J. Myers.
New Brunswick, U.S.A.: Transaction Books, c1987.
Editor: Myers, Robert John
Description: 184 p.: ill.; 23 cm.
ISBN: 0887386741 (pbk.) 088738143X (hard)
Notes: "Published for the Carnegie Council on Ethics & International Affairs." Includes bibliographies and index.
Subjects: International Monetary Fund. International finance--Moral and ethical aspects.
Series: Ethics and foreign policy; v. 3
LC Classification: HG3881.5.I58 P65 1987

Dewey Class No.: 332.1/52 19

The Poverty brokers: the IMF and Latin America / [edited by Martin Honeywell].
London: Latin America Bureau, 1983.
Editor: Honeywell, Martin.
Description: ix, 138 p.; 22 cm.
ISBN: 0906156173 (pbk.) : 0906156246 (hard)
Notes: Bibliography: p. 135-136.
Subjects: International Monetary Fund. International Monetary Fund--Latin America. Debts, External--Latin America.
LC Classification: HG3881.5.I58 P68 1983
Dewey Class No.: 332.1/52 19

The poverty of nations: a guide to the debt crisis from Argentina to Zaire / edited by Elmar Altvater ... [et al.]; translated by Terry Bond.
London; Atlantic Highlands, N.J.: Zed Books, 1991.
Editor: Altvater, Elmar.
Description: 282 p.: ill., maps; 23 cm.
ISBN: 0862329485 (Hb) 0862329493 (Pb)
Notes: Translation of: Die Armut der Nationen. Includes bibliographical references (p. [269]-271) and index.
Subjects: International Monetary Fund--Developing countries—Case studies. Debts, External--Developing countries--Case studies.
LC Classification: HJ8899 .A7613 1990
Dewey Class No.: 336.3/435/091724 20

The Problem of international debt / edited by Christopher A. Kojm.
New York: H.W. Wilson Co., 1984.
Editor: Kojm, Christopher A.
Description: 203 p.; 19 cm.
ISBN: 0824206967 (pbk.)
Notes: Bibliography: p. 196-203.
Subjects: International Monetary Fund. Debts, External. Debts, External--Developing countries. Banks and banking, International.
Series: The Reference shelf; v. 56, no. 1
LC Classification: HJ8083 .P76 1984
Dewey Class No.: 336.3/435 19

The proposed general capital increase for the World Bank : hearings before the Subcommittee on International Development Institutions and Finance of the Committee on Banking, Finance, and Urban Affairs, House of Representatives, One-hundredth Congress, second session, May 4, 11, 18, and 24, 1988.
Washington: U.S. G.P.O.: For sale by the Supt. of Docs., Congressional Sales Office, U.S. G.P.O., 1988.

Description: iv, 412 p.; 24 cm.
Notes: Distributed to some despository libraries in microfiche. Shipping list no.: 88-524-P. "Serial no. 100-62." Item 1013-A, 1013-B (microfiche) Includes bibliographies.
Subjects: World Bank. World Bank--Developing countries. Economic assistance, American. Loans, American--Developing countries. Debts, External--Developing countries.
LC Classification: KF27 .B547 1988
Dewey Class No.: 332.1/532 19
Govt. Doc. No.: Y 4.B 22/1:100-62

The Quest for economic stabilization: the IMF and the Third World / directed and edited by Tony Killick ; contributors, Graham Bird ... [et al.].
New York: St. Martin's Press, 1984.
Editor: Killick, Tony.
Description: ix, 340 p.; 23 cm.
ISBN: 0312660278 :
Contents: Introduction and summary of companion volume / Mary Sutton-- Extent, causes, and consequences of disequilibria /Tony Killick and Jennifer Sharpley -- The potential of domestic stabilisation measures / Jennifer Sharpley -- Balance of payments policy / Graham Bird – An introduction to the IMF / Tony Killick -- Relationships, resource uses and the conditionality debate / Graham Bird -- IMF stabilisation programmes; The impact of fund stabilization programmes / Tony Killick -- Towards a real economy approach / Tony Killick ... [et al.]
Notes: Companion vol. to: The IMF and stabilization. 1984. Includes indexes. Bibliography: p. [321]-331.
Subjects: International Monetary Fund. Economic stabilization--Developing countries. Balance of payments--Developing countries. Developing countries--Economic policy.
LC Classification: HG3881.5.I58 Q47 1984
Dewey Class No.: 332.1/52 19

The Rand McNally bankers directory.
Chicago, Ill.: Rand McNally, c1986-
Description: v.; 29 cm. Final 1986 ed. issued in 4 pts.; first 1987 ed.- issued in 3 pts.
Final 1986 ed.- 221st ed.- Ceased with 229th ed., published in 1990.
Current Frequency: Semiannual
Continues: Rand McNally international bankers directory 0360-7445
Continued by: Thomson bank directory 1057-8986
ISSN: 0895-4623
Notes: "The bankers blue book." SERBIB/SERLOC merged record
Subjects: Bankers--United States--Directories. Banks and banking--United

States--Directories. Banks and banking, International--Directories.
LC Classification: HG2441 .R3
Dewey Class No.: 332.1/025/73 19
Entry: Rand McNally bankers directory (Chicago, Ill.: 1986)
88-657016

The reform of public sector management: lessons from experience / Country Economics Department.
Washington, D.C.: World Bank, c1991.
Description: xii, 43 p.: ill.; 28 cm.
ISBN: 0821319345
Notes: Includes bibliographical references (p. 42-43).
Subjects: World Bank--Developing countries. Public administration—Developing countries. Administrative agencies--Developing countries--Management. Government business enterprises--Developing countries. Developing countries--Economic policy.
Series: Policy & research series; 18.
LC Classification: JF60 .R4 1991
Dewey Class No.: 350.007/09172/4 20

The role of exchange rates in the adjustment of international payments: a report / by the executive directors.
Washington: International Monetary Fund, 1970, 1973 printing.
Description: v, 78 p.: ill.; 28 cm.
Contents: Review and analysis.--Implications for policy.
Notes: Includes bibliographical references.
Subjects: Foreign exchange rates. Balance of payments.
LC Classification: HG3851 .I53 1973
Dewey Class No.: 332.4/5

The stakes of Bretton Woods, a statement by the Committee on international policy of the National Planning Association.
[Washington, 1945]
Description: 24 p. 28 x 22 cm.
Subjects: International Monetary Fund.
International Bank for Reconstruction and Development.
LC Classification: HG255 .N3

The struggle for accountability: the World Bank, NGOs, and grassroots movements / edited by Jonathan A. Fox and L. David Brown.
Cambridge, Mass.: MIT Press, c1998.
Editor: Fox, Jonathan A.
Description: xi, 570 p.: ill.; 24 cm.
ISBN: 0262061996 (hc: alk. paper) 0262561174 (pbk.: alk. paper)

Notes: Includes bibliographical references and index.
Subjects: World Bank. Economic development--Environmental aspects—Developing countries. Political participation. Non-governmental organizations. Social movements--Developing countries.
Series: Global environmental accords.
LC Classification: HD75.6 .S77 1998
Dewey Class No.: 332.1/532 21

The UN and the Bretton Woods institutions: new challenges for the twenty-first century / edited by Mahbub ul Haq ... [et al.].
New York: St. Martin's Press, 1995.
Editor: Haq, Mahbub ul,
Description: xi, 268 p.; 22 cm.
ISBN: 031212449X 0312124503 (pbk.)
Notes: Includes bibliographical references and index.
Subjects: World Bank--Congresses. International Monetary Fund--Congresses. United Nations Monetary and Financial Conference (1944: Bretton Woods, N.H.)--Congresses. International finance--Congresses. International economic relations--Congresses. Economic history--1990- --Congresses.
LC Classification: HG205 .U5 1995
Dewey Class No.: 332/.042 20

The World Bank and poverty in Africa: a critical assessment of the Bank's operational strategies for poverty reduction / Elling N. Tjonneland, project leader Henrik Harboe ... [et al.].
Oslo: Royal Ministry of Foreign Affairs, 1998.
Editor: Tjønneland, Elling Njål,
Description: 92 p.; 30 cm.
Notes: "Submitted to the Royal Norwegian Ministry of Foreign Affairs by the Chr. Michelsens Institute."
Subjects: World Bank. Economic assistance--Africa, Sub-Saharan. Poverty--Africa, Sub-Saharan.
Series: Evaluation report (Oslo, Norway); 98.7.
LC Classification: HC800 .W69 1998

The World Bank and the poorest countries: support for development in the 1990s.
Washington, D.C.: World Bank, c1994.
Description: ix, 53 p.: ill.; 28 cm.
ISBN: 0821327704
Notes: Includes bibliographical references.
Subjects: World Bank--Developing countries. Structural adjustment (Economic policy)—Developing countries. Debts, External--Developing countries. Economic assistance--Developing countries.
LC Classification: HC59.7 .I552 1994

Dewey Class No.: 332.1/532/091724 20

The World Bank at quarter century; highlights of the World Bank since Bretton Woods, by Edward S. Mason and Robert E. Asher.
Washington, Brookings Institution [1973]
Editor: Mason, Edward
Brookings Institution.
Description: 11 p. 23 cm.
Subjects: World Bank.
Series: Brookings research report 137
LC Classification: H62 .B714 no. 137 HG3881
Dewey Class No.: 300/.8 s 332.1/53

The World Bank group in Asia.
[Washington] 1967.
Description: 34 p. illus. 22 cm.
Subjects: World Bank--Asia. Loans, Foreign--Asia.
LC Classification: HG3881 .I57223 1967
Dewey Class No.: 332.1/53

The World Bank Group in Brazil.
[Washington] 1967.
Description: 12 p. illus. 22 cm.
Notes: Cover title.
Subjects: World Bank--Brazil. Loans, Foreign--Brazil.
LC Classification: HG3881 .I572235
Dewey Class No.: 332.1/53/0981

The World Bank group, multilateral aid, and the 1970s.
[Edited by] John P. Lewis [and] Ishan Kapur.
Lexington, Mass., Lexington Books [1973]
Editor: Lewis, John Prior, ed.
Description: xvii, 168 p. 23 cm.
ISBN: 0669905550
Notes: Originated as talks at a seminar held at the Woodrow Wilson School of Public and International Affairs, Princeton University, in 1971. Bibliography: p. 151-158.
Subjects: World Bank.
LC Classification: HG3881 .W593
Dewey Class No.: 332.1/53

The World Bank in Africa: hearing before the Select Committee on Hunger, House of Representatives, One hundredth Congress, first session, hearing held in Washington, DC, July 23, 1987.

Washington: U.S. G.P.O.: For sale by the Supt. of Docs., Congressional Sales Office, U.S. G.P.O., 1987.
Description: iii, 84 p.; 24 cm. Notes: Distributed to some depository libraries in microfiche. Shipping list no.: 87-690-P. "Serial no. 100-12." Item 1009-B-11, 1009-C-11 (microfiche)
Subjects: World Bank--Africa. Economic assistance, American--Africa. Africa--Economic conditions--1960-
LC Classification: KF27.5 .H8 1987i
Dewey Class No.: 332.1/532/096 19

The World Bank participation sourcebook.
Washington, D.C.: World Bank, c1996.
Description: xvi, 259 p.: ill., map; 28 cm.
ISBN: 0821335588
Notes: "Environmentally Sustainable Development."
Includes bibliographical references and index.
Subjects: World Bank. Economic development projects--Case studies--Handbooks, manuals, etc. Economic development projects--Citizen participation—Case studies--Handbooks, manuals, etc. Community development--Case studies--Handbooks, manuals,
LC Classification: HG3881.5.W57 W692 1996
Dewey Class No.: 338.9 20

The World Bank policy on disclosure of information.
Washington, D.C.: World Bank, [1994]
Description: 17 p.; 23 cm.
ISBN: 0821328077
Notes: "March 1994".
Subjects: World Bank. Disclosure of information.
LC Classification: HG3881.5.W57 W694 1994

The World Bank: governance and human rights.
Edition Information: 2nd ed., rev. and updated.
New York: Lawyers Committee for Human Rights, c1995.
Description: iii, 127 p.; 23 cm.
ISBN: 0934143781
Notes: "August 1995." Includes bibliographical references (p. 125-127).
Subjects: World Bank. Human rights.
LC Classification: HG3881.5.W57 W673 1995

The World Bank: governance and human rights.
New York, N.Y.: Lawyers Committee for Human Rights, c1993.
Description: iv, 82 p.; 23 cm.
ISBN: 093414365X

Notes: At head of Human rights and U.S. foreign policy. "August 1993."
Includes bibliographical references (p. 80-82).
Subjects: World Bank. Human rights.
LC Classification: HG3881.5.W57 W673 1993

The World Bank: lending on a global scale / edited by Jo Marie Griesgraber and Bernhard G. Gunter.
London; Chicago, Il.: Pluto Press, with Center of
Concern, Washington, DC, 1996.
Editor: Griesgraber, Jo Marie.
Description: xix, 240 p.; 22 cm.
ISBN: 0745310508 (hc)
Notes: Includes bibliographical references (p. 209-223) and index.
Subjects: World Bank. International finance--History. Economic development--History.
Series: Rethinking Bretton Woods; v. 3
LC Classification: HG3881 .R418 1995 vol. 3 HG3881.5.W57
Dewey Class No.: 332/.042 s 332.1/532 20

The World Bank's experience with post-conflict reconstruction / Alcira Kreimer ...
Washington, D.C.: World Bank, 1998.
Editor: Kreimer, Alcira.
Description: xix, 96 p.: ill.; 28 cm.
ISBN: 0821342908
Notes: At head of World Bank Operations Evaluation Department, OED.
"ISSN 1011-6984"--Verso t.p. Includes bibliographical references (p. 53-55).
Subjects: World Bank. Economic assistance--Evaluation.
Series: OED study series
LC Classification: HG3881.5.W57 W6949 1998
Dewey Class No.: 332.1/532 21

The World Bank's partnership with nongovernmental organizations / Participation and NGO Group, Poverty and Social Policy Department (PSP), the World Bank.
Washington, D.C.: World Bank, c1996.
Description: v, 38 p.; 27 cm.
ISBN: 0821336037
Notes: "May 1996." Includes bibliographical references (p. 25-26).
Subjects: World Bank--Developing countries.
Non-governmental organizations--Developing countries.
LC Classification: HG3881.5.W57 W695 1996

The World Bank's role in the electric power sector : policies for effective institutional, regulatory, and financial reform.
Washington, D.C.: World Bank, c1993.

Description: 84 p.: ill.; 23 cm.
ISBN: 0821323180
Notes: Includes bibliographical references (p. 78-84).
Subjects: World Bank. Electric utilities--Developing countries. Electric utilities--Developing countries--Finance.
Series: A World Bank policy paper, 1014-8124
LC Classification: HD9685.D452 W67 1993
Dewey Class No.: 333.79/323/091724 20

The World Bank's support for the alleviation of poverty.
Washington, D.C., U.S.A.: World Bank, 1988.
Description: 60 p.; 23 cm.
ISBN: 0821310879
Notes: Includes bibliographical references.
Subjects: World Bank--Developing countries. Economic assistance--Developing countries. Economic development projects--Developing countries. Poor--Developing countries.
LC Classification: HC60 .W67 1988
Dewey Class No.: 332.1/532/091724 19

The World Bank's treatment of employment and labor market issues / Arvil Van Adams with Gail Stevenson ... [et al.].
Washington, D.C.: World Bank, c1992.
Editor: Adams, Arvil V.
Description: viii, 64 p.: ill.; 28 cm.
ISBN: 0821321641
Notes: Includes bibliographical references (p. 36).
Subjects: World Bank. Labor market--Developing countries. Wages--Developing countries.
Series: World Bank technical paper, 0253-7494; no. 177
LC Classification: HD5852 .W66 1992
Dewey Class No.: 331.12/091724 20

The world payments situation: a series of charts with commentary presented to the Seventh Annual Meeting of the Board of Governors of the International Monetary Fund at Mexico City, September 8, 1952.
Washington, D.C.: International Monetary Fund, 1952]
Description: 54 p.: diagrs.; 28 cm.
Subjects: Balance of trade. Commercial statistics.
LC Classification: HF1016 .I65
Dewey Class No.: 382

The world's monetary system: toward stability and sustainability in the twenty-first century / edited by Jo Marie Griesgraber and Bernhard G. Gunter.

London; East Haven, CT: Pluto Press, 1996.
Editor: Griesgraber, Jo Marie.
Description: p. cm.
ISBN: 0745310524 (pbk.)
Notes: Includes bibliographical references and index.
Subjects: International Monetary Fund. International finance--History.. Economic development--History. Twenty-first century--Forecasts.
Series: Rethinking Bretton Woods; v. 4
LC Classification: HG3881 .R418 1995 vol. 4 HG3881.5.I58
Dewey Class No.: 332/.042 s 332.1/52 20

Third World debt legislation : hearings before the Subcommittee on International Development Institutions and Finance of the Committee on Banking, Finance, and Urban Affairs, House of Representatives, Ninety-ninth Congress, second session, March 12, 18, 19, and 20, 1986.
Washington: U.S. G.P.O., 1986.
Description: iii 294 p.: ill.; 24 cm.
Notes: Distributed to some depository libraries in microfiche. Shipping list no.: 86-555-P. "Serial no. 99-74." Item 1013-A, 1013-B (microfiche) Bibliography: p. 24.
Subjects: World Bank--Developing countries. Banking law--United States. Loans, American--Developing countries. Debts, External--Developing countries.
LC Classification: KF27 .B547 1986a
Dewey Class No.: 346.73/082 347.30682 19
Govt. Doc. No.: Y 4.B 22/1:99-74

Third World debt: public reaction to the Brady Plan : hearing before the Subcommittee on International Development, Finance, Trade, and Monetary Policy of the Committee on Banking, Finance, and Urban Affairs, House of Representatives, One Hundred First Congress, first session, April 5, 1989.
Washington: U.S. G.P.O.: For sale by the Supt. of Docs., Congressional Sales Office, U.S. G.P.O., 1989.
Description: iii, 140 p.: ill.; 24 cm.
Notes: Distributed to some depository libraries in microfiche. Shipping list no.: 89-407-P. "Serial no. 101-19." Item 1013-A, 1013-B (microfiche) Includes bibliographical references.
Subjects: World Bank--Developing countries. Debts, External--Developing countries. United States--Foreign economic relations—Developing countries. Developing countries-Foreign economic relations—United States.
LC Classification: KF27 .B547 1989b
Dewey Class No.: 336.3/435/091724 20
Govt. Doc. No.: Y 4.B 22/1:101-19

Third World debt: reports and the Brady Plan: hearing before the Subcommittee on International Development, Finance, Trade, and Monetary Policy of the Committee on Banking, Finance, and Urban Affairs, House of Representatives, One Hundred First Congress, first session, March 16, 1989.
Washington: U.S. G.P.O.: For sale by the Supt. of Docs., Congressional Sales Office, U.S. G.P.O., 1989.
Description: iii, 127 p.: ill.; 24 cm.
Notes: Distributed to some depository libraries in microfiche. Shipping list no.: 89-407-P. "Serial no. 101-14." Item 1013-A, 1013-B (microfiche) Includes bibliographical references.
Subjects: World Bank--Developing countries. Debts, External--Developing countries. United States--Foreign economic relations—Developing countries. Developing countries-Foreign economic relations—United States.
LC Classification: KF27 .B547 1989c
Dewey Class No.: 336.3/435/091724 20
Govt. Doc. No.: Y 4.B 22/1:101-14

Thomas, Vinod
Issues in adjustment lending / Vinod Thomas.
[Washington, D.C.]: Country Economics Dept., World Bank, [1988]
Description: 40 p.; 28 cm.
Notes: Cover title. "March 1988." Bibliography: p. 37-40.
Subjects: World Bank--Developing countries. Economic assistance--Developing countries. Loans, Foreign--Developing countries. Developing countries--Economic conditions.
Series: Policy, planning, and research working papers; WPS 2
LC Classification: HG3881.5.W57 T48 1988
Dewey Class No.: 336.3/435/091724 19

Toedtman, James
IMF, World Bank: Their Global Role -
Newsday Oct. 9, 1998

Trade policy reform in the countries of the former Soviet Union / prepared under the direction of Jack Boorman by an IMF staff team comprising Naheed Kirmani.[et al].
Washington, D.C.: International Monetary Fund, [1994]
Editor: Boorman, Jack. Kirmani, Naheed.
Description: iv, 73 p.; 28 cm.
ISBN: 1557753725 (pbk.) :
Notes: "February 1994." Includes bibliographical references (p. 71-73).
Subjects: Former Soviet republics--Commercial policy.
Series: IMF economic reviews; 1994, 2.
LC Classification: HF3626.5 .T716 1994

Dewey Class No.: 382/.3/0947 20

Transition, private sector development and the role of financial institutions: proceedings of a seminar held during the annual meeting of the European Bank for Reconstruction and Development, St. Petersburg, Russia, 17 April 1994 / edited by Steven Fries; contributions from Nicholas Stern ... [et al.].
London: The Bank, [1994]
Editor: Fries, Steven M.
Description: 46 p.; 21 cm.
Subjects: World Bank--Congresses. European Bank for Reconstruction and Development Congresses. Finance--Europe, Eastern--Congresses. Mixed economy--Europe, Eastern--Congresses. Post-communism--Europe, Eastern--Congresses. Privatization--Europe, Eastern--Congresses. Development banks--Japan--Congresses. Europe, Eastern--Economic conditions--1989---Congresses.
Series: Working paper (European Bank for Reconstruction and Development); no. 13.
LC Classification: HC244.A1 W67 no. 13

Tshuma, L.
The political economy of the World Bank's legal framework for economic development
Social & Legal Studies, 1999, Vol 8, Iss 1, pp 75-96
Over the last two decades there has been a renewed interest in the role of law in development. The major player in the new law and development movement is the World Bank which provides advice on, and funding for, law reform projects. The Bank's initial foray into law reform issues was through adjustment programmes intended to push back the state from the economy in developing countries in order to liberate markets. Despite the Bank's claim that adjustment programmes are technical and apolitical, they have a negative impact on the livelihoods of many social groups in he countries implementing them.

Twele, Cord, 1964-
Die Entwicklungspolitik der Weltbank-Gruppe vor dem Hintergrund der Schuldenkrise der "Dritten Welt" seit Beginn der achtziger Jahre / Cord Twele.
Frankfurt am Main; New York: P. Lang, c1995.
Description: xviii, 246 p.; 21 cm.
ISBN: 363148450X
Notes: Includes bibliographical references (p. 229-246).
Subjects: World Bank--Developing countries. Debts, External--Developing countries. Debt relief--Developing countries.
Series: Europäische Hochschulschriften. Reihe V, Volks- und Betriebswirtschaft; Bd. 1555.
LC Classification: HJ8899 .T84 1995

U.S. participation in ADB and IDA. Hearing, Ninety-third Congress, first session, on S. 2193 ... S. 2665 ... and S. 2666 ... November 19, 1973.
Washington, U.S. Govt. Print. Off., 1974.
Description: iii, 69 p. 24 cm.
Subjects: Asian Development Bank.
International Development Association.
LC Classification: KF26 .F6 1973r
Dewey Class No.: 341.7/51

U.S. participation in the multilateral development institutions: hearing before the Subcommittee on International Development Institutions and Finance of the Committee on Banking, Finance, and Urban Affairs, House of Representatives, Ninety-seventh Congress, first session, March 11, 1981.
Washington: U.S. G.P.O., 1981.
Description: iii, 258 p.; 24 cm. Notes: "Serial no. 97-5." Item 1013-A, 1013-B (microfiche)
Subjects: World Bank. African Development Bank. Economic asssistance, American.
LC Classification: KF27 .B547 1981
Dewey Class No.: 332.1/53 19
Govt. Doc. No.: Y 4.B22/1:97-5

U.S. policies toward the World Bank and the International Monetary Fund: a report of the Panel on International Financial Institutions of the Economic Policy Council of UNA-USA.
New York, N.Y.: Available from the United Nations Association of the United States of America, c1982.
Description: ix, 86 p.; 28 cm.
ISBN: 0934654409
Notes: "August 1982." Bibliography: p. 69-72.
Subjects: World Bank. International Monetary Fund. International Development Association. Economic assistance, American.
LC Classification: HG3881 .U645 1982
Dewey Class No.: 332.1/5 19

Ukraine: accelerating the transition to market : proceedings of an IMF/World Bank seminar / editors, Peter K. Cornelius and Patrick Lenain.
Washington, DC: International Monetary Fund, 1997.
Editor: Cornelius, Peter,
Description: xi, 291 p.: ill.; 23 cm.
ISBN: 1557756198
Notes: Papers presented at an IMF-World Bank seminar held in Washington, D.C. on July 9, 1996. Includes bibliographical references.
Subjects: Post-communism--Economic aspects--Ukraine--Congresses. Ukraine--

Economic policy--1991- --Congresses. Ukraine--Economic conditions--1991- --Congresses. Ukraine--Social policy--Congresses.
LC Classification: HC340.19 .U474 1997
Dewey Class No.: 338.9477/099/049 21

Un Fondo común para América Latina.
Edition Information: [1. ed.]
México, Centro de Estudios Monetarios Latinoamericanos, 1967.
Description: ix, 299 p. 22cm.
Notes: Bibliography: p. 273-278.
Subjects: Banks and banking, International. Latin America--Economic integration.
LC Classification: HG3883.L3 F6
Dewey Class No.: 332.1/5

United Germany, the first five years: performance and policy issues / Robert Corker
Washington, DC: International Monetary Fund, 1995.
Editor: Corker, Robert.
Description: vii, 74 p.: col. ill.; 28 cm.
ISBN: 1557754721
Notes: Includes bibliographical references.
Subjects: Germany--Economic policy--1990- Germany--Economic conditions--1990- Germany--History--Unification, 1990.
Series: Occasional paper (International Monetary Fund); no. 25.
LC Classification: HC286.8 .U555 1995
Dewey Class No.: 338.943 20

Valverde, G.A.
Democracy, human rights, and development assistance for education: The USAID and World Bank in Latin America and the Caribbean
Economic Development and Cultural Change, 1999, Vol 47, Iss 2, pp 401-419

Van De Laar, A.J.M.
The world bank and the poor / A.J.M. van De Laar.
The Hague: Institute of Social Studies, 1979.
Description: 25 p.; 21 cm.
Notes: Includes bibliographical references.
Subjects: World Bank--Congresses. Poor--Congresses.
Series: Hague. Institute of Social Studies. I.S.S. occasional papers; no. 70.
LC Classification: HG3881 .V332
Dewey Class No.: 332.1/532 19

Verspoor, Adriaan, 1942-
Lending for learning: twenty years of World Bank support for basic education /

Adriaan Verspoor.
Washingtion, D.C.: World Bank, 1991.
Description: 42 p.; 28 cm.
Notes: Cover title. Includes bibliographical references (p. 41-42).
Subjects: World Bank--Developing countries. Education--Developing countries--Finance. Educational assistance--Developing countries.
Series: Policy, research, and external affairs working papers; WPS 686
LC Classification: LB2826.6.D44 V47 1991
Dewey Class No.: 370.19/65/091724 20

Vetter, Artur
Die Bank für Internationalen Zahlungsausgleich;
Heidelberg, 1950.
Description: v, 124 l. 30 cm.
Subjects: Bank for International Settlements. Foreign-exchange.
LC Classification: HG3881 .V4

Vijftig jaar na Bretton Woods / onder redactie van W. Mak, H. Visser.
Utrecht: Lemma, 1994.
Editor: Mak, W. Visser, H. (Herschel),
Description: 195 p.; 23 cm.
ISBN: 905189385X
Notes: Includes bibliographical references.
Subjects: International Monetary Fund--History. World Bank--History. United Nations Monetary and Financial Conference (1944: Bretton Woods, N.H.)--History. International finance--History.
Series: Preadviezen (Koninklijke Vereniging voor de Staathuishoudkunde); 1994.
LC Classification: HG205 .V55 1994

Villegas, Edberto M.
Japanese capitalism and the Asian Development Bank / by Edberto M. Villegas.
Diliman, Quezon City, Philippines: Third World Studies Center, University of the Philippines, [1983]
Description: 42, [7] p.; 22 cm.
Notes: "December 1983." Bibliography: p. 38-42.
Subjects: Asian Development Bank. Corporations--Japan. Corporations, Japanese--Asia. Capitalism--Japan.
Series: The Philippines in the Third World papers; ser. no. 38

Villegas, Edberto M.
Reforms in the Philippine financial system and contradictions within US capitalism / by Edberto M. Villegas.
Diliman, Quezon City: Third World Studies, College of Arts and Sciences, University of the Philippines, [1982]

Description: 31, [21] p.; 28 cm. Notes: "July 1982." Bibliography: p. [32]-[36]
Subjects: International Monetary Fund--Philippines. World Bank--Philippines. Finance--Philippines. Philippines--Colonial influence.
Series: Research and working papers The Philippines in the Third World papers; ser. no. 31
LC Classification: HC451 .P58 ser. no. 31 HG187.P6
Dewey Class No.: 332.1/09599 19

Washington, D.C. Joint Library of the International Monetary Fund and the International Bank for Reconstruction and Development..
Current Frequency: Monthly
ISSN: 0363-3535
Notes: Holdings in 3x5 and visible files.

Watanabe, Takeshi
Ajia Kaigin S¯osai nikki. 48(1973)
Description: p. cm.
Notes: Romanized.
Subjects: Asian Development Bank. Underdeveloped areas--Finance.
LC Classification: HG4517 .W37 (Orien Japan

Weitzenegger, Karsten, 1964-
Die Umweltpolitik der Weltbank: Reform oder Rhetorik einer internationalen Organisation / Karsten Weitzenegger.
Münster: Lit, [1992]
Description: 90 p.: ill.; 21 cm.
ISBN: 3894734825
Notes: Includes bibliographical references (p. 76-90).
Subjects: World Bank--Developing countries. Environmental policy--Developing countries. Economic assistance--Developing countries.
Series: Politikwissenschaft (Münster in Westfalen, Germany); Bd. 15.
LC Classification: HC59.72.E5 W45 1992

Wellisz, S.
The World Bank: Its first half century, vol 1, History, vol 2, perspectives, by D. Kapur, J.P. Lewis, R. Webb
Journal of Economic Literature, 1999, Vol 37, Iss 1, pp 215-217

Welter, Erich, ed.
Die Reparationsbank,
Edition Information: 2. aufl.
Frankfurt am Main, Frankfurter societäts-druckerei g.m.b.h., 1930.
Description: 61 p. 22 cm.
Subjects: Bank for international settlements.

LC Classification: HG1997.I6 W4

West, Gerald T. 1944-
MIGA and foreign direct investment: evaluating developmental impacts / Gerald T. West and Ethel I. Tarazona.
Washington, D.C.: World Bank, 1998.
Description: x, 86 p.: ill.; 28 cm.
ISBN: 0821343467 (alk. paper)
Notes: Includes bibliographical references.
Subjects: Multilateral Investment Guarantee Agency. World Bank--Developing countries. Investments, Foreign--Developing countries. Economic development projects--Developing countries.
LC Classification: HG3881.5.W57 W47 1998
Dewey Class No.: 332.1/532 21

Wharrad, H. and Robinson, J.
The global distribution of physicians and nurses
Journal of Advanced Nursing, 1999, Vol 30, Iss 1, pp 109-120

What has the IMF in store for South Africa?: Proceedings of a symposium held on 27th July 1991 at the Soweto College of Education /contributors, Kevin Davie...[et al.]
[Braamfontein]: Institute for African Alternatives, [1991]
Editor: Davie, Kevin.
Description: 27 p.; 30 cm.
Subjects: International Monetary Fund--South Africa--Congresses. South Africa-Economic policy--Congresses.
LC Classification: HC905 .W44 1991
Dewey Class No.: 338.968 20

Whitehead, A. and Lockwood, M.
Gendering poverty: A review of six World Bank African poverty assessments
Development and Change, 1999, Vol 30, Iss 3, pp 525-555
Since the late 1980s, Poverty Assessments have emerged as the most important statements by the World Bank about poverty in particular countries. This article examines, in some depth, a set of Assessments from four sub-Saharan African countries from a gender perspective. These Assessments display an enormous variation in the extent to which gender is present, and they also show a sharp contrast between the treatment of gender issues in the measurement of poverty, particularly in the participatory elements of the Assessments, and their absence in the policy sections of the documents. The article goes on to analyse why the inclusion of gender in these World Bank country-specific poverty documents has been so problematic.

Williams, D.
Constructing the economic space: The World Bank and the making of Homo Oeconomicus
Millennium - *Journal of International Studies*, 1999, Vol 28, Iss 1, pp 79+
The World Bank is engaged in constructing market economies in developing countries. Part of the justification for this activity is that market-based economic arrangements are, at base, 'natural' because they are the product of an economic rationality inherent in all persons. An examination of the practices of the World Bank, however, reveals that the economy is a 'constructed' space not simply in ten-ns of the need for the 'right' economic policies, or a 'good' institutional and regulatory environment, but because economic rationality itself must be constructed.

Wilson, Dick, 1928-
A bank for half the world: the story of the Asian Development Bank, 1966-1986 / by Dick Wilson.
[Manila]: Asian Development Bank, c1987.
Description: 392 p., [8] p. of plates: ill.; 24 cm.
ISBN: 9711240025
Notes: Bibliography: p. [377]
Subjects: Asian Development Bank--History.
LC Classification: HG3881.5.A75 W55 1987
Dewey Class No.: 332.1/53/095 19

Witteveen, H.J.
Economic globalization from a broader long-term perspective: Some questions and concerns
Economist, 1998, Vol 146, Iss 4, pp 539-554
This article considers economic growth in view of a diversity of risks. These concern economic shifts between developing and developed regions with serious global implications. Some examples are labour and capital flows, attended by increasing instability, but also risks of international tax competition and environmental deterioration on a global scale. Moreover, the article addresses spiritual concerns about the materialistic and egoistic attitude encouraged by economic globalization and the strife for material wealth. The main conclusion is that perhaps a shift in emphasis from materialistic concerns towards spiritual values should be stimulated in the Western world.

Women and development: articles, books, and Research papers / indexed in the Joint World Bank-International Monetary Fund Library, Washington, D.C.
Boston, Mass.: G.K. Hall, 1987.
Description: 181 p.; 29 cm.
ISBN: 0816104646
Subjects: Joint Bank-Fund Library--Bibliography--Catalogs. Women in

development--Bibliography--Catalogs. Women--Economic conditions--Bibliography.
LC Classification: Z7963.E18 J65 1987 HQ1240
Dewey Class No.: 016.3071/4/088042 19

Workshop on Asian Development Bank (ADB) projects, 25th January 1983, New Delhi: [Background papers]
New Delhi: Association of Indian Engineering Industry, [1983]
Description: 59 p.; 28 cm.
Summary: Role of Asian Development Bank, 1977-1981.
Subjects: Asian Development Bank--Congresses. Economic development projects--Asia-Congresses.
LC Classification: HC412 .W629 1983
Dewey Class No.: 332.1/53/095 19

Workshop on Asian Development Bank Projects, 25th January 1983, New Delhi: summary and conclusion.
New Delhi: Association of Indian Engineering Industry, [1983]
Description: 68 p.; 29 cm.
Subjects: Asian Development Bank--Congresses.
Economic development projects--India--Congresses.
LC Classification: HG5993 .W67 1983
Dewey Class No.: 332.1/53 19

World Bank and poverty alleviation: hearing before the Select Committee on Hunger, House of Representatives, One Hundred First Congress, second session, hearing held in Washington, DC, June 20, 1990.
Washington: U.S. G.P.O.: For sale by the Supt. of Docs., Congressional Sales Office, U.S. G.P.O., 1990.
Description: iii, 94 p.: ill.; 24 cm.
Notes: Distributed to some depository libraries in microfiche. Shipping list no.: 90-667-P. "Serial no. 101-21." Item 1009-B-11, 1009-C-11 (MF)
Subjects: World Bank--Developing countries. Economic assistance, American--Developing countries. Loans, American--Developing countries. Poor--Developing countries. Economic development.
LC Classification: KF27.5 .H8 1990c
Govt. Doc. No.: Y 4.H 89:101-21

World Bank Delays China Loans Move Follows Bush Bid To Hold Up Funds
Pat Wechsler. Newsday Staff Correspondent - June 27, 1989

WORLD Bank Funds For Poland
Newsday Feb. 23, 1990

World Bank in 1992: progress in poverty alleviation : hearing before the Select Committee on Hunger, House of Representatives, One Hundred Second Congress, second session, hearing held in Washington, DC, June 3, 1992. Washington: U.S. G.P.O.: For sale by the U.S. G.P.O., Supt. of Docs., Congressional Sales Office, 1992.
Description: iii, 81 p.; 24 cm.
ISBN: 0160393167
Notes: Distributed to some depository libraries in microfiche. Shipping list no.: 93-0223-P. "Serial no. 102-32."
Subjects: World Bank--Developing countries. Economic assistance--Developing countries. Loans--Developing countries. Poor--Developing countries.
LC Classification: KF27.5 .H8 1992k
Govt. Doc. No.: Y 4.H 89:102-32
Report No.: Serial no. 102-32 (United States. Congress. House. Select Committee on Hunger)

World Bank To Cut Staff, Reorganize
Newsday May 6, 1987

World Bank, IMF On 'Trial,' Accused Of War In 3rd World
Newsday Sep. 271988

World Bank: $1.2B for Palestinians
Newsday May 3, 1994

World economic outlook: a survey by the staff of the International Monetary Fund. Washington, D.C.: The Fund, [1980-
Description: v.; 28 cm. May 1980-
Current Frequency: Semiannual, Sept. 1984-<Oct. 1995>
ISSN: 0256-6877
Notes: Has occasional updates called: Interim assessment. SERBIB/SERLOC merged record Interim assessment for 1998 issued with the interim assessment for 1998 of: International capital markets. Staff studies for the World economic outlook (OCoLC)14956614 (DLC) 86646901 International capital markets 1085-6374 (DLC) 5649765 (OCoLC)7829564
Translated as: World economic outlook (International Monetary Fund). Arabic. Aføaq al-iqtisøad al-`øalamøi (DLC) 6648379 (OCoLC)35595208
Subjects: Economic history--1971-1990--Periodicals. Economic history--1990---Periodicals.
Series: Occasional paper (International Monetary Fund) World economic and financial surveys.
LC Classification: HC10 .W7979
Dewey Class No.: 338.5/443/09048 19
Entry: World economic outlook (International Monetary Fund)

Washington, D.C. 84-640155

World Fund and Bank journal.
[Savannah, Ga.] [n.d.]
Description: 9 no. in 1 v. 32 cm.
Notes: Serial.
LC Classification: HG3881 .W6

World progress through international banking: the Twenty-second Annual United Nations Ball: Friday, October 10th, 1980, Waldorf-Astoria, New York.
[New York, N.Y.: United Nations Association of the United States of America], 1980.
Description: 110 p.: ill.; 28 cm.
ISBN: 0934654298 (pbk.)
Subjects: World Bank. United Nations Association of the United States of America. Banks and banking, International.
LC Classification: HG3881 .W64
Dewey Class No.: 332.1/5 19

World recession and the food crisis in Africa / edited by Peter Lawrence.
London: Review of African Political Economy; Boulder,Colo.: Westview Press, 1986.
Editor: Lawrence, Peter R., 1
Description: 314 p.; 24 cm.
ISBN: 081330511X (Westview: pbk.) :
Notes: Cover World recession & the food crisis in Africa. Includes index. Bibliography: p. 300-311.
Subjects: International Monetary Fund--Africa--Congresses. World Bank--Africa--Congresses. Food supply--Africa--Congresses. Economic assistance--Africa--Congresses. Recessions--Africa. Africa--Economic conditions--1960---Congresses.
LC Classification: HD9017.A2 W67 1986
Dewey Class No.: 363.8/526/096 19

World summary of international transactions, 1967-972 / prepared by Balance of Payments Division; approved by Arie C. Bouter.
[Washington]: International Monetary Fund, Research Dept., 1974.
Description: 125 p.; 28 cm.
Notes: Tables. Includes index.
Subjects: Balance of payments--Statistics.
LC Classification: HG3882 .I57 1974
Dewey Class No.: 382.1/7/0212

Yamin, Kafil
Bigger U.N. Clout Sought in World Economy.
Inter Press Service Aug. 11, 1998, pn.p.

Yasutomo, Dennis T.
Japan and the Asian Development Bank / Dennis T. Yasutomo.
New York, N.Y., U.S.A.: Praeger, 1983.
Description: xi, 210 p.; 25 cm.
ISBN: 0030633494 (alk. paper) :
Notes: Includes index. Bibliography: p. 192-200.
Subjects: Asian Development Bank--History. Japan--Foreign economic relations.
Series: Studies of the East Asian Institute.
LC Classification: HG3881.5.A75 Y37 1983
Dewey Class No.: 332.1/53 19

Young, Mary E., 1955-
Investing in young children / Mary Eming Young.
Washington, D.C.: World Bank, c1995.
Description: x, 48 p.; 28 cm.
ISBN: 082133171X
Notes: Includes bibliographical references (p. 46-48).
Subjects: World Bank--Developing countries. Child care services--Developing countries. Economic assistance--Developing countries.
Series: World Bank discussion papers; 275
LC Classification: HQ778.5 .Y68 1995
Dewey Class No.: 362.7 20

Zanini, Gianni, 1954-
Philippines: from crisis to opportunity: country assistance review / Gianni Zanini.
Washington, D.C.: World Bank, 1999.
Editor: World Bank. Operations Evaluation Dept.
Description: xv, 57 p.: ill.; 28 cm.
ISBN: 0821342940
Notes: At head of World Bank Operations Evaluation Department. Includes bibliographical references (p. 35-37). Pref. and summary also in French and Spanish.
Subjects: World Bank--Philippines. Economic assistance--Philippines. Philippines--Economic policy. Philippines--Economic conditions--1986-
Series: OED study series
LC Classification: HC453 .Z36 1999
Dewey Class No.: 338.9599 21

Zwi, A.
Policy forum: The World Bank and international health - Introduction
Social Science & Medicine, 2000, Vol 50, Iss 2, pp 167-168

WEBSITES

About the International Monetary Fund, IMF, Introductory Information

Financial Statements of the IMF • Financial Resources...

www.imf.org/external/about.htm

BBC News - World Trade Wars

Conflicts among nations and industries over world trade including history of WTO

http://news1.thls.bbc.co.uk/hi/english/business/the_eco...

BBC News Economy Reports: The IMF and World Bank

James Morgan explains the IMF and World Bank.

http://news.bbc.co.uk/hi/english/business/the_economy/e...

IMF and International Economic Policy

IMF And International Economic Policy

www.house.gov/jec/imf/imfpage.htm -

IMF Financing: A Review of the Issues

www.house.gov/jec/imf/imf.htm -

IMF International Monetary Fund Home Page (IMFRN)

IMF News Releases Publications Country Information...

www.imf.org/

IMF/World Bank Protest New!

Site designed to raise public awareness of the negative impact of International Monetary Fund and World Bank programs have on the world's poorest countries.

http://humanrights.about.com/newsissues/humanrights/lib...

IMF--Dissemination Standards Bulletin Board--SDDS and GDDS
Reference Site (dsbb.imf.org/

Stop the World Bank Resettlement Project! New!
http://diamond.net.udel.edu/events%20online/Conferences...

Stop World Bank Loan to Exxon for Chad-Cameroon Pipeline New!
http://www.economicjustice.org/chadCameroon.html

TechNet: The Technology Network of the World Bank
science, technology and information in development.
http://www.worldbank.org/html/fpd/technet

The World Bank and the Environment- Environment New!
Site is concerned with the negative aspects environmental policies of the World Bank.
http://environment.about.com/newsissues/environment/lib...

The World Bank Group Countries: Angola
The World Bank's country brief for Angola. Angola is a potentially wealthy country, with a population of over 12 million and substantial natural resources.
http://www.worldbank.org/html/extdr/offrep/afr/ao2.htm

The World Bank Group in Kazakhstan
History, structure, and overview of the World Bank activities in Kazakhstan. Description of projects funded by the World Bank Group. Languages: English, Russian.
http://www.worldbank.kz

The World Bank Group
Banking guide to the Maldives.
http://www.worldbank.org/html/extdr/offrep/sas/mv2.htm
The World Bank Group
The World Bank Group offers loans, advice, and resources developing countries
http://www.worldbank.org

The World Bank Office in Warsaw
Information on the activities of the World Bank in Poland.
http://www.worldbank.org.pl

The World Bank Resident Mission Croatia
World Bank office in Croatia
http://www.worldbank.hr

World Bank Development News

Daily online news and information from the World Bank. Includes news and analysis on global debt issues.

http://www.worldbank.org/developmentnews

World Bank Group - Nicaragua

Includes country overview, details of active projects and document search facility.

http://wbln0018.worldbank.org/External/lac/lac.nsf/54a7...

World Bank Prospects for Development

Monthly, quarterly market analysis; price, stock, trend forecasts on 46 major world commodities with 3 global summaries and news, highlights, graphs and data.

http://www.worldbank.org/prospects

World Bank to Support Reconstruction Efforts in Tajikistan

Index of Previous Releases

http://www.worldbank.org/html/extdr/extme/1627.htm

World Bank/IMF: World Bank / IMF Fact Sheet

www.globalexchange.org/wbimf/facts.html -

It's Time for the World Bank to Close its Doors New!

Site dedicated to the citizens' groups who feel the World Bank is causing social harm throughout the Third World.

http://www.nextcity.com/main/article/pi2/96-10-22-devel...

World Bank/IMF: World Bank / IMF Questions and Answers

www.globalexchange.org/wbimf/faq.html –

AUTHOR/EDITOR INDEX

C

D

E

F

G

H

I

J

K

L

M

N

O

P

Q

R

S

T

U

V

W

Y

Z

SUBJECT INDEX

E

F

G

H

I

J

K

L

M

N

Z